AF522680

SOCIAL PROBLEMS AND DEVELOPMENT ISSUES OF YOUTH

Edited by

Dr. Keshao Shankar Patil

M.S.W., Ph.D.

&

Dr. Robin D. Tribhuwan

M.A., M.Sc., PGDM, Ph.D.

DISCOVERY PUBLISHING HOUSE PVT. LTD.

NEW DELHI-110 002

Published by:
Tilak Wasan

DISCOVERY PUBLISHING HOUSE PVT. LTD.
4383/4B, Ansari Road, Darya Ganj
New Delhi-110 002 (India)
Phone : +91-11-23279245, 43596064-65
Fax : +91-11-23253475
E-mail : discoverypublishinghouse@gmail.com
sales@discoverypublishinggroup.com
parul.wasan@gmail.com
web : www.discoverypublishinggroup.com

***First Edition:* 2014**

ISBN: 978-93-5056-449-3

Social Problems and Development Issues of Youth

Printed at:
Aditi Fine Art Press
Delhi

Preface

In his book captioned, "India My Love," Osho (1994:50) has stated that old age has its own dignity. If a person becomes truly mature, old age has its own beauty – which can never be found in a young person. In youth, there is excitement, but no serenity, no coolness of the moon in it. Beauty is like a slowly flowing river, and youth is full of energy, that there is a great impatience to use it.

Youth can never be mentally stable says Osho (1994). Mentally a youth is in a restless mind. Young minds are vibrant and full of energy. They are curious and always want to try out new things. Some youngster are focused, carrier minded and are socio-economically and educationally useful and productive. On the other hand, socio-economic, psychological or other circumstances push some youth into several problems. Youngsters of the 21st century became victims of several social, economic, educational, health, occupational and other problems. The contemporary problems of the youth today are very different from what they were five decades ago.

This book throws light on the contemporary social problems and development issues of the Indian youth. Authors from varied academic fields such as Anthropology, Sociology, Social Work, education, economics, journalism, health, etc. have contributed papers.

This book will be of immense use to students, research and teachers from the fields of social work, sociology, anthropology, tribal studies, economics, education and other social sciences. It will also be useful to N.G.Os., policy makers and general readers as well.

Dr. K.S. Patil
M.S.W., Ph.D.

Dr. Robin D. Tribhuwan
M.A., M.Sc., P.G.D.M., Ph.D.

Contents

PART - THREE
Educational Issues of Youth

PART - FOUR
Alcoholism and Drug Addiction

Contributors

Dr. **K.S Patil**, Principal, Tirpude College of Social Work, Civil Lines, Sadar, Nagpur - 440001, (M.S.), (India) *e-mail:* keshaopatil1@gmail.com, Mobile: 91-9890171364

Dr. **Robin D. Tribhuwan,** Anthropologist & Development Experts, 9, Krishnakunj, Vikas Nagar, Wanawadi, Pune - 411040 (M.S.) (India) *e-mail:* drtribhuwan@hotmail.com, Mobile: 91-9822329819

Dr. **Joy C. Kurian,** Ph.D., D.Sc. is Dean, Faculty of Science, Asia-Pacific International University, MuakLek, Saraburi - 18180, Thailand, *e-mail:* jckurian@apiu.ed

Laurie Anderson, Feminist, 4927, Varalum place NW: Calgary, Alberta, Canada, T3 AOJ 9.

Dr. **Usha Varghese**, Associate Professor, Social Sciences Center, Bharti Vidyapeeth, Erandwane, Pune - 411 004 (M.S.) (India).

Dr. **Jyoti S. Gagangras**, Vice Principal & Head, Department of Sociology, Modern College Ganesh Khind Post, Pune - 411 007, (M.S.) (India).

Dr. **Amrita V. Nadkarni**, Sociologist, 202, Anmol Pride, Excel estate, off S.V. Road, Opposite Patel Auto, Goregaon West, Mumbai -400 062 (M.S.) (India).

Dr. **Jayshree V. Kharche**, Asst. Professor, Department of Sociology, Modern College, Ganesh Khind Post, Pune - 411 007 (M.S.) (India).

Dr. **Pranali K. Patil**, Asst. Professor, College of Social Work, Kamptee, District Nagpur, (M.S.) (India). *e-mail:* patilpranali2012@gmail.com

Dr. **Kasturi Pesala**, Assistant Regional Director, IGNOG, Regional centre, Port Blair, Andaman & Nicobar Island, (India)
e-mail: pesalakasturi@gmail.com, Mobile: 91-9474214027

Dr. **Pandit R. Fulzele**, Head of Department of Sociology, Ramabai Ambedkar College of Arts, Saoli, District Chandrapur - 441 225, (M.S.) (India).

Dr. **M.L. Santhanam**, Retired Professor, National Institute of Rural Development, Rajendra Nagar, Hyderabad, Andhra Pradesh (India).

Girish Sarode, Project Officer, Integrated Tribal Development Project Nagpur, Adivasi Vikas Bhavan, Opposite, RTO Office, Giripeth, Nagpur (M.S.) India.

Anjali Gawande, 134, Chhatrapati Nagar, Wardha Road, Nagpur - 440 015, (M.S.) (India).

Swati S. Kadam, Research Scholar, Department of Sociology, Tilak Maharashtra Vidyapeeth, Mukund Nagar, Gultekdi, Pune - 411 037, (M.S.) (India).

Adv. Lalsu Narote, At post Juvvi, Taluka Bhambragad, district Gadchiroli, (M.S.) (India).

Sadashiv S. Shende, Sociologist, 203, Sanivarpeth, Pune - 411 030, (M.S.) (India).

Rohit Sharma, F5/12, Salunke Vihar, Kondhva Post, Pune - 411 048, (M.S.) (India).

Shailesh Wadekar, Sarhad, Behind Bharti Vidyapeeth, Oppiste Rajaram Gas Agency, Katraj, Pune - 411 046, (M.S.) (India), *e-mail*: shwadekar@yahoo.co.in

Azimuddin F. Sherkar, Anthropologist, Tribal Research & Training Institute, 28 Queens Garden, Pune - 411 001, (M.S.) (India) *e-mail*: afsherkar@yahoo.co.in, Mobile: 91-9371235492

Insha Khan, Journalist, Babla Cottage, Ground Floor, Girgaum, Mangalwadi, Nest Gaywadi, Mumbai - 400 004, (M.S.) (India).

Miss **Avanti Patwardhan**, 55/4, Erandwane, Ashok Path, Pune - 411 004 (M.S.) (India).

Melanie Fedyk, 22, Armour Street, Regina SK, S4 R4 G3, Canada.

Ms. **Beena Rajan**, Deputy Director Technical, Lokya Manya Medical Fondation, Chinchwad, Pune.

Part – I

Youth Cultures, Movements, Social Problems and Development Issues

Social Problems and Development Issues of Youth *An Overview*

– Dr. **Robin D. Tribhuwan**

What is a problem ?

A problem is a difficulty or an obstacle that needs to be resolved. It is a question raised for consideration or solution. It is an pooprtunity that prepares a platform to answer a question. It makes one difficult to achieve a desired goal, objective or purpose. Finally, it is an unplanned or unexpected deviation from a predefined standard or expectation (MSBTE, 2008)

Every individual, couple, family, group, community or a country comes across one or more problems. Problems may be psychological, social, economic, educational, physical, spiritual, political or nutritional.

People in problems make efforts to understand the meaning of the problem, its root cause and try to find various strategies to resolve the same. Problems vary from one society to another.

Social Problems and Social Disorganisation

According to Madan G.R.(1965), "social problems are behaviour patterns or conditions that are considered objectionable or undesirable by many members of the society." A social problem to one society, may not be a problem in another society. Drinking toddy among the Warlis may be a social problem to an outsider, but from an insiders point of view it may be a way of life.

Madan G.R.(1965) reveals the ro-relation between social problems, individual, family and social disorganisation. He states that when an individual, a family or a group is disorganized and is not functioning according to the norms lai down by the society the social problem is in existence.

As aptly defined by Elliot and Merrill, "social disorganisation represents a break down in the equilibrium of forces, a decay in the social structure, so that old habits and forms of social control no longer function effectively." Gillin and Gillin (1951) point out – "by social disorganisation, we mean such maladjustments between the various elements in the total cultural confidugration as to endanger the survival of the group, or as seriously to interfere with satisfaction of the fundamental desires of its members with the result that social cohesion is destroyed.

Why study problem of youth ?

As rightly pointed out by Kennedy Robert (1966), that, this world demands the qualities of youth : not a time of life, but a state of mind, a temper of the will, a quality of imagination, a predominance of courage over timidity, of the appetite for adventure over the life of ease."

Youth of any nation are an asset. Their sound physical, mental, spiritual and social well being is very essential for the progress of the nation. Quality of youth determines the future of a nation. The developing countries are very conscious of population explosion, small family norms, quality of life, and formal education, social and economic status and so on.

Poverty, ignorance, illiteracy, misery, dependence, superstitious beliefs, economic differences and social hierarchy have adverse impact on the quality of life of an individual, family, group, community or a nation as it were.

Youth who become victims of the above mentioned forces cannot have quality life. In fact, they become victims of several social, economic, educational, psychological, physical, occupational and political problems. This does not mean that the youth belonging to the upper and middle class do no have problems.

Research and documentation of problems and development issues of youth, will certainly contribute in furnishing valuable data for the policy makers, Government, national and international NGOs to plan and execute need based programmes for children, adolescent and youth of a country.

The problems, needs and development issues of youth certainly vary from one society to another and from one country to another. A country like India has diverse cultural and ethnic groups, certainly would pose multiple and group specific problems of male and female youth. Understanding problems and development issues of youth will also contribute in pointing out solutions.

Contemporary Problems of Youth

Interviews with youth, their parents, economists, sociologists, anthropologists, employers, including review of literature revealed that some of the contemporary problems of youth are:

1. Unemployment;
2. Drug abuse and alcoholism;
3. Individual and family disorganisation;
4. Obstacles in education;
5. Poverty;
6. Gambling, smoking and consumption of abusive substances;
7. Health and nutritional problems;
8. Accidents due to rash driving;
9. Crime among the youth;
10. Occupational problem and hazards;
11. Prostitution;
12. Domestic violence;
13. Sexual harassment at work place;
14. Social and economic insecurity among young labourers in informal sector;
15. Child rearing: A problem of young working couples;
16. Living in encroached land: a problem of youth belonging to nomadic and semi nomadic groups;
17. Impact of mixed marriages on the lives of young couples;
18. Stress among the working youth.

One can go on listing the problems of the youth. What is equally important is to know, why these problems arise? What are the root causes of these problems? And what can be done to resolve them? Researchers must make efforts to explore why certain development programmes for youth click, while others don't?

What are the failures or gaps in the development programmes? What strategies should be developed to make these programmes successful?

Development Issues of Youth

Some of the developmental issues that emerged through focused group and informal interviews regarding the development of youth were as below:

1. Counseling and guidance centres

The youth being vibrant and full of energy need counseling and guidance in many aspect of life including:

- Choosing a career;
- Significance of studies;
- Leadership;

- Communication;
- Sex education;
- Personality development;
- Talent search;
- Physical fitness;
- Patriotism;
- Choosing a life partner;
- Time management etc.;

2. **Training**

Every youth needs training before he or she takes up a job, business venture or even educational career for that matter.

3. **Employment opportunities**

It is the responsibility of the state to create opportunities of employment for the youth.

4. **Awareness**

There is an urgent need to create awareness among various classes, castes, tribes and nomadic groups regarding the human and constitutional rights. The youth especially should be made aware of this.

5. **Balancing ecological, economic and social systems**

The youth should be made aware of the urgency of balancing ecological, economic and human resources. The need to conserve forests, animals, birds and biodiversity, should be taught to them. They should be made aware of the threats that are causing ecological disturbances.

6. **Fight corruption**

The youth should be inspired to fight and prevent corruption.

7. **Promote communal harmony and national integration**

Youth should be involved in promoting communal harmony and national integration.

8. **Adopt small family norms**

It is estimated that India would over ride China, as regards the population size within the next two decades or so. The youth should be taught up to take up small family norms after they get married.

9. **Education, career and employment**

Youth should be made aware of the significance of education, career and employment.

10. **Focus on quality of life**

The vision of youth, especially in the developing countries is to focus on quality of life.

Concluding Remarks

Youth of any country are an asset to their nation. Understanding their problems and development issues is an imperative need. It is the moral responsibility of a state to educate, train, counsel and guide its youth towards progress.

Youth Movements in India
An Overview

– Dr. **Amrita V. Nadkarni**
– Dr. **Robin D. Tribhuwan**

Introduction

Throughout history, the generations with an exceptionally high youth ratio have created socio-political movements that have shaken the systems and have left a profound impact on society.

e.g. America's baby boomers, all the 79 million people born between 1946 and 1964, led the change in the civil rights movement and the sexual revolution.

e.g. In China, the present charismatic leaders have emerged out of the stormy cultural revolution and they have taken China to great heights of prosperity and power.

The question is – Will India follow the same path? Will the youth of India take their country to the heights of glory, prosperity and power?

The recent Anti – Corruption movement in India, led by an aged Gandhian, but joined by thousands of youth, the movement against the sexual assault of women; all these are *Signs of a Rising Youth Movement in the country.*

Nearly 70 per cent of India's population is under the age of 40 years. 600 million Indians are below the age of 25 years. The problem is a 4 decade gap between the median age of India's population and the political leaders. The decision makers thus have views that differ considerably from the youth.

According to *Vibhuti Acharya,* the youth of India are the saviours of democracy. They are the powerhouse of energy and this power should be used carefully to make India more powerful. The youth has the power to present a new face of India in the global market and the talent to make India a developed country.

This chapter is an attempt to trace youth movements in India before and after Independence. It presents an overview of the participation of the Indian youth in the movement towards the growth and change of their country. A brief outline of social movements has been given and the involvement of youth across movements has been studied.

Youth in India are not given the due importance they deserve. They are the new face of India in the global market and they comprise the most creative segment of our society. They need to be encouraged as the torch bearers and active participants in the eradication of the evils that cloud our social system today.

It is rarely that people in India remember the fervent young patriots who fought so gallantly against the British Rule in India. Names like *Bhagat Singh* figure in history books of students today, but for how many young students is Bhagat Singh a role model? Is Bill Gates who is not even an Indian, the preferred role model?

Besides Bhagat Singh, who was 22 years old when he was sentenced to the gallows, there were several other young men who died fearlessly for the nation. Their names are hardly read in any of the books. But all of them took part in nationalist activities against the British Rule in India.

E.g. *Arur Singh* – died at the gallows at the age of 26 years.

Ashfaqullah Khan – sentenced to death and hanged in Faizabad jail in 1927. He was only 27 years old.

Avadh Bihari – sentenced to death and hanged in Ambala Central jail. He was only 26 years old.

Azad Chandra Shekhar – died fighting the British. He was betrayed by a friend and faced a large troupe of British soldiers all alone with revolvers in both hands. He fought till his last breath. He was only 25 years.

Barhat Pratap Singh – led a revolutionary movement against the British. He was captured and tortured to death. He refused to divulge the names of his fellow patriots. He was only 24 years old.

Such were the youth of the pre-independence period; fearless, direct, fiercely patriotic and selfless. Today's youth is a generation with a difference. In this day and age of globalization, the Indian youth are giving priority to education; they are carefully diplomatic, strategic and calculative in approach. The generation X as they are called, are highly ambitious, eager to grow and angry at being unnoticed and fully capable of bringing change in society.

Since pre-independence, India has witnessed the youth playing a major role in the various social movements in different time periods. Before going into these details, it is necessary to understand the meaning of social movements, how they originate, the types of social movements that exist and their lifecycle. These are points that have to be discussed before moving into the discussion of youth movements in India.

The term Social Movement first came into use in the early 19th century. At that time, it had a very specific meaning. Viz. it referred to the movement of the new industrial working class who had socialistic, communistic and anarchistic tendencies. Today, however, social movements are no longer identified only with the labour movement. The meaning widens to incorporate independence movements in colonial countries, peasant and farmers movements, womens movements, environmental movements etc.

Definitions of Social Movements

Herbert Blumer (1939) - Social Movements are "collective enterprises to establish a new order of life".

Rudolf Heberle (1949) – Social Movements are "collective attempts to bring about a social change".

According to *Francis Abraham* (2006) – "A Social Movement is a form of collective behaviour in which a large number of people are united in an attempt to promote or resist change".

International Encyclopaedia of Social Sciences – states that "the term social movement is used to denote a wide variety of collective attempts to bring about a change in certain social institutions or to create an entirely new order".

Further, it states that the term is also used when differentiating between varied movements e.g. religious and political. As also, it is used to differentiate between movements among particular groups. E.g. the Women's Movement, the Youth movement. Thus, since all these movements occur in society and directly or indirectly affect the social order, the term Social Movements may be applied to all of them.

There are several schools of thought on the origin of social movements. The historical theories along with other ideologies like the cyclical and linear theories all have varied views on the origin of social movements.

Historical Theories:

1. **The Mass Society Theories** – are of the view that *due to lack of an intermediate structure, people in the mass society are not integrated. This leads to alienation, tension and ultimately to protest.* Propounders of this theory like *Kornhauser* (1959) state that in the mass society, individuals are not related to one another by a variety of groups but by their relation to a common authority. E.g. the state. In the mass society, there is an absence of independent groups and associations. So people lack the resources

to ward off the threat to their autonomy. They also lack the resources to restrain their own behaviour as well as that of others. Strong feelings of alienation and anxiety emerge. All this leads to them engaging in extreme behaviour to escape from these tensions.

2. **The Theory of Status Inconsistency** – states that *the objective discrepancy between peoples ranking and status (i.e. education, income, occupation) generates subjective tension in society*. This leads to cognitive dissonance, discontent and protest. Proponents of this theory are *Lenski* (1954), *Broom* (1959). These scholars feel that if the state of status discrepancy is severe, it leads to subjective dissonance and tensions. *Geschwender* (1971), is of the view that the set of circumstances described by the status inconsistency hypothesis, would produce varying degrees of dissonance and dissonance – reducing behaviour.

3. **The Structural Strain Theory** – Has been propagated by *Smelser, Lang and Lang* and *Turner* and *Killian*. *This theory suggests that any severe structural strain can help manifest social movements*. Smelser is of the view that the more severe the strain, the more likelihood of social movements. It is argued that there are sequences leading to the manifestation of social movements. These sequences move from structural weakness in society to psychological disturbances and ultimately to social movements. There are a variety of reasons for the strain. Smelser suggests that individuals experience strain out of disruption in the normal functioning of society. This disruption could be caused by varied processes like industrialization, urbanization, migration, unemployment etc. Thus in general, this theory views social movements as collective relations to strains that create severe tensions, some of which may reach "boiling point", triggering social emergency. This theory emphasizes more on the psychological effect than on the political goal. *James Davies* (1992), *proposed a strain theory which is based on the gap between expectations and the capacity to achieve these expectations*. If people's expectations continue to rise and their levels of satisfaction continue to decline, or if their opportunities are blocked somehow, then there will be a considerable strain leading to collective action.

4. **Relative Deprivation Theory** – propounded by *David Aberle* (1966), who says that "relative deprivation is a necessary condition for precipitating social movements. *Relative Deprivation refers to disadvantage which a group experiences in comparison* with a *reference group*. Relative deprivation is not measured by objective standards but always in reference to another group. E.g. the economic situation of school teachers may be improving. But no matter how big a pay raise they get, they will still feel deprived if they see other non-gazette government employees getting better salaries. *There is also a gap between people's aspirations and their achievements*. E.g. In many agrarian societies which won freedom from colonial rule,

people's expectations shot up. Exposure to mass media, political participation and the spirit of nationalism led to a revolution of rising expectations. But there was no corresponding improvement in their standard of living. This leads to frustration and a call for concerted action. This theory has been given a prominent place in the study of social movements. In Marxian analysis, *Economic Deprivation* has been identified to be the prime cause of social conflict among two antagonistic classes viz. the haves and the have – not's. *According to Aberle, deprivation also has a non-material base*. E.g. Status, privileges, worth etc. *Gurr* (1970), has perceived a deprivation as a gap between expectations and perceived capabilities, involving three generalized sets of values viz. Economic conditions, political power and social status.

5. **Resource Mobilization Theory** – According to Francis Abraham, only widespread discontent is not enough to launch a social movement. There must be a leader or leaders who can mobilize the resources viz. people, money, channels of communication and commitment of time. Such leaders formulate specific goals, provide the ideology and deliver the messages in such an effective manner that they resonate with the right people. At times, an organized format also is necessary to recruit large numbers of people, to assign duties and responsibilities and to allocate resources. The Resource Mobilization Theory is helpful in explaining several contemporary movements. The women's movement, student movements in Assam, the Narmada Andolan and various religious revivalist movements demonstrate the importance of resource mobilization.
6. **Collective Identity Theory** – as expressed by *Meyer, Whittier* and *Robnett*. According to these theorists, collective identity emerges from interaction within movements as participants transform their sense of themselves. *Collective Identity is grounded in the group's social location* viz. its structural position, its common experiences and dominant definitions of the group. It is shaped by forces external to the movement, but it is never a straightforward result of a shared social location. Collective identity is thus an interpretation of a group's collective experience; who the members of the group are, what their attributes are, what they have in common, how they are different from other groups and what the political significance of all this is.
7. **Discourse Theory** – This theory grows out of the effort to understand how the powerful control meanings, even as there are openings for dissent and opposition. The State and other powerful institutions construct particular discourses, but movements and others dispute them. Discursive change is an important goal for social movements. Such discursive change entails telling new stories about the operations of institutions, challenging the legitimation of power and the production

of identities that are part of the dominant discourse. Discourses thus provide a way of seeing and interpreting information, categorizing individuals and events and justifying power relations.

Two Theories that are also of sociological significance are:

1. **The Cyclical Theory** – such a theory of social movements assumes that social movements occur for similar reasons and have similar destinies. E.g. The conceptual framework that explained the emergence of the labour movement in the 19th century is equally valid to explain the emergence of the green movement in the early 1970's (*Kumar Lalit* 2010). *Alan Touraine* views social movements in terms of political cycles. According to him, social movements strive for political power at the national level. However, in the process of reaching that power, they are co-opted. Thus, national social movements arise e.g. the green movement. These are seen as the equivalent in a post – industrial society of old social movements such as labour movement in an industrial society.
2. **The Linear Theory** – This theory states that whenever social movements emerge, they are unique and must be viewed as such. A movement's uniqueness is tied to the fact that the process of industrial development is linear and produces unique societal effects. *Claus Offe* views social movements as a means to help the political system evolve and adjust to the new requirements that industrial development places upon it. According to Offe, the key to managing the process of industrial development and its societal consequences is the political system (the nation state). The political system may be viewed as the regulator between the economic system on hand and civil society on another. *Habermas* states that social movements refer to the conflict between the social world and nature. He takes the example of the National Socialist Movement in Germany of the 1930's. According to him, technical rationality renders a society unhealthy because it destroys a society's capacity to critique and reflect. It alienates people and diminishes a society's ability to learn and master its own evolution and future. Habermas' theory views a political system (which is like a national system) and social movements try to restore the autonomy of this system.

Social Movement has a number of Characteristics:

1. **Members share a sense of unity and subscribe to a common goal.** A social movement is a collective enterprise. The members experience a sense of membership along with other people who share the same dissatisfaction with the present state of affairs and the vision of a better order. Thus, it is a collectivity with a common goal and shared values.
2. **Members follow certain codes of conduct and patterns of behaviour.** They may have their own insignia, badges, colours, slogans and even

dress codes. This sense of membership suggests that the individual is subject to some discipline. Along with shared values, a movement possesses norms which prescribe behaviour that will symbolize the member's loyalty to the social movement, strengthen his commitment to it and set him apart from non-members. These norms prohibit behaviour that may go contrary to the movement and strengthen commitment through group activity.

3. **They are inspired by an ideology that justifies their action**. The movement provides guidelines as to how members think. The ideology provides these members with a readymade and presumably authoritative set of arguments. It provides them with the strength and vision to collectively move towards the change that they want to bring about.
4. **A social movement is characterized by relatively long term duration.** This is one of the defining characteristics of a social movement. Some movements may last for decades and enlist thousands of members e.g. The Jharkhand Movement. Other movements may take place within the boundaries of a specific group viz. a religious association or a local community and may enlist only a few hundred members.
5. **Movements use a variety of approaches to recruit people.**
6. (a) Enlisting the support of influential people.
   (b) Getting the attention of the media.
   (c) Mobilizing political support.

   These are the 3 key processes involved in the development of the movement.
7. **Social Movements are characterized by a semi – formal structure.** It does not possess the fully developed formal structure of an association (like a club or a corporation). The leaders do not possess legal authority or legitimate power and members are not formally recruited. This absence of formal decision making procedures places a premium on the part of members. Not all members display the same loyalty. There is no legal obligation to the movement. Hence, commitment to the movement and its values becomes one of the most important sources of control.
8. **Social Movements are characterized by a varied motivation to join.** The motivation of individuals joining a social movement has a wide range. It may vary from rational belief in the movement's aim to pure opportunism. Very often, the decision to join is more emotional than rational. E.g. the Baiga of Orissa protecting their trees which they believe are their gods abode. E.g. the Dongria Kondhs of Orissa protecting their Mountain God on the Niyamgiri Mountain. Thus, rationalization gets tied up with emotions. When a movement has existed for so long, it becomes traditional. The nature of the movement changes as a new

generation grows into it. The new generation consists of people who have experienced the movement in the formative years of their lives and they develop some rational ideology to give it momentum.

9. **Movements Network with other agencies for continued support.** Many movements seek the help of other organisations and agencies for their continuous development and funding. Not all movements are able to garner such support in a big way. At times, if the movement is causing upheaval, the support system may be poor. But if the movement is bringing reform for the betterment of society, the support is easier to obtain.
10. Yet another important characteristic of contemporary social movements is that the bureaucratic form of the institutional movement survives as a formal organisation. Once the movement becomes institutionalized, the functions, rules and regulations become fixed and the movement grows into organisations. E.g The Environmental Movement has led to several formal NGO's springing up all over the world and they are supported by Government departments for environment today.

Types of Social Movements:

Many different types of social movements have been identified. These have been listed below:

1. **Alterative Social Movements:** these seek to alter or change some specific behaviour. E.g. the prohibition movement in India was designed to make people stop drinking and to force governments to enforce the dry law.
2. **Reformative Social Movements:** these advocate fundamental reforms. E.g. movements against untouchability, sati, child marriage, dowry etc.
3. **Transformative Social Movements**: are revolutionary movements. They aim at a total transformation of society. E.g. French, Russian and Chinese Revolutions. Nationalist Movements, farmers' movements and labour movements which try to bring about systemic changes are also transformative movements. They can also be called Mass Movements. These are the 'classical' movements which attain historical importance.
4. **Reactionary Social movements**: these embrace the values of the past or some fundamental tenets of faith and want to return general society to yesterday's values. These are revivalist in nature. E.g. Arya Samaj. Even some fundamentalist religious movements come under this category.
5. **Expressive Social Movements**: simply express personal feelings of satisfaction and general well being and people join these for mutual support and togetherness. They choose alternative lifestyles and subscribe to a different set of values. E.g. the Hare Krishna Movement, the Osho Movement and the Hippie Movement of the 1960's.

6. **Transnational Social Movements**: these are global in their orientation. Many ideologically based social movements transcend national boundaries. E.g. the Environment movement.
7. **Small Group Movements:** are more like protest movements. They may also try to redress grievances of certain groups. E.g. Tribal rebellions, Dalit movement in India. These are limited in spatial expansion and are mostly local, regional and maybe at times national in character. The tribal movement to conserve their sacred groves in Thane District appears to fall under this type.
8. **According to Dr. Robin Tribhuwan** – Social Movements can also be classified as Issue – Based Movements. These, he states revolve around a particular issue for e.g. Freedom, Human Rights, Environment, Gender related etc. The level of intensity of the movement would depend on the importance the issue is given.

Lifecycle of Social Movements

Social Scientists have analyzed social movements in terms of various stages and models. *Armand Mauss* – has identified 5 stages through which a typical social movement passes. They are as follows:

1. **Incipience** – refers to the prevalence of *some discontent or frustration among a large number of people.* Such relative deprivation and discontent usually occur during times of economic crisis, war and major technological changes. Then *there emerge leaders who can channel the frustration of affected people,* give a voice to their frustration, define the message and tell the people that change is possible. But are unable to mobilize the required support or resources or effectively convince people that change is possible. Thus, many social movements fail at this stage.
2. **Coalescence** – During this stage, interest groups form around leaders and formulate programmes. They network with other groups and likeminded individuals. They look for the support from well connected and well known personalities. They also mobilize other resources such as money, goods, people's skills and time as well as the attention of the mass media.
3. **Institutionalization** – If the movement attracts large numbers of people, it can no longer depend on the charismatic qualities of the leader. Then the movement will need a formal organisation with a full time staff, functional division of labour, a budget and its own publications. When the movement becomes institutionalized, there is always the danger that it will become "just another organisation."
4. **Fragmentation** – During this stage, conflicts occur over a number of issues, leadership style, doctrine, bureaucratization and even the message. Rebel groups emerge and claim that the organisation no longer represents the original goal or mission of the movement.

5. **Demise** – This is the end of the social movement. The organisation created by the movement may survive, but many of the goals of the original movement may have been accomplished.

ROLE OF YOUTH IN THE VARIOUS SOCIAL MOVEMENTS IN INDIA: AN OVERVIEW

Role in Reform Movements

During the 18th century and post that period, a great challenge swept over India. The impact of Westernization opened people's minds to several social evils. This triggered into motion social reforms which began to discard traditional beliefs and practices which were dysfunctional to society. These were the beginnings of a new awareness that was taking expression. Right from *Raja Ram Mohan Roy's "Brahmo Samaj", Swami Dayanand Saraswati's "Arya Samaj", Swami Vivekananda's "Ramakrishna Mission", Annie Besant's "Theosophical Society" and Mahatma Gandhi's "Sarvodaya"*, all such movements served not only to eradicate social evils, but to enlighten people about the changing value system.

The Youth in many of the above mentioned movements were responsible for introducing new ideas. E.g. Keshab Chandra Sen played a major role in introducing the concept of "God – Force" in the Brahmo Samaj, to express devotion to the 'Universal Spirit'. He was also instrumental in initiating the birth of the *Prarthana Samaj* in Maharashtra in 1867. This movement was then taken over by other young leaders like M.G. Ranade and Dr. Atmaram Pandurang.

Swami Dayanand Saraswati is called *'The Martin Luther of Hinduism'*. Though his was a revivalist movement, he strongly opposed and attacked orthodoxy in Hinduism and encouraged the meeting of Western Science and Eastern Philosophy. The youth members of the Arya Samaj played a very active role in establishing a network of schools and colleges in India and later, Arya Samaji's like Lala Lajpatrai joined the Freedom Movement.

The greatest contribution of the *Ramakrishna Mission* was the shaping of a disciple like *Swami Vivekananda*. He was a radical thinker, a forceful orator and a staunch nationalist. He stressed the need for social action and declared 'Vedanta' as a rational system of thought. He emphasized the urgent need to save Hinduism from becoming a 'religion of cooking pots and touch me not's. The patriotic and spiritual impulses mingled together to uplift India and place her among the nations of the world.

The Theosophical Society of India, under the leadership of *Mrs. Annie Besant*, stood for the development of a national spirit among the Indians. She played a very significant role in launching the *"Home Rule Movement"* and the creation of awareness about "Swarajya". She founded the 'Central Hindu School' in Benares, which later became the "Banaras Hindu University".

Role of Indian Youth in the Non-Brahmin Movement

The '*Satya Shodhak Samaj*' was established by *Mahatma Phule*, whose fight against Brahminic Supremacy and campaign for social equality was taken up by several youth (including Brahmins) of the time. This was the first Backward Classes Movement of its kind. After Mahatma Phule's death, this movement was taken up by Chhatrapati Shahu Maharaj of Kolhapur. Crowned at the age of 20 years, the efforts of Shahu Maharaj and his supporters enabled the movement to spread to other parts of India.

Shri Narayan Guru Dharma Paripalana Yogam (*SNDP Yogam*) in Kerala was meant to be a casteless organisation open to all people. Its two important programmes were:

1. Encouragement of Education by starting schools and colleges.
2. Building temples and simplifying rituals.

It also was opposed to the practice of Untouchability. Several youth from Kerala joined this movement, but after the death of Sri Narayan Guru, the movement took a political turn. It became divided and one section comprising of middle classes supported the Congress and the other section comprising of the lower classes supported the Communist party.

Backward Classes Movement started in India in the early 20th century. It was started by the lower caste youth who realized that they were unable to avail of admission to post – graduate and professional courses. Also, they were not able to get good jobs in government services due to upper cast monopoly. This movement became political when these lower castes began demanding a separate electorate. This movement was a big blow to the social and cultural domination of the Brahmins. It was an attempt to achieve social mobility.

The politics pursued by the British widened the gap between the Brahmins and the non-Brahmins. At the same time, the new modern education introduced helped them to challenge Brahminic supremacy. *Dr. Babasaheb Ambedkar* played a major role in forwarding this movement and he got the support of a large section of youth in his effort.

Role of Indian Youth in Agrarian/Peasant Movements

Agrarian unrest has been in India for the past two decades. In pre-independence period, peasant movements were influenced by the struggle for national freedom. They were targeted against the zamindars, the money-lenders and the government. Some of the significant peasant movements were:

1. The Santhal Insurrection (1855-56).
2. Peasant Revolt in Punjab (1930)
3. Champaran Movement – Bihar (1917-18)
4. Kheda Peasant Struggle (1918)

5. The Bardoli Satyagraha (1920)
6. Moplah Rebellion in Malabar (1921)

After independence, the significant peasant movements were:

1. Telangana Peasant Struggle (1947-51)
2. Naxalbari Peasant Struggle (1967)

Peasant struggles are still widely prevalent. They are controlled by well established organisations and powerful leaders. A large number of youth are involved in these organisations e.g. Shetkari Sanghatana in Maharashtra. Two peasant agitations in which the youth were actively involved were:

1. **The Indigo Growers Agitation in 1860:**

   Indigo farmers of Bengal got together, Hindus and Muslims alike against the exploitation of indigo farmers by the British. There was no violence, but the British, not wanting a repeat of the Santhal insurrection gave in to the demands of the indigo farmers. This was a big victory for the farmers.

2. **The Naxalbari movement in 1967:**

   This movement was launched in March, 1967 in a village called Naxalbari in West Bengal. Various tribals were also involved e.g. Santhals, Oraons, Mundas. Totally, around 42,000 people took part in this violent agitation. The dissatisfaction of peasants in more than 60 villages in West Bengal culminated in this revolt. The idiom of this movement was that power came from the barrel of a gun and not by slogans or by non – violence. The target of the movement was the big farmers, landlords, government officials and the jagirdars.

At a later stage, this movement took on an ideological flavor. Young Naxalite leaders like *Charu Majumdar, Kanu Sanyal, Kumar Kishan, Punjab Rao, Jungal Santhal, Jail Singh, Vinod Mitra* and *others* played a key role here. The main feature behind this movement was that the farmers began to fight for political power.

The Naxalbari movement became a specific ideological struggle oriented to Marxist Socialism. However, it was not really successful, due to vested interests of certain communist leaders, too much use of violence and lack of consensus among the leaders themselves.

Today, the Naxalites are still carrying on their struggle in different parts of the country especially in forested belts, which are now known as 'red belts'. They are not agrarian struggles anymore. Their tactics are almost equivalent to terrorism and they are a proscribed section of society.

Tribal Youth Involvement in Movements to Save their Ecosystems is not a new phenomenon. Such movements date right back to the 18th century in India.

The Chipko Movement

In 1730, in Khejarli Village of Rajasthan, the original Chipko Movement was started by the Bishnoi tribe of Rajasthan. A large group of villagers, led by a lady called Amrita Devi, laid down their lives in an effort to protect the Khejri Trees which they regarded as sacred, from being felled on the orders of the Maharaja of Jodhpur. After this incident, the Maharaja gave a strong royal decree preventing the cutting of trees in all Bishnoi villages.

1793-1915: was a period of open revolt. The British imposed the Bengal Permanent Settlement Regulation Act and land was then subjected to taxation. The respective tribal chiefs became agents of revenue collection for the British. This led to internal strife and division among the tribals. It resulted in a series of uprisings which were initially ethnic in nature but later became regional.

1. The first Santhal revolt of 1793 was under the leadership of Tilka Manjhi.
2. 1798 – The Bhumij revolt of Manbhum took place.
3. 1810 – The Chero uprising of Palamu led by Bhukan Singh.
4. 1819 – 20 – The Munda uprising of Tamar led by Rudu and Konta.
5. 1833 – The Kol rebellion led by Singhrai and Binrai Manki
6. 1834 – The second Bhumij revolt led by Ganganarayan.
7. 1855 – The second Santhal Rebellion led by the Santhal brothers, Sidhu, Kanu, Chaud and Bhairao.
8. 1857 – The Sepoy mutiny led by Bisnath Sahi, Ganpat Rai, Sheikh Bhikhari and Bir Budhu Bhagat.
9. 1875 – 95 – The Sardar Movement
10. 1895 – 1900 – The Birsa Munda Movement
11. 1914 – The Tana Bhagat Movement under the leadership of Jatra Oraon.

The Bihar State Reorganisation Bill of 2000 asked for a separate state Vanachal or Jharkhand.

The Dongria Kondhs of Niyamgiri Hills in Orissa – have been fighting a long battle from 2005 onwards to save their beautiful Niyamgiri Mountain from the clutches of a mining company. This struggle began when a Kondh Village at the foothills of the Niyamgiri Mountain was bulldozed by the Vedanta Open Pit Mining Company to make way for the refinery.

The Kondhs realized that if this open pit mine began functioning, it would destroy their forests, disrupt the rivers and spell the end of the Dongria Kondhs as a distinct people.

To the Dongria Kondhs, Niyam Dongar hill is the seat of their God, Niyam Raja. But for the Vedanta Company, this mountain is a $ 2 billion deposit of bauxite.

The Dongria Kondhs have lived on the Niyamgiri Hills for thousands of years. Today, they are about 8000 people residing there. Their lifestyle and religion have helped to nurture the areas dense forests and unusually rich wildlife.

In 2007, India's Supreme Court denies Vedanta permission to mine the Niyamgiri Hills, but invites its subsidiary Sterlite to apply for a license.

In 2009, the U.K. Government stepped in and condemned the Vedanta treatment of the Dongria. Their representative was Joanna Lumley who made a film on the Dongria Kondhs. The U.K. Government demanded a change of state of affairs in favour of the Kondhs.

In 2010, India's Environment Minister blocks Vedanta's proposed mine.

In 2011, The Ministers decision is challenged in the Supreme Court.

The struggle continues........

In the Sunday Times of India of 15th April, 2012 an article featured written by Lemuel Lall of TNN.

The Baiga Tribe living in Dindori District of Madhya Pradesh have picked up their Bows and Arrows to stop the felling of their trees by the Forest Department.

The Baiga are a dwindling tribe living in the remote jungles of Ranjara in Madhya Pradesh. The lush jungles have been their home for generations and their trees are their Gods. So, armed with lethal bows and arrows, they stand guard for their gods. All of them, men, women and children are involved.

The local village Panchayat had held frequent meetings to protest against the forest department's policy of cutting trees. Finally, they ran out of patience and asked every able man, woman and child to take up their traditional arms to ensure that not a single tree is felled.

Though the Forest Department states that they have been cutting only dead wood and that if they ignored this it would lead to illegal logging as had happened in Uttarakhand.

But the Baiga are in no mood to listen to any arguments. They are nature worshippers and say that the trees are their gods and felling them would devastate the ecology. They have vowed to die or be jailed for saving their gods.

Forest officials were stunned by the sudden and stiff resistance and are now trying hard to "thaw" the "differences" over tree felling.

Students Union Movements

There are several student unions in India. Before independence, they fought against the British. Today, they fight for many social and community causes. They appear to be much more interested in affiliation with political parties than with the raising of academic standards.

The vast majority of students unions are backed by political parties. Only a handful does not have any political backing.

Table indicates that all political parties in India have a student wing attached to them. This student wing is responsible for involving the youth in various activities related to education and community problems. However, there is a tendency for the youth to become so political in approach that academics take a backseat.

Students Union	Affiliated to
NSUI (National Students Union of India)	Indian National Congress
Trinamool Chhatra Parishad	Trinamool Congress
Bharatiya Vidyarthi Sena	Shiv Sena
Gorkha Janmukti Vidyarthi Morcha	Gorkha Janmukti Morcha
All Assam Students Union	Asom Gana Parishad
All India Students Federation	Communist party of India
Chhatra Rashtriya Janata Dal	Rashtriya Janata Dal
Maharashtra Navnirman Vidyarthi Sena	Maharashtra Navnirman Sena
Muslim Students Federation	Indian Union Muslim League
Samajwadi Chhatra Sabha	Samajwadi party

At this juncture, it is necessary to mention that there are student unions like SIMI (Students Islamic Movement of India). This is an Islamic Fundamentalist Organisation which advocates "liberation of India", by converting to an Islamic Land. It has contacts and links with organisations outside of India, who are generously funding all its unlawful activities. This movement has been proscribed under the Unlawful Activities (Prevention) Act, 1967.

Youth Involvement in Women's Empowerment and Feminist Activities

Women's empowerment is a central concern of the women's movement. It refers to the general process through which women gain knowledge about the structures that oppress them. It is also the process through which people try to change the power imbalances in society.

There have been waves of women's empowerment starting with the US. In the first wave, it was directly linked with political power in the form of voting rights. In the second wave, it was linked with issues such as reproductive rights, workplace rights, and freedom from men's violence. Between the 1960's and 1970's, it took the form of awareness raising groups. It has also led to several controversies for women's sports and self defense courses.

Recently, the concept of empowerment factored heavily in development discourse and practice, particularly among the NGO's (non – government organisations). One of the ways in which women's empowerment is being pursued in developing countries is through micro-credit lending.

Women's movements can become feminist when it concerns survival in their families or when they are faced with situations wherein they are considered subordinate to men.

The feminist movement beginnings were seen in India from the time of the social reformers. The crusade against 'Sati' and 'Child Marriage' has been taken up. Maharishi Karve is called 'The First Feminist of India".

The feminist movement continues in India with a large number of youth to support it, fighting issues like domestic violence, sexual harassment etc.

Concluding Remarks:

1. In the present set up of our democracy, there is an urgent need for the youth to unite and work to restore the faith of the common man in democracy.
2. The youth together can be a very powerful movement towards the overall development of the country.
3. The youth movement will spearhead a new face of India. They are the new generation X in whose hands the future of the country lies. However, this has to be channelized in the right direction.
4. Both urban as well as rural youth are ambitious. Opportunities should be given equally to both.
5. Can the Indian Industry create 40 million jobs by the end of the decade to absorb the huge increase in the youth work force?
6. Channelizing the youth and involving them fruitfully is a huge challenge before the nation.

REFERENCES

Abraham Francis: Contemporary Sociology, an Introduction to Concepts and Theories, Oxford University Press, New Delhi, 2006.

Meyer David S., Whittier Nancy, Robnett Brenda: Social Movements, Identity Culture and the State, Oxford University Press, New York, 2002.

Rao Shankar C.N.: Sociology of Indian Society, S. Chand and Co., New Delhi, 2008 Ed.

Singh K.S. Manohar: Tribal Movements in India, New Delhi, 1983.

The Blackwell Encyclopedia of Sociology, Ed. By George Ritzer, Blackwell Publishing, Australia, 2008, Vol. X.

The International Encyclopedia of Revolution and Protest: 1500 to the Present. Ed. By Immanuel Ness, Wiley – Blackwell, UK, 2009, Vol. V.

Internet References

http://en.wikipedia.org/wiki/chipko_movement

http://en.wikipedia.org/wiki/list-of-student-organisations-in-india

http://www.satp.org

http://www.thehindubusinessline.in/2005/11/15

http://www.merinews.com/article/youth-movement-vital-for-sustaining-democracy

http://india.blogs.mytimes.com/2012/08/27-is-a-youth-revolution-brewing-in-india

http://www.aicc.org.in

Changing Attitudes of Youth Towards Preservation of Sacred Groves

– Dr. **Amrita V. Nadkarni**
– Dr. **Robin D. Tribhuwan**

Introduction

This chapter proposes to study Youth Culture and the approach of youth towards environmental conservation in Thane District. The authors have studied youth over 9 talukas of Thane District living in and around the Sacred Groves of 11 villages. Their responses have been indicative of their approach towards the preservation of the sacred groves that are so important to the tribal and rural community, since all their agricultural activity begins after collective worship of the deities of the grove.

Youth Culture has been traced sociologically, looking at the various schools of thought that have laid the foundations of the modern sociology of youth culture. Adolescence and alienation have also been studied briefly. Following this, the changing attitude of the youth towards the sacred groves of Thane District has been studied.

Are the youth of Thane District getting alienated from their culture which aims at preservation of the sacred groves?

Is theirs a 'sub – culture' of resistance?

Are they learning to reconcile the images of popular culture with the realities they face in Thane District?

Can the youth be viewed as a source of power to create a new identity for the people of tribal and rural Thane?

The Sociology of Youth Culture

According to *Bennet Andy* (2000), the sociological study of youth culture is long and complex. Over the years, youth culture has undergone several stylistic and aesthetic changes. Also, the analytical tools and theoretical perspectives that sociologists' use, in trying to interpret youth culture are changing over time.

According to *Epstein Jonathon* (1998), both social scientists and cultural critics have long been intrigued and confused by youth. Young people sometimes seem like a completely different species from adults. Their habits and idiosyncrasies have always mystified grownups.

There have been several views on youth culture and often those interested in the topic have been baffled to the extent of declaring adolescence itself to be the problem.

From all the Sociological and Cultural studies on youth - three distinct periods of scholarship emerge.

1. The Chicago School (US) – began in the 1920's and 1930's
2. The Birmingham School (England) – began in 1920's and 1930's
3. The Culture Critics of the US (from 1990's till date).

The Chicago School (in the 1920's), laid the foundations of the modern sociology of youth culture. This school constructed a model of Juvenile Delinquency, arguing that when studied in its own context, juvenile delinquency can be shown to be a normal response emerging out of cultural norms. Several studies were made to this effect.

'Street Corner Society' by *Whyte* (1943), wherein he studied the "gangs" who developed the social norms and codes they would need to survive in the town he called 'Cornerville'.

Howard Becker (1963) argued that deviant behaviour was a product of labeling.

Cohen (1964) studied how the 'mods' and 'rockers' were representative as 'folk devils' and caused moral panic which led to a demand for law enforcement and keeping police vigil in the area.

Hall and Critcher (1978) studied how 'mugging' was associated with the Afro – Caribbean males who became the mugging problem.

Cashmore (1984) adopted Merton's means – goals model and argued that there is a gap between the goals of consumption and the channels through which such goals could be achieved. This led to Inter – City Riots where youth battled police and looted shops to seize consumer items like fashion wear, records and stereo equipment.

All the above authors were focusing on the fact that the youth develop a 'Sub-culture of Resistance' to normal codes of conduct.

The Birmingham School, England (Centre for Contemporary Culture Studies) (CCCS) took up the term 'sub-culture' which then became associated with the study of youth. With the publication of CCCS research, British studies of youth culture began to change in two significant ways:

1. The focus moved from youth gangs to style based youth culture. Thus, Teddy Boys, Mods, Rockers, Skinheads rapidly became an integral part of everyday British social life.
2. A Sub-cultural Model of explanation of youth culture was adopted. This sub-culture of the youth had to be understood as a collective reaction of working class youth to the structural changes taking place in British post-war society.

CCCS Theorists like *Willis* (1978) explained homology through The Biker Culture. In this culture there was a homological relationship between the physical features of the bike and the gang. *Hebdige* (1979) explained polysemy through the Tel Quel Group who advocated the Punk Culture, wherein art represented the transformation of commodities and values on the site of the body.

The Cultural Critics of the US focused mainly on Adolescence and Alienation of the youth form the mainstream. *Donna Gaines* (1990) studied adolescent culture and the concept of alienation of adolescents from the mainstream. She conducted an ethnographic study of the lives of adolescents. Her work began with teen suicides and the youth were portrayed as America's forgotten generation. *Henry Giroux* (1983, 1994) is a pragmatic who feels that the alienation can be empowered as 'resistance'. Locations of resistance are the schools and the streets. These are viewed as arenas of struggle, as places where domination by hegemonic culture can be challenged.

Mention also needs to be made of *Liechty* (1995), who conducted a study of youth culture in Kathmandu, Nepal. According to him, Nepali youth culture is a space that is still being created and genuinely contested between younger people, their parents and commercial interests. Developing youth cultures of Kathmandu occupies a tenuous space between village and external modern metropolis. The youth of Kathmandu, says Liechty, are learning to reconcile the Western image with the realities they face in Nepal. This new cultural territory that the youth are discovering is acting as a source of power to create a new cultural identity.

How can all the above literature be applied to the youth of rural and tribal Thane District?

A sacred grove is "A patch of forested land, maybe small or large, dedicated to a local deity or deities, generally believed to be fierce, left untouched by the local people for socio-religious reasons. This patch may have rare trees, medicinal plants and endemic species of birds or animals. Such patches, in their pristine condition, which the local people want to conserve, contribute immensely to the bio diversity of the nation."

To a Sociologist , the Sacred Grove is very closely tied up with the social life of the local people for varied reasons:

1. They feel protected, inspired and healed by them.
2. The local deity reigns completely. E.g. Gaondevi is the village goddess all over the tribal area in their sacred groves in Thane District and she owns all the trees and the rocks and flora and fauna around.
3. Tabooes and traditions are followed for fear of invoking the anger of the deity. These traditions and social values have been followed by the local people for generations and they have helped to conserve the groves.
4. Annual rituals, ceremonies and sacrifices are performed by the villagers to appease the protecting deity and for the benefit of the village.
5. The grove is very much entwined with the socio economic, cultural and religious life of the tribal people. It defines their cultural identity in many ways. These groves are cared for by the local community as they consider them to be of fundamental value.
6. The Sacred Grove is a meeting point for many tribal communities. It pulls them together and establishes a bond between varied communities.

Today, the pace of modernization has begun to deplete the groves and alter the traditional systems protecting them. Values are changing and along with this, so is the 'aura of sacredness' around the groves. The younger generation of the rural and tribal people has developed new ideas which are not conversant with traditional conservation. For them, the profit motive and commercialization of the grove is becoming more important than the reigning deity inside the same. This is not completely because their faith is dying out, but it is their way of combating poverty and ensuring survival.

The threats that the sacred groves face are several viz.

Destruction of Groves for dams, roads, highways and industries

Government ignoring the local community's traditional management and allowing commercial forestry operations to develop.

Groves thrown open to pilgrims and tourists.

Land on which groves are is not declared as forestland

Political interference in the sacred groves.

No effective legislation with respect to sacred groves

Illegal felling of trees.

Impact of Idol worship.

No separate government department or fund for preservation, promotion and maintenance of sacred groves.

Dumping industrial waste into the forest area

Unrestricted drawing of well water by tanker companies

"Booking" of trees by non-locals for commercial purposes

Encroachment for trees having medicinal value

Depletion due to construction of Public Toilets

Threat due to Stone quarrying and mining and Brick Kilns

In the face of the above threats which loom large, and which are leading to the depletion of the sacred groves in Thane district, the youth hold their own ideology with respect to the preservation of sacred groves.

Based on primary and secondary data, the Objectives of the paper are as follows:

1. To understand the concept of sacred groves as perceived by the youth of rural and tribal Thane.
2. To unveil their changing attitudes towards preservation and threats to sacred groves.
3. To present a Model to revive the respect, the values and the aura of sacredness, beliefs and practices those surround the sacred groves in Thane District.

Methodology

A Pilot Study was conducted covering 85 sacred groves out of 11 talukas. Out of the total 85 groves covered by the authors, 11 sacred groves were selected through random sampling method taking every 8th grove over 9 talukas. The total number of houses covered was 2472 and the total number of people over these houses was 7610. Of these, youth were totally 2511 (33%) of the total.

Target Population thus was the youth from the 9 Talukas chosen by random systematic sampling.

The Research Tools used were mainly:

- **Focused Group Discussions:** 10 focused group discussions were held with the youth aged between the ages of 13-19 years. They were given questions to discuss and the discussions were recorded on paper as they spoke.
- **Informal Interviews** were held with the youth and also with the adult population. This was done to find out the attitude of reverence held by the youth towards the sacred groves. All these interviews were conducted in the homes of the youth, in the sacred groves and the fields, as and where the authors could locate them.
- **Observation method** was also used to gather and crosscheck written and recorded data.

Photography was also used to give a clearer picture of the youth.

Main Findings

Summary of the 10 focused group discussions and informal interviews with the youth over 9 talukas of Thane district revealed that 60 per cent of the youth are moving away from the reverence and sacred beliefs associated with the sacred groves. The "aura of sacredness" as it was earlier, is declining today. The threats faced by the sacred groves are not impacting them so much. Reasons for this may be outlined below:

1. **The Power Relations web is very strong.** Government officers, Forest Officials, Industrialists, Contractors and owners of Stone Quarries form a very powerful nexus. The tribal and rural youth do not show any inclination to revolt against such a strong network.
2. There is a tendency among the youth to work **as daily wage laborers or as permanent or temporary workers.** They work at Brick kilns, Sand Mines, Stone Quarries etc. and are away from their homes for long stretches. Their main concern is to earn a large sum of money.
3. **Land Fragmentation.** Ancestral land gets fragmented over the generations as the clan gets enlarged. Thus, there are more cultivators and less share of the agricultural output. The land gets subdivided into smaller pieces generation after generation. E.g. In Rajatpada of Raitali Village, Dahanu Taluka, the ancestral land of the Sutar Clan was subdivided into small fragments to give each son an equal share of the property.

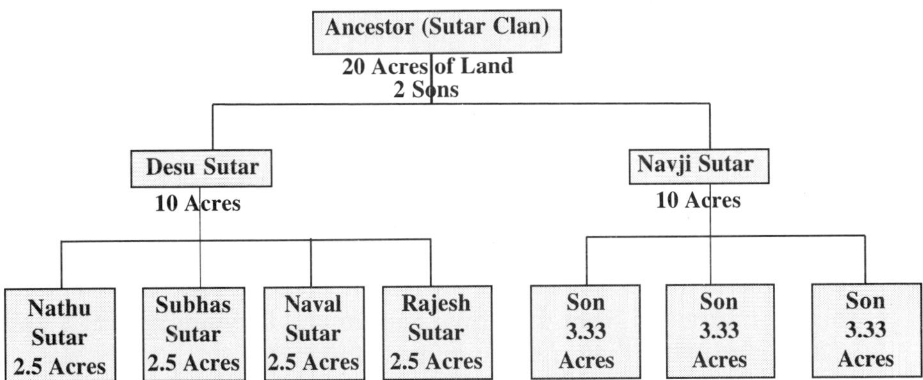

Just as the land of the Sutar Family got fragmented, other families have got even lesser share after fragmentation i.e. a few gunthas which gives them an annual produce that will last only for 2-3 months.

In such a situation, the youth do not harbor any sentiment for the land of their ancestors. Their desire to conduct ancestor worship in the sacred groves also declines. They are thus willing to sell it or rent it out to other families for a sum of money.

4. **Migration for Jobs in the cities.** 60 per cent of the youth interviewed stated that they wished to go to the cities to avail of better opportunities. As per their discussion, they would like to complete good degrees which cannot be done in their village and get good jobs which would ensure a brighter future for them. They were of the opinion that the village

which did not even have a secondary school, nor proper water facilities nor adequate transport would not help them in any way to earn well and have a bright future.

55 per cent of the youth stated that even if they wished to go to the cities, they would like to improve the conditions of their village i.e. they would want to have more bore wells made, to introduce solar cookers and heaters, Solar Electricity and have better vehicles for transport. All this, they emphasized could not be done if they remained in their villages.

5. **Cash vs. Groves** 35 per cent of the youth interviewed were willing to sell the groves if the need arose. The owner of Gaondevi Mandir at Savroli Village, Vikramgad Taluka, Thane, had sold the entire grove of about 5 acres of land to a Christian gentleman by the name of Mr. D'costa who had started his poultry farm there. Some of the youth of Savroli village were employed at the poultry farm.

Allowing encroachment at a price is also something that the youth are willing to consider. They are willing to allow outsiders to "book" trees that give good produce of commercial value. E.g. Chincha (Tamarindus indica), Khajuri, Tadgole (Phoenix sylvestris), Mahua (Madhuca indica). Karvanda (Carissa carandas). The cash that this "booking" rakes in is of greater value to them than the sacred grove.

Concluding Remarks

1. Tribal and Rural youth today are getting educated. They are aware that there are better opportunities outside their villages and that they have a right to go in search of the same.
2. The youth wish to make use of these available opportunities. As Donna Gaines mentions, the concept of alienation is felt by them at this point. They feel alienated from their own culture and they are not yet a part of the culture that they want to migrate to.
3. Among almost 50 per cent of the youth, the fear element is still prevalent with respect to the sacred groves. Even if this fear is declining, it is important to generate the "feeling of sacredness" about the grove. Thus, 50 per cent of the youth still fear the shamans and their prophecies about the deities and about conservation. This aura of reverence needs to be nurtured and strengthened.
4. If there are 30 per cent of the youth who state that they wish to do something for the village, then this desire must be encouraged. They can be made to feel a part not only of their own culture, but also of the place they wish to move to for higher studies.
5. If there is an activist element among the youth of the tribal and rural areas to conserve, it must be encouraged. This will help to garner support and spread awareness about the need for preservation of sacred groves.

Recommendations

1. It is necessary to target Ashram Schools. There are 1,130 Ashram Schools in Maharashtra, both Government and Aided. Sacred grove preservation can be promoted here with the help of Zilla Parishad schools and colleges and NGO's. Awareness can be created among the youth about the necessity to preserve sacred groves.
2. Preservation of Sacred Groves can be one of the major topics for practical work in the Environmental Education programme at school and college level. Project work worth 30 marks is entrusted to students. Both rural/ tribal and urban students can play a role in the promotion of reforestation through the EVE Programme.
3. Sacred Grove Forestry should be funded by the Forest Department and through Integrated Tribal Development Projects (ITDP). This funding can be for:
   (i) Social forestry in and around the schools.
   (ii) Social forestry in and around respective farms
   (iii) Social forestry in and around grazing lands owned by the village
   (iv) Social forestry in and around the sacred groves.
4. The Traditional and Statutory Panchayat has Gram Sabha and Statutory rights. The support of the Panchayat must be sought if the youth are to be involved in Joint Forestry Development Programmes.
5. NGO's can play a very important role by lending their valuable ideas and their support to rope the youth into reforestation programmes.

REFERENCES

Abraham Francis: Contemporary Sociology, An Introduction to Concepts and Theories, Oxford University Press, New Delhi, 2006.

Bennet Andy: Popular Music and Youth Culture: music, identity and place, Macmillan press, London, St. Martin's Press Inc., New York, 2000.

Bennet John W. and Tumin Melvin M.: Social Life, Structure and Function, An Introductory General Sociology, Alfred A Knopf Inc., New York, U.S.A., 1949.

Epstein Jonathon S: Youth Culture: identity in a post modern world, Blackwell Publishing Ltd. 1998.

J.J.Roy Burman: Sacred Groves among Communities, Mittal Publications, New Delhi, 2003

Vartak et al: Focus on Sacred Groves and Ethno botany, Prism Publications, Chembur, Mumbai, 2004.

Man and his Gods: Encyclopedia of the World's Religions, Ed. Geoffrey Parrinder, Hamlyn Ltd. 1974.

Encyclopedia of World Religions, Octopus Books Ltd., London, 1975.

Internet References

http://en.wikipedia.org/wiki/sacred_grove
http://asiatribune.com
www.mahaforest.nic.in
www.thaneforest.org

Age Roles of Youth and Societal Expectations *A Conceptual Note*

– Dr. **Robin D. Tribhuwan**

Age Roles: Cross Cultural Comparison

Age roles are often determined by ones own age. Once age stratum changes as one ages from childhood, through adolescence, youth, adulthood to old age. Every human society develops clearly recognizable signs, rituals and ceremonies surrounding the passage of persons from one age boundary to the next. These are called rites of passage.

"Munj" ritual among the Brahmins of Maharashtra is a male passage rite. Among the Muslims circumcision is a male passage rite. Baptism by immersion is a rite of confirming the membership of an youth in the church among some Christian communities. Tribal societies world over have elaborate rituals, boys or girls must go through to be called youth and adults.

Age roles are culturally determined. The elderly people in the family especially in rural and tribal India are respected. Every society assigns certain roles to its members. Expectations of a society regarding age roles vary. For example, older people are treated as elder statesmen, who deserve all the respect and best in life without working as in Samoa. In other cultures, they are required to do all the work younger members do not want to do.

Role of Youth: Societal Expectations

There was a time, when youth were expected to work in the house, on the farm, at work sites, or in the forest to earn money or gather natural resources for the family.

In the tribal societies, fishing, hunting, honey collection, fetching timber etc. was a job of male youth. The youth in tribal dormitories had several social responsibilities. On the other hand, young girls in tribal societies were assigned the job of collecting Mahua flowers, leaves, fruits, fuel wood, fetching drinking water, cooking food, child rearing and so on.

In the modern societies, parents expect their children to go to schools, colleges, universities and other educational institutes to gain knowledge, a degree or diploma, so as to gain the right kind of employment or business skills. The businessmen expect their youths to learn skills of managing their family business. An actor expects his son and/or daughter to carry on his profession.

Youth, Occupation and Social Responsibilities

Tribhuwan Robin and Kharche Jayshree (2013) have revealed that among the vulnerable groups in the unorganized sector, the children, the adolescent and the youth hardly enjoy these significant phases of life. Their life starts as child laborers or household workers and ends as bonded labourers. The children and youth of the vulnerable groups in unorganized sector are deprived of their rights and privileges. Their parents are helpless and hence their children do not get to enjoy the freedom of the economically well to do families. The parents of the vulnerable groups only expect their children to work, beg or gather resources for survival.

In their book captioned, *"Streets of Insecurity – A Study of Pavement Dwellers"*, Tribhuwan Robin and S. Rangnhild (2003) have observed that the poor pavement dwellers get their daughters married off into another family at an early age to shift their economic responsibility. They hardly spend any money on the wedding. Some times it is a mere ritual of worshipping a photograph or a statue of a deity, before the couple starts living as husband and wife. In doing so the young couple takes responsibility as adults, at an early age.

Contrary to youth in unorganized sectors and tribal societies, we find youth in the Information Technology (I.T.) sector delay marriages adopt small family norms for the sake of occupational and economic stability.

Khatereh A. (2012) in her study captioned, "Life style of I.T. personnel" observed that the I.T. youth get married late, and produce a child or two for the sake of occupational and economic stability. In fact, getting a job first, an apartment first, be it owned or rented, and getting married has become a priority of most youth in urban areas.

Live in Relation

Hasnain Nadeem (1987) has reported about a form of marriage in some tribal communities, namely, marriage by probation, wherein a boy and a girl are allowed to live in the village together, till they decide to formally get married. Tribhuwan Robin and Finkenauer Maike (2003) observed this form of marriage among few Warli couples. Subash Nathu Sutar, lived in Rajadpada of Raitali village, in Dahanu block of Thane district, with his wife for three years, produced a daughter and was formally married. He had another son after he was formally married.

Live in relations are very common in the West. Young boys and girls live together have pre-marital sex and get married whenever they are convinced that their marital relations will work in future. This concept is creeping amongst the migrant students and youth who do not get accommodation in the hostels. They live in an apartment with one or more males or females.

Change in Age Roles

The age characteristics of the world's population have changed drastically over few decades. Globalization, urbanization, modernization and technological advancement are no doubt influencing the people's traditional concept of age roles.

Youngsters and children are looking at life differently. There is an urgent need to carry out social science research on how youth from various sections of Indian Societies look at life and their changing role. The impact of various forces that influence the changing roles of youth.

The Poverty of Youth

Wallace and Wallace (1945:32) have pointed out that, low income is a problem that the elderly share with the young. Today's youth, especially those without educational training, have a high rate or unemployment. When they can find jobs, they are often discriminated against in salary. Knowing that they are hungry for jobs, employers often pay less to wolrkers in the sixteen to twenty four year old group. The situation is getting worse.

Studies by Breman Jan (2000) Panjiar Smita (2007), Tribhuwan Robin and Patil Jashree (2008), Tribhuwan Robin and Kharche Jayshree (2012), Tribhuwan Robin and Shende Sadashiv (2013) have revealed that the youth and adults in the informal sector work hard and are paid very less, in India.

Concluding Remarks

As economic and social needs change, the roles and statuses of youth change. In the western countries gender roles and age strata are changing to accommodate new information and new ways of living. This trend is on a slower pace in rural areas of developing countries.

REFERENCES

Tribhuwan Robin & Kharche Jayshree, 2013, Child Labour and Rights Issues: A Study of Migrant Labourers, Discovery Publishing House, New Delhi.

Tribhuwan Robin & Kharche Jayshree, 2012, Hard Labour: Poor Pay in Changing Trends in Employment in India, Pragati College, Dombivili.

Tribhuwan Robin and S. Rangnhild (2003) Streets of Insecurity, Discovery Publishing House, New Delhi

Tribhuwan Robin & Patil Jayshree, 2008, Stone Quarry Workers, Discovery Publishing House, New Delhi.

Tribhuwan Robin and Shende Sadashiv (2013).

Panjiar Smita 2007, Locked Homes, Empty Schools, Zuben, New Delhi.

Tribhuwan Robin and Finkenawer M. 2003 Threads Together, Discovery Publishing House, New Delhi

Breman Jan & Das Arvind, 2003 Down and Out: Labouring Under Global Capitalization, Oxford University Press, New Delhi

Wallace R.C. and Wallace W.D., 1945 Sociology, Allyn and Bacon, Inc.Boston.

Tribal Youth Associations and Organisations
A Potential Base for Development

– Dr. **Robin D. Tribhuwan**
– Dr. **Jayshree V. Kharche**

Introduction

Development is all about people. It is an anthropocentric concept, that advocates maximum participation of people in planning, implementing, monitoring, following up and evaluating development programmes. It is a process that provides choices to free ignorance, illiteracy, dependence, poverty, misery and servitude.

Most development experts across the globe firmly believe in advocating people centered development approach. Development modules by international and national development experts, activists and N.G.O.s advocate the concept of building on what is available with people. Helping people to help themselves, searching their "talent bank", potential, human and natural resources.

This chapter throws light on the various youth associations and organisations in tribal societies. The occasions that bring and bind the youth together. The development potentials, these youth associations and organisations have. Finally, this paper gives suggestions to use these youth groups for promoting development and welfare of the tribal's.

Youth Associations and Organisations

Research studies by Anthropologists, Ethnographers and Sociologists have revealed that some of the major tribal associations and organisation are as below:

1. Youth Dormitories

In his book captioned, "The Muria and their Ghotul," Elwin Verrier (1947:269) states that the concept of village youth dormitories are distributed throughout the world. Peal S.E. (1893) was one of the first writers to examine the communal barracks of primitive races.

Hutton Webster (1908) wrote on Primitive secret societies. E. Westermarck (1938) has written on Three Essays on sex and Marriage." Malinowski in his book, "The sexual life of savages" (1932) writes about bukumatual a decorated bachelors house in the Trobiand Islands, V Fric and Paul Radin (1906) have written about village youth dormitories in many parts of America, Haimendorf (1938) has written on the Morung system of the Konyak Nagas.

All the studies on Ghotul (youth dormitories) reveal that there are two types of dormitories namely; uni-sex (male or female) or bi-sexual (male & female) dormitories. The functions of these dormitories are to socialize the youth on social, cultural, political familial and sexual life.

2. Dance Troops

In their book captioned, Tribal dances of India (Tribhuwan Robin and Tribhuwan Preeti (1999) have reported serveral dance forms of tribals in India. Some of the major ones are as below:

Table 5.1: Tribal Dance Forms

Sr.No.	Tribe	Dance Forms	Status
1.	Naga	1. Horn Bill Dance 2. Honey Bee 3. Ho-Dance	Nagaland
2.	Gond	4. Rela Dance	Maharashtra
3.	Warli	5. Tarpa dance 6. Kambad dnace 7. Gaurie Dance 8. Dhumsa	Maharashtra
4.	Bhil	9. Dhol dance 10. Chhibali	Maharashtra Madhya Pradesh

Most of the participants in the tribal dance troupes are youth. These dance troupes are a potential base for launching development programmes. There is a need to promote and preserve these dance forms as well.

3 **Music troupes**

Tribal music troupes consists of musicians, who play wind, string, rhythm and side rhythm instruments. Singers are also part of the same. The Koli Mahadev, Koli Malhar, Kokna, Warli etc. tribes of Maharashtra have "Bhajan Mandals" who sing bhajans using pakawas, tabla, nal (rhythm instruments) harmonium and cymbals. The members of the musical troupes are a source of planning development and educational programmes.

4. **Drama troupes**

Some of the famous drama troupes among the Bhils and Koknas of Thane are Bohada and Songadya troupes. Dandar drama troupes are seen among the Gonds. Majority of the characters or actors, who are part of these drama parties are male youth.

Adv. K.C. Padvi the member of Legislative Assembly, Government of Maharashtra used Songadya drama as a medium to create awareness regarding health, development programmes impact of alcoholism on the lives of tribals etc. This traditional folk media proved to be effective. Drama troupes hence are a potential base for creating awareness of development, programmes.

5. **Financial Associations**

In his book captained, Fairs and Festivals of Indian Tribes Tribhuwan Robin (2003) has shown that there are traditional organisation and associations among tribals that are responsible for handling accounts during fairs, festivals and dramas. The Traditional Panchayat prominently takes the lead in most situational; however these are financial associations who keep a track of tribal and non- tribal traders and take money from them for the space provided to them during fairs and festivals. These financial associations are important assets to base development programmes upon.

6. **Associations of the Artisans**

Traditional paintings of the Warli, Gond, Rathwa, Bhil and Soara tribes have gained commercial significance, since the last 3 decades. The paintings of these tribes are in great demand, both in India and abroad. These painters have visited several metropolitan cities in India for exhibition and sale of their paintings. Some of them have gone abroad as well.

Even other artisans involved with wooden craft, metal craft, mask making, bamboo craft etc are earning in cash. Most of these artisans have formed financial associations. Now these associations of the artisans should be targeted to base development programmes and schemes.

7. **Other Associations**

Besides, the associations mentioned about, there are several other associations that need to be studied and exposed through social science research.

The Binding Force

What binds the youth together into traditional organisations and associations? As aptly pointed out by Anthropologists that, culture is historically developed, learnt and shared behavior, it is the totality of socially transmitted behaviour. Roles and responsibilities of youth are governed by cultural laws, norms, rules and traditions. Tribal youth respect and rever these norms and play their roles in different cultural situations and contexts to fulfill the expectations of their society.

They perform their roles as per the demands of cultural norms in different situations. Thus, the Warli males perform Kambad Dance in times of famine, to please the goddess of food grains Kansari.

The youth both males and females are expected sing; dance throughout the night, at the same time guard the village from thieves and wild animals. Tribal youth come together due to other reasons as well. These are as below:

1. For hunting games
2. During Sports
3. Dancing, Singing and Playing music
4. Festival and Fair celebrations
5. For drinking mauha liquor, toddy, madi, rice beer etc.
6. For discussing personal, familial and communal problems
7. For chewing tobacco, smoking or chewing kharra
8. For swimming cdlecting minor forest produce etc.

Tribal Youth Organisations and Development Programmes

Experiments to use tribal youth associations and organisations to plan and implement development programmes have been successful. The Bhartiya Agro Industries Foundation (BAIF) under the leadership of Dr. Ashwini Ghorpade, launched the micro-credit finance programme among the Warli tribal women, using their traditional association called 'Wavli' meaning a group of women who save money and do not reveal the saved amount to their husbands. As per the traditional norms the husbands do not enquiry about the amount saved nor quarrel with their wires. Dr. Ashwini Ghorpade was successful in combining the concept of self help group of young women with that of the Wavli tradition.

A Pune based NGO captioned Institute of Development Educational Activities and studies supported the young Warli female artists to market their paintings. Padmabhushan late Dr. Rajnikant Arole trained Traditional Birth Attendants regarding maternal and child health case on scientific lines.

The Academy of Development Science launched the grain bank programme with the help of Traditional Panchayats in tribal communions of Raigad district.

Concluding Remarks

Youth of any nation are an asset to their country. Nine per cent of India's population is tribal. The quality of the life of tribal youth is significant. Efforts should therefore be made to study the potentials and talents of tribal youth, understand their problems explore the behavioral patterns that exist in their traditional associations and organisations. Then build on what is available. Given below are few recommendations.

Recommendations

1. **Reforestation/Plantation**

   Provide financial incentives in the form of schemes to tribal youth to plant trees, medicinal herbs, bamboos and vegetables in their kitchen garden in their village on their farms, on fallow land and in their school and college premises.

2. **Folk media**

   Involve the youth by giving financial assistance or incentives in kind for preparing songs, dramas, poems proverbs in their dialect to pass on health and development related themes and messages.

3. **Employment and carrier guidance**

   Create awareness of employment, self employment and career guidance among the youth organisation.

4. **Self-help Groups**

   Use youth organisation to start SHGs in tribal areas for both males and formals.

5. **Talent Search**

   Efforts should be made to search talents among tribal youth, by identifying their association and organisation and each youth should be followed up to develop his talent.

6. **Traditional Medical Practitioners**

   Tribhuwan Robin (1998), has classified seven types medical practitioners among the Thakars. It is recommended that the young boys and girls, that is the educated children of the traditional medical practitioners the shamans, bone setters, herbalists masseurs and traditional midwives be trained on scientific lines and observed in primary health care as Health workers, I.C.D.S workers, helpers, ANM's etc.

7. **Sports Potentials**

   Dr. Jaiprakash Duble. former district sports officer, Gadchiroli, identified 400 tribal youth who were good in swimming, running, fast walking, shorting, archery, high jump etc. He trained them and about 300 youth were able to participate in state and national level sports events. Similarly tribal youth in the country having sports potential should be identified trained coached and sent for representing state and national level sports events.

8. Career Guidance

Career guidance and trainings should be compulsorily organized in 11th, 12th grades and colleges in tribal areas.

9. Preservation of music songs and dance forms

There are 14 Tribal research and Training Institutes in the country. These institutes should make efforts to preserve tribal music, songs and dance forms by working with tribal youth associations and organisation.

10. Co-operatives of the youth

Efforts should be made to form co-operatives of tribal youth, especially those vulnerable groups working in the unorganized labour sector as brick kilns, salt pan, stone quarries workers.

REFERENCES

Peal S.E. (1859:3) The Communal Barracks of Primitive Races JASB Vol. LXI.

Hutton Webster (1908), Primitive Secret Societies New York.

Westermarck, 1938, Three Essays on Sex and Marriage, London.

Malinowski, 1932, The Sexual Life Savages, London.

Elwin Verrier, 1997, The Muria and their Ghotul, Oxford University Press, Delhi.

Vidyarthi L.P. & Rai B.K (1985), Tribal Cultures of India, Concept Publishing House, New Delhi.

Tribhuwan Robin & Tribhuwan P. 1999, Tribal Dances of India, D.P.H. New Delhi.

Tribhuwan Robin (2003), Fairs & Festivals of Indian Tribes, Discovery Publishing House New Delhi.

Cornered in the Shadows

– Ms. **Insha Khan**

Amidst progressive and developing nation building, there is a growing concern of women safety and security. In India where on one hand women are awarded the Padmashrees and Padma Vibhushans for their contribution and on the other side the same is ravaged brutally sometimes in the form of bride burnt alive for Dowry or a modern college going girl gang raped in Broad day light. There is no doubt that the country is walking in the right direction for a brighter tomorrow where infrastructure, Trade and commerce, scientific advancement and many more fields are flourishing but holistic societal welfare is being compromised.

Months pass by after the unfortunate death of a 23 year old who was Gang raped in the capital by six men in a running bus and the Anti-rape Law is juggled between political parties and their never ending ideological differences. It took no time in spite of all the outrage and uproar for ten or more cases of rape, murder and molestation to appear as a proof to the nation, shouting and shaking each one of us from the roots to stop watching and start reacting. Women from all spheres marched on the roads of different cities and states of the country condemning the pseudo empowered status of women where she is portrayed to be independent economically and not socially.

Candle light marches or peace rallies are not sufficient because even in these procession women are rubbed and touched indecently where men purposely join the crowd to feel or molest girls. Many a times cases go unreported due to unwillingness on the part the families and women as well who fear the consequences. Laws are formulated and implemented but it is no guarantee or certificate of confirmation to prevent anti-social activities carried by unpredictable mind frames settled in various corners of the country. One cannot blame or allege a particular group or party responsible for the atrocities being pushed on women, be it the Khap Panchayat which functions as the self-appointed moral guardian of forming senseless and oppressive rules or diktats to protect females. The Khaps may believe that a woman is to be protected by hook or by crook but under Universal Declaration of Human Rights every person has equal liberty to life and freedom. Under no circumstances can a girl be forced to marry a man forty years elder to her or due to his higher caste to improve the status of the girl and her family.

Equipping women with concepts of equality and freedom is not the solution. The larger issue of the unfair attitude towards a girl not just in rural India but within educated urban masses as well is a matter of grave concern. Why is a woman always asked to be keep quite when a man is speaking?, how is it that a woman gets beaten up by her in laws in the city and nobody complains?, what is the mistake of those young girls whose mother could not bear a boy child and she is brutally burnt in broad day light?, how can women with a group of friends be molested by a mob and people just watched like a street show?. These are some pivotal questions posed on the society of those who claim to be its moral guardians every day but they seem to go unheard.

Launching a campaign or setting up NGO's is not enough in the struggle of washing away the deep rooted prejudices against women. Basic mentality of a layman has to be altered and not just of the intellectual class who already are involved in the issue. Gathering socialites and requesting a celebrity to address the public in a five star hotel only deviates from the main topic. To empower the woman of our country we need to step out in the field sparing sometime from our regular routine to teach and convince a woman about the significance of her existence.

Constructing platforms or forums to eradicate this inequality calls for independence of women with responsibility and stop making ineffective policies to impress the nation or its citizen time to time. In a town of western Uttar Pradesh a Dalit lady is set ablaze by men from the upper caste only because her son was accused of eloping with a girl of another caste. Cases of such heinous crime against women in the country are countless but there have been very few actions taken to curb or fight it from the core as the matter vanishes gradually from the media's agenda and public view.

Not all women in urban areas are strong to voice their opinion in an indirect male dominated world. Here men claim to consider women a part of the decision making and there in the rural lands men openly suppress her unsaid ideas on potential matters of growth and development. A woman in ancient India had a very different role to play compared to women in the western world. She was held in high esteem like a Devi and mata who exhibited energy and positivity for the survival of mankind. The scenario today has not changed much but the only thing that has evolved is the outlook. Earlier also women goddess were worshiped and even now. The behaviour and intentions towards a woman in real life is very different compared to the dedication and affection expressed to a woman in the form of a goddess.

They say that Durga and Saraswati are the epitome of piousness then why does the society lack the wisdom to extend basic right of freedom to a woman who deserves to live in an equal environment. A woman's ultimate goal is not always to surpass men but live in a surrounding which allows them to breadth fresh air of equality and no subjugation. With education comes broad-mindedness which blesses a woman with independence from all types of oppressions and instils in her the self-confidence to construct a pathway to a brighter future. To many of us it sounds a myth that even today in well to do families a boy's preference is taken to be a priority and a girl's choices are listed to be secondary.

Till we don't get rid of our 'forget it' attitude, we will never be able to challenge a typical patriarchal society. We have to realize that India is not just about modern men in the metropolitan cities but majorly about men who daily suppress their women directly or indirectly. Unfortunately even education at times fails to clear their minds and the entire purpose of shaping change is defeated.

Generally when a woman opposes eve-teasing on the road by collecting some attention for people to realize the issue, she is considered to be a woman who likes to attract limelight. When she approaches her father or brother regarding the trouble the suggestions given to her are very discouraging. They recommend her to avoid the cheap attitude of men and move on without understanding the consequences. If every woman sat at home assuming that her cause to fight injustice has no future then India in hundred years would never had given birth to feminist movements and its glorious success could never been a part of the world history.

Part – II

Social and Economic Problems of Youth

Exploitation of Migrant Labourers of Alang-Sosiyo Recycling Shipyard
A Case Study

– Dr. **Robin D. Tribhuwan**
– Mr. **Sadashiv S. Shende**

Introduction

Alang and sosiyo are two coastal villages, situated in Talaja tahasil in Bhavnagar district in the state of Gujarat, is one of the five largest recycling shipyards in the world. The village is 50 kms. away from the main Bhavnagar district head quarters. The other four recycling ship yards are in the world are at:

- **Chitgaon** – in Bangladesh
- **Gedani** – in Pakistan
- **Aliaga** – in Turkey
- **Giangin** – in China

There are 183 plots spread over in an area stretching upto 15 to 20 Kms. along the coast of Arabian Sea. Each plot has around 180-200 labourers who are paid by the contractors and have no communication or interaction with the owners of the plot. The owners pay a deposit of Rs. 10,00,000/- called *"Pagdi"*, which is non-refundable. This money is paid to the Gujarat Mari Time Board, by the owners. The Gujarat Mari Time Board is a Government under taking organisation that runs the yard at Alang . Besides, the deposit, the owners pay six monthly rent of 10,00,000/- as well.

The owners mostly belong to Marwari, Jain, Yadav and Guajarati communities from Gujarat, Uttar Pradesh, Bihar and Jharkhand. They buy passenger, navy, army, goods etc. ships from different countries, dismantle them in the recycling ships yard and sell the new and old items of the ships in Alang & other markets.

On an average each company owners purchases a ship for 16 millions US dollars and makes an approximate profit of 5 to 8 million US dollars. With in a span of six months, he makes an approximate profit of 15 to 25 million US dollars. It's a huge business and hence there is a though competition among the owners.

The Migrant Labourers

As mentioned earlier, each plot is owned by a owner, who has to his disposal 150-200 migrant labourers. It is estimated that there are 30 to 35 thousand labourers, in Alang-Sosiyo recycling ship yard. Like ants devouring a dead animal the ship yard workers use blow torches to cut a part the ship. Most of these labourers are from Bihar, Jharkhand, Orissa and Uttar Pradesh. Around 80 per cent of the labourers are youth belonging to the age-group 18-35 years of age. Almost all the labourers are males, with few exceptions of female labourers. They live in the recycling ship yard for 8-9 months and go back home for a period of 3-4 months.

Classification of Labourers

The authors have classified these labourers into four categories namely:

1. Batli wala – Cylinder transporters
2. Cylinder wala – Cylinder operators
3. Jodidar – Electricians, who remove wiring network from the ship.
4. Mazdoor – Helpers, who help other labourers and transport goods from the ship to the trucks.

Mukerdams: The Middlemen

The owners of the scrap ship companies, bank heavily on the mukerdams who extract maximum work from the migrant labourers for very less payment. They are supported by the goons, who see to it that no unions of laborers are formed. That,no one voice their opinion against social and economic exploitation, That no demonstrations, agitations take place. The poor and in secured migrant labourers are aware of the "power and power-relationship of the mukerdams and their owners" hence prefer to be silent about their rights and exploitation.

Settlements of the Migrant Labourers

The labourers live in temporary houses of 300-500 sq ft. These houses are made up of ply wood walls and temporary roofs of tin, cement sheets or tiles as it were. In every house there are 10 to 15 labourers from their respective states. Usually relatives, friends and labourers belonging to the same village, district or state live under a roof. They take turns to cook food, fetch fire wood, water, clean the house and so on. Some of them fix the responsibility of house hold work to the younger fellows.

Facilities and Civic Amenities

There is no electricity, tap water, drinking water, drainage, toilet and bathroom facility in their houses. The Gujarat Mari Time Board provides them drinking water. Every house gets 20 liters of water per week. Water supply is a big problem. The labourers take bath in the open. Since there are no individual public toilets the labourers go out on the shore for defecation Medical & health facilities are prevalent in Alang town.

Research Methodology

The method of collecting data, analyzing it, interpreting and presenting the same is given below:

1. **Locale of the study**

   The present Study was carried out in Alang, recycling ship yard, situated in Talaj, block of Bhavnagar district, in the state of Gujarat, India.

2. **Target population**

   Migrant labourers belonging to the age group 18 to 35 were the main respondents. Besides, the labourers, the mukerdams, restaurant & grocery shop owners too were interviewed. The private & Government Doctors practicing in Alang were randomly interviewed to understand the health problems of the labourers.

3. **Method of data collection**

   The researchers collected both primary & secondary data. Primary data was gathered using an interview guide. Relevant secondary sources were read & incorporated in relevant portions of the paper.

4. **Research tools**

   Since the data was qualitative in nature, an interviews guide was designed for the migrant labourers, the murkerdams, the doctors and other key informants. The data was gathered by conducting informal & focused group interviews.

5. **Analysis**

   The data was analyzed manually, as it was qualitative in nature.

Major Findings

Based on the observations, focused group discussions and informal interviews with respondents including photography, the main findings of the study are:

1. **Long hours of hazardous work**

   The labourers work for 12 to 14 hours a day in hazardous situation. Labourers, who operate gas cylinders get exposed to the hot flames & the gas. The helpers and other labourers have to work in extreme hot &

humid climates. The electricians & gas operators have to climb on heights to remove the wire & do soldering work. There are often risks of falling from heights.

2. **Health Problems**

The labourers revealed that they suffer from following health problems:

(a) **Respiratory problems** – Due to inhalation of gas & poisonous smoke that is liberated while soldering, they become victims of respiratory problems.

(b) **Burns** – while, handling flames.

(c) **Eye problems** – Due to constant eye contact with flames, and working in heat, they suffer from eye problems.

(d) **Skin disorders** – Due to exposure to humid climate, constant sweating and not taking having regular bath, unhygienic conditions, not washing clothes regularly etc, they become victims of skin disorders.

(e) **Digestive disorders** – Such as ulcers of intestines, cirhosis of the liver etc are caused due to excess drinking.

(f) **Sexually Transmitted Infections** –

The young & married labourers also revealed that majority of them are males and live in the recycling ship yard for nine months. On Sunday they go to the brothel centers and street based sex workers. Some of them also revealed that young lads in a group also become victim of homo sexuality.

It is quite possible that the prevalence of HIV among these migrant labourers must be high. There in an argent need to conduct medical and health check-up of these labourers so an to get accurate statistics on health problems of these workers.

3. **Hard labour – poor pay**

As aptly pointed out by Tribhuwan Robin & Kharche (2012), Tribhuwan Robin & Shende Sadashiv (2012), panjiar Smita (2007), Tribhuwan Robin & patil jayshree (2013) in their research studies, that most labourers in the unorganized labour sector work very hard for long houses to get poorly paid.

The migrant labourers of the Alang recycling ship yard ore no exception to this rule. They work for 12 to 14 hours in hazardous environment and are poorly paid. On an average a labourers gets Rs. 60 to 250/- per day, but that us on paper. The labourer's attendance muster Is maintained by the mukerdam, who sees to it that the labourers work for 2 months and get a salary of 15 days only.

The murkerdam decides, how much money the labourers should get monthly and also by the end of his tenure of 8-9 months every year. He decides the amount of loan to be given to the labourer, while returning home. In case of accidents at work place, the murkerdam decides, whether the labourer has to be hospitalized or sent to a private practitioner. The labourers also revealed, that they do not get any financial compensation for accidents, injuries and even death, while at work. They are deprived of their social & economic security as daily wage labourers.

On an average a labourer who gets Rs. 60/- per day works for 200 days in a year should ideally get Rs. 27,000.00/-. However, he only gets 15,000/- because he has to give some bribe to the murkerdam so that he gets salary on time out of the 27,000/- rupees, he spends on himself Rs. 7500/- and the balance 7500/- is sent home by money order. Thus, by the end of the season, he is felt with nothing. He then borrows money (loan) from the contractor (murkerdam) an interest . When he returns back to the recycling yard, the murkerdam subtracts the amount along with interest per month. The labourers does not understand, why & how his interest & corpus loan amount gets cut every month. This hooks him into the vicious cycle of bonded labour.

4. **Bonded labour** – While holding focus group discussions with the labourers, it was observed, that a majority of them borrow loan and are indebted, therefore they are hooked into the vicious cycle of bonded labour.

5. **Muscle power versus bonded labour**

The murkerdam have strong men from the rabari (nomadic) community to control the labourers, at place of work. They too have goons in the native villages & blocks of the labourers. If a labourer who takes loan and does not come back for work, is pressurized & threatened in his place of original & is forced to be in the recycling ship yard. The poor bonded labourers have to bow down before the muscle power.

6. **Vigilant watch over labourers**

The murkerdam, his supervisors and the muscular men hired by the murkerdams keep a vigilant watch over the labourers so as extract maximum work with in a span of 10 to 14 hours a day. They get 15 minutes break twice a day and 30-40 minutes lunch break. The labourers are not allowed to go out of the recycling ship yard during work hours. If he comes late, he is marked absent. If he is sick, he is not paid for that day.

7. **Attendance Musters –** It was observed that the attendance muster are kept in the custody of the murkerdam Even the records of loan & its interest are with the murkerdam.

8. **No labourer union**

It is surprising to note that there is no single union of labourers to voice their opinion against exploitation & injustice done to them. The murkerdam & the owners keep a strict check on this.

9. What attract the labourers to Alang and sosyo ?

Despite of indebtedness, bonded labourer, socio-economic exploitation, social, economic and political insecurity, the youth migrate to Alang and sosyo away from their families for 8 to 9 months, because survival without job, food & proper shelter back home is a dream and mirage for them and their families.

10. How do their family members survive ?

The family members of these labourers survive on the little amount of money sent by them. Their family members work as daily wage labourers, beg, collect Minor Forest Produce and some how manage to survive.

11. Risks at the recycling ship yard

An article captioned Toxic watch – Alliance Against corporate crimes and pollution, posted by Krishnaat and translated by Christopher Sultan from the German, reported following facts about the Alang-sosyo recycling ship yard (http:/www.spiegel.de)

1. **Ships dismantled in 2012**

   According to the above mentioned article, a record number of more than 1,000 ships were scrapped world wide, in 2012 India accounted for the largest number, 527, followed by Bangladesh, Pakistan and china
2. European ship owners prefer to dump their defunct ships in south Asia, where there are few environmental problems and occupational security regulations, but where steel is all the more valuable. The scrapping companies pay about us dollars 400 per ton for the ships. The high-quality steel used to make the vessels is in great demand as a resource. Recycling ships currently satisfies 9 per cent of India's demand for steel.
3. The 6 kilometer road to the world's largest ship grave yard is like a giant bazaar. Pots, beds, TV sets ... every thing that crews of the scrapped ships once used on broad ... are stacked up for sale in this bazaar.
4. In Pakistan, more than 20 ship yard workers died and more than 150 were injured in 2011. In Allang, 173 workers have died in more than 170 ship yards since 2011, killed by falling steel parts or burn to death in explosions. Workers are some times bare foot as they climb over the ships, and toxic waste is often incinerated on the beadle. On October 6th, 2013, six workers died in a fire in Alang as they were dismantling the oil tanker namely Union Brave on the beach.
5. The ship scrapping company, owners claim that they leave a "green pass", which confirms compliance with ISO environmental standards. The author if this article reviewed say, never the less, these is still no valid international standard specifically for the scrapping industry.

Concluding Remarks

The ship scrapping company owners of south Asian countries are literally fighting and competing for every ship, because of the valuable steel which fetches them high amounts of money. The people of China, already the world's largest ship builders, are vigorously establishing scrapping operations. They need the out-of-commission ships badly. They have invested a lot of money in new facilities and new the price of steel in the country is falling, they have there fore to fight for every ship.

The Indian ship scrapping companies negotiate over the price of steel portion & offer more to the ship sellers. This is possible because the labourers are paid less as compared to the labourers in china. In china the workers wear helmets. When toxic material or asbestos are disposed of, the workers in China put on protective suits and gas masks. Well, these preventive and protective measures are not implemented for the ship recycling labourers in India and hence the degree of physical, social & economic in security among the migrant Indian labourers at the ship yards is high.

It is high time that the labour unions in Gujarat & even in other states take a note of this, and help there labourers to lead a misery free life at the ship yards.

Occupational Shift Among the Kanphate Gosavi Youth

– Dr. **Robin D. Tribhuwan**
– Ms. **Swati S. Kadam**

Introduction

In his paper captioned "Gosavi", that was published in the People of India, Maharashtra, volume XXX, part one, Mandal H.K. (1993: 754-759), presented a brief ethnographic profile of the Gosavi of western Maharashtra. The members of this caste are principally found in Thane, Pune, Satara, Sindhudurg and other districts. Mandal H.K.(1993: 754-759), states that although they call themselves Gosavi, but to others they are known by several synonyms such as Goswami, Gosai, Nath, Jogi etc.

They claim that they are followers of Gorakhshnath and belong to the shaivite sect., Mandal H.K. (1993),states that they belong to the shudra varna. The Gosavi are divided into following sub-groups: Raj-Giri, Bharat, Puri, Jogi, Giri, Nath, Daori, Kanphata, and Sanyasi. These sub-groups were formed based on different occupations of the community people.

The Raj Giri and Bharti were engaged in worshiping acts as priests of the temple. The Mahanta (religious chief) is selected from them. The Puri were cultivators. The Jogi, Giri and Nath used to beg in different forms. The Daori were also traditional beggers and begged with a damru & trishul from door to door.

The "Kanphata" or "Kanphate" roamed from door to door to pierce the ears of children and young girls. They are very adept in their techniques. The Sanyasi are those who abandon the desire of the world and body. Among these groups are the Raj-Giri and the Bharati hold higher status. (Russell R.V & Heeral R.B, 1916)

Mandal H.K (1993) and several other researchers are of the view that the poor socio-economic condition and frequent tendency to migrate has resulted in the integration of their family structure forming nuclear ones and that they are mostly sporadic in the multi-ethic & caste village.

Objectives of the Study

Given the above background, the present study aims to unravel:

1. A brief profile of the traditional life of the Kanphate Gosavi.
2. The problems faced by the youth of this community.
3. The occupational changes that have taken place among the Kanphate youth.

Research Methodology

The present study has been conducted in eight villages and four tahsils in Satara district of the state of Maharashtra. Researchers interviewed 100 youth. Focused group discussions using an interview guide were conducted. A survey of 200 households was conducted. Both qualitative and quantitative data was analyzed scientifically. Since the focus of the paper was on occupational shift the other statistical data was not projected.

Traditional Life of the Kanphate Gosavi

Origin of their Name

The term Kan-means, ears and phate means one who pierce ears. The traditional occupation of the Kanphate Gosavi was to pierce ears of children, young girls & women. They would go from door to door to pierce ears of children & teenagers. In return, they would get food grains, vegetables, pulses, or cooked food. Sometimes, they received money as well. During the "fairs", they would earn more than the normal days.

Besides piercing ears, they begged for food & money. Fishing & hunting was yet another source of earning their lively hood. Interestingly, we observed that majority of the Kanphate Gosavi living near farms or outskirts of the village had trained dogs that are used for hunting cats, hare, jackals, wild boars, deer etc. In times of crisis, even now these dogs are used for hunting. The dogs are also useful in guarding their houses at night, watching & guarding the fish and crabs caught by them.

Native Place

The respondents interviewed said they migrated from Rajasthan, their native place.

Dialect

The Kanphate Gosavi speak a different dialect called "Gosavi" which is a mixture of Hindi, Marathi, Gujarati & Marwari.

Clans

The Kanphate Gosavi revealed that their original clan names are different from what they have adapted after settling down in Satara.

These clans names are as below:

Rajasthani Clan	Maharashtrian Surname
1. Rathod	1. Patole, Jadhav, Atole.
2. Umat	2. Chavan, Umat
3. Padiyar	3. More, Shelke
4. Solanki	4. Salunke
5. Gohil	5. Gole
6. Ghatad	6. Ghadge
7. Kale	7. Kale
8. Pawar	8. Pawar
9. Mangale	9. Mangale
10. Makwane	10. Makwane
11. Bamani	11. Jadhav

Among themselves, they give importance to their traditional Rajasthani Clans. While fixing marriages, they first consider their original Rajasthani Clans. On enquiring, why they shifted to Maharashtrian surnames. They revealed that they wanted to be identified with Maharashtra. The Kanphate Gosavi do not marry among the same clan.

Festivals

Dasara & Holi are their main festivals. They do not celebrate these festivals with other settlements. Each clan has its own rituals. During Holi an elderly person of the Thana (hamlet) lights the Holi. He is known as "Mankari". They offer chicken to the burning fire. Holi is celebrated for 3-5 days. On the fifty day, they distribute sweets, prepared from jaggery, gram, wheat and dry coconuts, etc. This sweet is known as gode ghugari.

Fairs

Traditionally, they participated in every fair in their region.

Nomadic Life

They led nomadic life traditionally. Most of them have settled on encroached lands. Semi-nomadic life is still seen among them.

Panchayat

Their traditional panchayat is known as "Jat panchayat" or "Phad". The decision makers are known as "panch ganga". Every clan is represented by one "panch". The traditional panchayat decides disputes of family and the community.

Marriage

Monogamy is the most common form of marriage. Widows and widowers can re-marry. The custom offering Rs. 12 to the bride, to fix marriage is prevalent among them. Bride price is given by the groom to the girl's parents.

Death Rituals

The kanphate bury their dead. They also perform the soul migration rituals.

Problems Faced by the Youth

Focused group discussions with youth revealed that the major problems faced by them are:

1. Un-employment
2. Ill-literacy
3. High dropout rates
4. Poverty
5. Alcoholism, tobacco chewing etc.
6. Food crisis
7. Social branding as criminals thieves
8. Social discrimination and exploitation
9. Watch over them for ill-legal hunting.

The occupational shift has been due to ban on hunting and social stigma as criminal groups and beggars. The Kanphate youth have taken up new occupations mostly in the unorganized sectors as:

1. Daily wage labourers
2. Agricultural labourers
3. Scrap collection & sale
4. Sale of plastic toys & ornaments
5. Selling bangles
6. Collecting human hair of females
7. Selling old cloths
8. Working in restaurants
9. Fishing
10. Small pan and grocery shops
11. Sugarcane cutting etc.

Major Findings

1. Out of the 100 respondents selected, 50 were boys and 50 girls ranging between the age of 18 to 35.
2. 20 per cent of the male respondents were married while 46 per cent of girls were married.
3. **Literacy:** 63 per cent of the youth were ill-literate, while 17 per cent studied up to primary, 14 per cent up to High school and 6 per cent up to Higher secondary level.
4. **Unemployment:** Almost 100 per cent of the youth studied were unemployed .They did not have permanent or temporary jobs in private and government sectors.
5. **Living Conditions:** Most of them lived in temporary houses, with a few exceptions.

Concluding Remarks

The Kanphate Gosavi are one of the most vulnerable groups among the Gosavis. Those ones living near farms, on the outskirts of the village, on fallow or encroached land, are the most dispossessed, socially discriminated, exploited, educationally and economically most backward group.

There is a need to free them from poverty, misery, illiteracy, ignorance and dependence. They need to be provided housing employment and a better status in the society.

REFERENCES

H.K. Mandal, 1993, Gosavi, in Singh K.S. (ed.), People of India, Maharashtra Vol. xxx, Part One, Oxford University Press, New Delhi.

Russel R.V. & Heeralal R.B. 1916, Tribes & Castes of the Central Provinces.

The Sorrow of Loosing the Joy of being a Youth *Case Studies of Labourers in Unorganized Sector*

– Dr. **Robin D. Tribhuwan**
– Dr. **Jayshree V. Kharche**

Introduction

Growth and development in the life and development of human beings, mark important biological mile stones such as birth, infancy, childhood, adolescence, youth, adulthood, old age and death. The rites of passage including birth, puberty, marriage, death and soul migration rituals have socio-cultural significance and vary from one society to another.

Similarly, celebrations, care, socialization, and rearing of children, teenagers and youth vary from one society to another.

There are societies in the world wherein parents take maximum precautions to provide enough care, support, recreation, nourishment, amusement, clothes and other needs of children, adolescent and the youth till they become responsible adults to get married, handle a job/business or other responsibilities of adulthood. On the other hand, there are societies that include vulnerable groups that are deprived of their rights to health, nutrition, recreation, education, etc.

This chapter throws light on youth of four vulnerable groups of laborers belonging to the unorganized sector who are deprived of their rights of enjoying childhood, adolescence and youth. There four vulnerable groups are as below.

1. The Katkaris, working as indebted and bonded labourers at the brick kilns.
2. The Bhil sugarcane cutters working as Doki Centre labourers in the sugar cane fields.
3. The Lamans
4. The Wadars, the stone quarry labourers.

Before getting into the determinants and causes of the sorrow of losing the joy of being a youth among the above mentioned vulnerable groups in the unorganized labour sector. It is necessary to understand:

(a) The methodology of studying the concept.
(b) The concept of childhood, adolescence and youth
(c) The socio-economic, educational and housing background of the respondents including the conditions in which they live.
(d) The push and pull factors that drive them to the brick kilns, sugarcane fields and stone quarries.
(e) The factors that are responsible for pushing their children into child labour. The reasons, why they are deprived of their rights to enjoy their childhood, adolescents and youth.

Methodology

The present study was carried out among the Katkari brick kiln labourers of Raigad, the Bhil sugarcane cutters of Nandurbar and the Lamans, Wadars stone quarry workers of Pune districts respectively. Table number presents district, tahsil and tribe caste wise number of respondents selected for the study.

Table 9.1: District, Tahsil, Tribe and Caste wise Number of Respondents

Sr. No.	Tribe/Caste	District	Tahsil	No. of Respondents
1.	Katkaris (Tribe)	Raigad	1. Pen	48
			2. Khalapur	52
2.	Bhils (Tribe)	Nandurbar	1. Shahada	50
			2. Taloda	50
3.	Lamans (VJNT)	Pune	1. Moshi	51
4.	Wadars	Pune	1. Moshi	62
	Total			**313**

The research tools administered to gather quantitative data were interview schedules, interview guides, case study method, observations and photography. The qualitative data was entered in excel software to prepare relevant tables that were analyzed and interpreted. Focused group interviews were taken wherever necessary.

The Concept of Childhood, Adolescence and Youth

Childhood, adolescence and youth are three biological stages of growth and development of youth. Given below are definition and concepts of the same.

(a) Childhood

Childhood is the age span ranging from birth to adolescence (i) In developmental psychology, childhood is divided up into the stages of toddler hood (learning to walk) early childhood (play age) middle childhood (School age) and adolescence (puberty through post puberty) The concept of age range of childhood varies from one society to another and from one continent/country to another.

(b) Adolescence

The term is derived from a Latin word namely 'adolescere' meaning to grow up. It is a transitional stage of physical and psychological human development generally occurring during the period from puberty to legal adulthood. The concept of adolescence too varies from one country to another and from one society to another.

Tribhuwan Robin and Finkenauer Makie (2003), have revealed that a warli girl starts taking small scale household responsibilities such as fetching water, cleaning vessels, rice, pulses, house, washing clothes etc since the age of seven.

(c) Youth

Youth is generally the time of life between child hood and adult hood (maturity)[2, 3]. Definitions of the specific age range that constitutes youth vary. Youth is also defined as the appearance, freshness, vigor, spirit etc characteristic of one who is young[4]. Youth is the term used to people of both the sexes, male and female. Around the world, the terms, "youth", "adolescent", "teenager", "kid" and "young person" are interchanged, often meaning the same thing, occasionally differentiated. Youth refers to a time of life that is neither child hood nor adult hood, but rather somewhere in-between[5]. The term youth is also related to being young[6]. The term also refers to individuals between the ages 18-24[7]. In India youth are considered to individuals between the age 15 to 35.

As aptly pointed out by Kennedy Rebert[8], "This world demands the qualities of youth: not a time of life, but a state of mind, a temper of the will, a quality of imagination, a predominance of courage over timidity, of the appetite for adventure over the life of ease."

– Robert Kennedy

Konopka[6] further points out that youth is an alternative word to the scientifically – oriented adolescent and the common terms of teens and teenagers. Another common title for youth is young person or young people.

Youth is the stage of constructing self concept [10]. The self-concept is influenced by several variables such as peers, life styles, gender and culture[10]. It is this time of a person's life in which they make choices which will affect their future[11].

It is pertinent to note that in the case of the children of the vulnerable families of the communities mentioned above, it was observed that:

1. They have no choice of freedom, nor can they enjoy child human and constitutional rights, at the place of destination (work place) because their parents are forced to go to the brick kilns, sugar cane fields and stone quarries.
2. They are forced to live in poor working conditions, in extreme heat, cold, dusty situations, temporary houses etc.
3. They cannot enjoy their child hood, adolescence and youth like other citizens of the country.
4. They are forced into child labour and house hold responsibilities at an early age.
5. Girls are married of at an early age by their parents, in order to shift their economic responsibility to another family.
6. They become victims of the sorrow of losing their joy of being a child, adolescent and youth as well.
7. They are forced and pushed into adulthood responsibility while in their youth.
8. They become victims of child labour, bonded labourers and debt at an early age.
9. They become susceptible to exploitation, social discrimination, and economic insecurity.
10. Undernourished girls get married, become mothers and produce malnourished children.
11. They are deprived of civic facilities and amenities such as toilets, bathrooms, electricity, and drinking water and so on at the place of destination.
12. They live in misery, servitude, and poverty both at the place of origin and destination.
13. They are cut off from their respective community who are at back home.
14. Children who go to schools too are forced to help their parents to complete weekly or monthly targets of work. We call this child labour.
15. They spend their child hood, adolescence and youth in house hold and commercial work without enjoying life.
16. Birthday celebration, toys, new clothes, picnics, children's parties, sweets, holidays, return gifts, music, songs, sports and other recreations are a dream to the children, teenagers and youth of the above mentioned vulnerable groups.

17. Their potentialities of sports, imaginations, vigour, talents, courage, appetite for creativity, programmes, development, adventure and success is shattered.
18. They become more and more dependent on their employers, the mukadams, and the middlemen for employment, loan (Uchal) and weekly monthly expenses (Kharchi) and above all for survival.

The socio-economic and educational background of the respondents:

Primary data gathered from the field on the social, educational and economic status of the youth studied revealed following facts:

(a) Social Status

The respondents of the four communities studied belonged to the unorganized labour sector. They worked as brick kiln labourers, sugarcane cutters and stone-quarry workers. Majority of them were victims of indebtedness and bonded labour. They were deprived of Government, individual and family development schemes at their places of destination. They lived in poor and temporary houses. They were susceptible to exploitation and discrimination. The Katkaris especially, are categorized at the lowest rank by both tribals as well as non-tribals because they eat field mice, bandicoots, monkeys, foxes etc. Hence, they are considered socially impure. Hunting of animals and birds is not seen among the Katkaris as there is a ban on hunting.

(b) Educational Status

Table 9.2 given below highlights the educational status of the youth studied.

Table 9.2: Educational Status of the Youth Studied

Sr. No.	Educational Status	Katkaris	Bhils	Lamans	Wadars
1.	Ill-literate	81	77	74.50	77
2.	Primary	07	10	04	16
3.	High School	12	08	06	05
4.	Higher Secondary	–	03	–	02
5.	Undergraduate	–	01	–	–
6.	Graduate	–	–	–	–
7.	Masters	–	01	–	–
8.	Ph.D.	–	–	–	–
9.	Diploma courses	–	–	15.7	–
	Total	**100**	**100**	**100**	**100**

(c) Annual Income

Table 9.3 present the status of B.P.L. families among the youth studied.

Table 9.3: B.P.L. Status of the Families Studied

Sr. No.	Income Range	Katkaris	Bhils	Lamans	Wadars
1.	Up to Rs. 20,000	90	65	–	1.6
2.	20,001 to 40000	08	29	12	24
3.	40001 to 60000	01	05	35	58
4.	60001 to 80000	01	01	25.5	11
5.	80000 and above	–	–	27.4	05
	Total	**100**	**100**	**100**	**100**

(d) Housing conditions of the respondents

The size, type and conditions of the houses of Katkari brick kiln labourers, Bhil Sugarcane cutters, and the stone quarry workers varied. Given below is the description of the same.

(i) Houses of the Katkaris Brick Kiln laboures

The laboures of the Katkaris at the brick kilns were temporary. They were made up of different material and varied from each other.

- Houses with an area of 80 to 150 sq.ft., with stick walls and thatched roofs and a hight of 5 to 8 feet.
- Houses with an area of 80 to 150 sq.ft. with piled up brick walls and thatched, plastic or tin roofs.
- Houses with grass and stick walls with thatched roofs.

(ii) Houses of the Bhil Sugar cane cutters

The houses of the Bhil sugarcane cutters in the fields too varied. Given below is the descriptions of the same.

- *Khopis* - is a small hut made up of bamboo mat, wherein the sugarcane cutters keep their belongings and use them for sleeping. (Panjiar Smita; 2007), (Dhamankar Mona)
- *Plastic tents* - Houses of 50 to 100 sq.ft. size, made up of plastic tents in the sugarcane fields is a common feature of their settlement.
- *Huts of dry sugar cane*

  It was observed, that some sugar cane cutters use dry sugar canes to make walls and sugar cane leaves to make the roofs of their temporary houses.

(iii) Houses of the stone quarry workers

- Houses having an area of 100 to 200 sq.ft. with piled stone walls and thatched or tin sheet roofs.

- Houses with an area of 80 to 150 sq.ft. having walls of cement blocks, with plastic, thatched or tin roofs.
- Houses of plastic walls and roofs.

Some of the salient features of the houses of these vulnerable groups were as below :

1. Temporary and poor
2. Small and less heighted
3. Houses without ventilation (windows) flooring, bathroom toilet and electricity.
4. Houses with a minimum area of 50 sq.ft. and maximum area of 150 sq.ft.

The Push and the Pull Factors

Tribuwan Robin and Kharche Jayshree (2012) and (2013) have classified major push and pull factors that drive the labourers of unorganized sector to the brick kilns, stone quarries and sugar cane fields, these are as below:

(a) Push factors:

1. Poverty
2. Landless or marginal farmers status
3. Economic food and debt crises
4. Indebtedness
5. Unemployment
6. Temporary and poor housing
7. Unskilled labour
8. Illiteracy
9. Social and economic insecurity
10. Absence of economic assets

(b) Pull factors

1. **Kharchi** - Weekly or monthly expenses given to the labourers.
2. **Uchal** - The loan taken by the labourers, before they leave to their native place.
3. **Employment Guarantee** - The promise of giving employment, to the labourers for the next season

These push and pull factors drive them into bonded labour. Further, heavy workload targets and less adult manpower in the family and the socio-economic status of parents hooks children into child labour.

Concluding Remarks

The innocent children, who are dependent on their parents, have no choice but to migrate with them at the work site, be victims of the poor living conditions, get deprived of their rights, get exposed to household and commercial work at an early age and finally loose the joy of being a child, an adolescent and youth. The moment they become teenagers they take up responsibilities of a young adult. They get paid by the contractor/owner. Once they get used to working, the parents get them married off. In this struggle for survival, they get deprived of enjoying their rights of children, adolescent and youth.

REFERENCES

1. Childhood – Wikipedia. The Free Encydopaedia (en. Wikipedia/org/wiki/childhood) the website
2. Macmillan Dictionary of Students, Macmillan Pub. Ltd. (1981) page 1155, retrieved 2010-7-15.
3. Youth- Merriam- Webster.http://www. merriam-webster.com/dictionary Youth Retrieved, November 6, 2012.
4. Youth.dictionary.reference. com. http://dictionary. reference.com/browse Youth. Retrieved November 6, 2012.
5. 2004) Webster's New World College Dictionary, Fourth Edition.
6. Konopka G (1973), Requirement for "Healthy Development of Adolescent Youth" Adolescence, VIII (31) P2.
7. Altschuler D. Strangler G. Berkey K and Burton L., 2009. Supporting Youth in Transition to Adulthood: Lessons Learned from Child Welfare and Juvenile Justice.
8. Kennedy Robert (1966). Day of Affirmation, University of Cape Town, South Africa, June issue.
9. Thomas A. 2003), Psychology of Adolescents, Self Concept, Weight Issues and Body Images in Children and Adolescents, p. 88.
10. Wing John, Jr. 2012), Youth, windsor Review: A Journal of Arts 45 1(2012) 9T Academic one File, web 24, October 2012.
11. Tribhuwan Robin and Finkenauer Maike (2003), Threads Together, Discovery Publishing House, New Delhi.
12. Tribhuwan Robin & Kharche Jayshree, 2012, Hard Labour: Poor Pay.
13. Tribhuwan Robin & Kharche Jayshree, 2013, Child Labour and Rights Issues, DPH, New Delhi.

Cyber Crime and Youth

– Dr. **K.S. Patil**
– Dr. **Robin D. Tribhuwan**

The Problem

The present age of advance technology & information has provided enough entertainment and electronic facilities to children, adolescent, youth and the adult as well. Twitters face book, emails, websites, games etc facilities on the internet often divert the attention of teenagers and youth to activities related to computer crime. Some youngsters, foolishly reveal too much personal information only to find themselves being black mailed into financial, sexual and psychological problems, caused by the once-amiable 'friend' they have made over the internet. These hunters or online predators, mostly men between 18 to 60 years old –know how to lead their prey into the trap. They confuse girls especially over love and sex. And they can be putting the moves on many victims at the same time.

This article is written for the youth to be aware of the dangers on line. It also provides basic concepts and terminologies associated with cyber crime. The youth need to be careful, when engage in on line activities and should knew how to protect themselves from falling prey to cyber crimes.

What is computer crime?

Moore, R., (2005) refers computer crime to any crime that involves a computer net work. David Mann and Mike Sutton, (2011) have defined net crime as criminal exploitation of the internet. Holder and Jaishankar, (2011 define cyber crimes, as offences that are committed against individuals or groups of individuals with a criminal motive to intentionally harm the reputation of the victims or cause physical or mental harm to the victim directly or indirectly, suing modern telecommunication net works such as Internet (Chatting rooms, emails, notice boards and groups), mobile phones (SMS/MMS). Such many threaten a nation's security and health. Issues Surrounding these types have become high-profile, particularly those surrounding cracking, copy right infringement, child pornography and child grooming. There are also problems of problems of privacy, when confidential information is lost or intercepted, lawfully or otherwise.

The Wikipedia – the free encyclopedia classifies the activities of computer crime into two broad categories namely:

1. Crime that primarily target net work or devices include:
   - Computer virus
   - Denial - of - service attacks
   - Malware (Malicious code)
2. Crimes that use computer net work or devices to advance other ends include:
   - Cyber staking
   - Fraud and Identity theft
   - Information warfare
   - Phishing scams

In the light of the above background, it is advisable that the youngsters should not get involved in computer crime. Given below are following tips to youth to prevent themselves from getting involved into cyber crime related activities.

1. Avoid computer fraud

Remember that altering, destroying, suppressing or stealing data output is illegal. Altering or missing existing system tools, software packages, altering or writing code for fraud purposes is a crime. The other forms of fraud may be facilitated using computer system, including bank frauds, identity thefts, extortion and thefts.

2. Be aware of spam

Spam or the unsolicited sending of bulk mails for commercial purpose is unlawful in some jurisdictions.

3. Obscene or offensive content

The content of websites and other and other electronic communications may be distasteful, obscene or offensive for a variety of reasons. In some instances these communications may be illegal. Youth must be aware of such communications.

4. Cyber bulling or harassment

The youth should be aware that any comment that may be found derogatory or offensive is considered harassment. Using a computer, cell phone or computer network to communicate obscene, vulgar, profane, lewd, lascivious or indecent language or make any suggestion or proposal of an obscene nature, or threaten any illegal need not involve any thing of a sexual nature is a cyber crime.

5. Stay away from mails and messages related to drug trafficking

Some drug traffickers are taking advantages of the Internet to pass on information or messages related to drug trafficking. It is suggested that we sty away from mails and massages related to the same. Do not indulge in communicating with such personnel.

6. Do not fall prey to sexual predators

Sexual grooming refers to the deliberate action taken by an adult to form a trusting relationship with a minor, with the intent of later having sexual contact. Typically, this is done to gain a teenage girl's trust. On line predators take advantage of the confused teenagers over love and sex. It is advice the teenagers as well as young girls not to fall prey to such kind of predators. You need to protect yourself against sexual grooming because you will expose yourself to danger and being sexually assaulted, raped and molested if you do not take precautionary measures.

If you knew of a friend who may be at risk of meeting such people or exhibiting such behaviour, you must alert her parents, teachers, family members and of course the police.

Concluding Remarks

Cyber or computer crime is a vast subject. A common man is hardly aware of such kind of crimes. However, as parents, teachers and citizens of this country it is our duty to read about this concept, the laws and punishments or penalties associated with it and educate our children & youth to prevent getting into it. In fact the schools and colleges in collaboration with the police and crime branch must organize awareness programmes in the schools, colleges and even in housing societies.

REFERENCES

Moore R., (2005), Cyber Crime: Investigating High Technological Computer Crime, Cleveland, Mississippi, Anderson Publishing Company.

David Mann and Mike Suttan, (2011), Net Crime, Bic Oxford Journals org. Retrived 2011-11-10.

Halder D & Jaishanker K. (2011), Cyber Crime and Victimization of Women: Laws, Rights and Regulations, Hershey, P.A. U.S.A., IGI Global, ISBN 978-1-6096-830-9.

Web Sites

(i) http://amumsworstnightmare.blogspot.com/2007/12/just-what-is-sexual-grooming.html

(ii) Computer Crime-Wikipedia the Free Encyclopedia.

(iii) Cyber Crime & Youth- Wikipedia the Free Encyclopedia.

Gambling
Habit that Shatters Personal and Family Life

– Dr. **Robin D. Tribhuwan**
– Ms. **Melanie Fedyk**

Gambling is often confused and associated with other forms of activities involving risks, investments, buying and selling, games of chance and transactions. While gambling encompasses a range of activities, in some instances it seems to develop like any other pastime, where more time and money is invested in the recreation, as a result of more experience, skills of sorts and knowledge. However, while gambling and other games or business may have some of the same elements, it is the further involvement, the sanction and encouragement of certain expectations and behaviors. The central role of money and the additional liabilities that distinguishes gambling from other hobbies, Gambling also involves a deliberate appeal to chance. To distinguish gambling more so from other similar activities. Perkins outlines certain elements. Such elements, he says, include the exchange of money which takes place without any equivalent value, material or personal, the possession of money determined solely by luck, the gain of the winners made possible solely by the loss of the losers and the unnecessary or often artificial risk involved (Cornish, 1978, p. 3). To further clarify gambling, G.R. Madan states that to game or gamble as an activity means, to use cards, dices or other instruments according to certain rules with a view to win money or other things waged upon the issue of the contest (1981, p. 183). One of the activities taken up in the city slums is gambling, an activity which not only affects the individual, but the family and society at large. A closer look at this undertaking reveals its circumstances, divesting effects, and dire personal, social and economic consequences.

Although there are different classifications, those who gamble can mainly be categorized into two types : the occasional and the habitual gambler. The casual gambler may gamble for recreation and leisure, with no intention other than entertainment. This type is the average person who gambles for diversion or distraction and can stop gambling at will.

Characteristics of the habitual gambler, as put forward by Edmund Bergler, include gambling as a typical, chronic and repetitive experience – this activity absorbing all of the person's other interests. The habitual gambler is pathologically optimistic about winning, and never "learns his lesson" when losing; he cannot stop even when winning, and no matter how great his initial caution, the true gambler eventually risks more than he can afford. Finally, the habitually gambler seeks and enjoys an enigmatic thrill which does not lend itself to logic. (Madan, 1981, p. 184).

Other types of gamblers include the professional gambler who earns a living from gambling, and the neurotic gambler who is driven by certain unconscious wants or needs and who is unable to stop his involvement in gambling. Ultimately gamblers themselves deliberately create unnatural and unnecessary risks in order to acquire some sort of financial return. In gambling, someone must assume the risk, as it is also necessary for commercial expansion of the industry.

According to Madan, "Of purely gambling activities the simplest are those for which the circumstances of chance may be reestablished easily and frequently at the will of the participants and in which the elements of skill and foreknowledge of the outcome are reduced to a minimum" (1981, p. 183). In the Indian context, the forms of gambling engaged in the slums include lottery tickets, playing cards for money, playing the carom board for money, playing marbles for money, drawing lucky numbers which takes different forms as "soral" and "matka".

Importantly, gambling is engaged in by a wide range of different groups in the society, depending on social class and subsequent levels of income, location and existing facilities and resources. In the slum areas, lottery tickets are a typical form of gambling as ticket prices range from Rs.10 to Rs. 100. Such tickets are usually purchased whenever the individual has money to spend. However, other forms of gambling are pursued and ultimately all forms have similar reaction or results. It is mostly males who gamble in the slums.

Affecting the individual, gambling leads to personal disorganisation. It tends to promote idleness, dishonesty and other vices and thus a damaging influence on the character of those who partake in it. In its many forms, gambling can lead to financial ruin, debts, poverty, extortion and murder for money. According to Madan. "It drags the person into extreme moral degradation and ultimately into extreme poverty, which leaves him no alternative, but a recourse to evil means (1978. p. 186). Comparable with other addictions, gambling takes over an individual's life, and can ultimately result in derelict status, being further outcast from society. Featured in Durkheim's theory of delinquency is the state of anomie, or cultural alienation, whereby the individual neglects or becomes indifferent to the norms in the society, ultimately threatening the solidarity of the society? It can be argued that gambling is one endeavour conducive to such a state, leaving the individual in disarray.

Disorganisation of the family is also linked to gambling. This habit and its ill effects spill over into the lives of those around the gambler, namely family members who are subject to its consequences. Gambling is passed on to younger members of the society, as this activity becomes part of the socialization process. Other problems associated with gambling and the family include poverty, conflict, divorce and ultimate disorganisation (Madan, 1981, p. 187)

The social disruption that comes about as a result of gambling arises in connection with other offenses included criminal activity. Certain crimes may be committed by the gambler in order to pay off debts. A large number of people in a state of disorder causes problems for the society, and it is the society in turn that eventually places a stigma on the individual.

In researching the problems and effects of gambling on the family in slum areas, basic inquiries were made by way of observation and interviews, interviewing the victims themselves, family members and essentially all those affected by this activity. Observations were also made as this inquiry involves a full 14 years experience in dealing with slum problems, its people and issues. The case studies presented here depict instances of gambling and how it affects the foundation of the family. For the most part, these case studies illustrate the progressive and leading nature of gambling, the linkage of habits and other activities connected to gambling. However, most importantly these cases outline the consequences of gambling: how gambling shatters personal and mental peace of an individual and his family.

CASE STUDIES

Case Study - 1

Mr. A.C. left school when he was just nine years old; teachers were fed up with him as he fought and quarreled with his classmates using abusive language. A.C.'s parents were also tired of his behavior. Eventually everyone gave up on him. At the age of 10, A.C. started smoking bidis (local cigars), teasing and making fun of girls, watching women taking a bath, learning about sex, gambling, watching movies and stealing. Although his parents were aware of these habits, they could not do anything as they were out selling papers the whole day.

As the focus of this case study is gambling, it is essential to highlight the different types of gambling games. A.C. was involved in : playing cards, combining marble games with gambling, lottery, "sorat" which involved drawing a lucky number Mr. A.C. has become a professional gambler. He steals more valuable items and spends most of his money in gambling.

Case Study - 2

Mr. S., age 55, from Shantinagar, is a mason by profession who has been playing the lottery game for the last 15 years or so. Every week he gets Rs. 1000 out of which nearly Rs. 200 goes towards buying lottery tickets for all the seven days. In one week. Rs. 200 is spent on alcohol, Rs. 200 on non-vegetarian food, additional money is also spent on bidis, tobacco, etc. Providing his work is regular, on average Mr. S. spends nearly Rs. 2400 out of the Rs. 4000 he earns a month on such items.

Following the same behavior as their father, his sons Sachin and Shashi started playing cards and buying lottery tickets. This has not only shattered the economic and educational base of the family, but also has given rise to fights, and quarrels between husband, wife and children as well.

Case Study - 3

Shortly after Mr. R.K. dropped out from 6th grade, his father expired. Both R.K. and his mother were left to bear the economic responsibilities of the home. Since R.K. was not educated, he chose painting as his profession and worked hard enough to become one of the best painters in Ambedkar slum in Aundh road region of Pune. Painting, however, is a seasonal job and it was during break periods, that he started getting frustrated as there was no money, slowly he started cheating the clients, his fellow painters and the contractors he came in contact with. When cheating ceased to work, he started gambling; that is, playing cards, lottery and matka. Sometimes he would win a fair amount, but soon he would again lose it. Today, gambling has become part of his life.

The frustrations he felt from losing money pushed him into drinking. At times he would drink and play cards, which led to the activity of fighting. He then started keeping knives and swords with him, and became a gangster. He is always found playing cards, carom, or matka (drawing a lucky number). He beats his mother for money.

Gambling as an activity, which not only affects the individual and family members, has larger social consequences. There is a need to approach this problem with concern as it is passed on to succeeding generations, causing all sorts of personal, social and economic hardship. Although it is difficult to regulate given its commercial expansion and addicting nature, habitual gambling occupies the lives of those economically disbanded, with little employment opportunities and little much else to do. All of these factors are equally detrimental.

Approaches to solving the problem of gambling in the slum setting can be found in providing forms of recreation for children and adults in the slums, providing further education for all not only in the formal schools, but also in the voluntary organisation based non-formal educational programmes. Regarding socio-economic development employment schemes to provide better opportunities for employment would be beneficial. Also, support systems set up for those addicted to gambling would assist in treatment. To look at what has been by way of study and recognition of the gambling problem in the slums, let alone support and treatment for this phenomenon, is minimal. Although people may gamble alone, or in groups, society places a stigma on those who gamble as they ultimately affect those around them. There is a need to conduct in-depth research on this issue in slum settings so as to understand the practice of gambling multidimensionally. This database will certainly contribute in planning programmes to control and prevent gambling at least in the younger generations.

REFERENCES

Cornish, D.B. (1978) Gambling: A Review of the Literature and its Implications for Policy and Research. London: Her Majesty's Stationary Office.

Madan, G.R. (1981). Indian Social Problems. (Volume 1, Third Edition). Bombay: Allied Publishers Private Limited.

Encroachment on Forest Land *Consequences Faced by Kaikadi Youth*

– Dr. **Robin D. Tribhuwan**
– Dr. **Pandit R. Fulzele**

Introduction

There are several interpretations regarding the origin of Kaikadi. Singh K.S. (1993) stated that in some parts of Maharashtra the Kaikadi are referred to as Gadhwe Sonar. Enthoven R.E. (1922) believes that the Kaikadi are migrants from Telangana. One derivation of Kaikadi is from Tamil, i.e. Kai – meaning hand and kudi – meaning basket, as they are considered to be basket makers. In Vidarbha, they are concentrated in Akola, Buldhana, Amravati, Chandrapur and Gadchiroli.

Singh K.S. (1993) has opined that the traditional occupation of the Kaikadis was basket making and stone cutting. In earlier days pig and donkey rearing were also considered major economic pursuits. Even now pig and donkey rearing is the main occupation of the respondents studied.

Some of the major clans of the kaikadi reported by Singh K.S. (1993) are Jadhao, Gaikwad, Parkey, Mule and Mane. Marriage within the clan is strictly prohibited. A person may marry his father's sister daughter or mother's brother's daughter. Polygyny is permitted but majority of them are monogamous.

Research Methodology

The present study was conducted in Kaikadi Vasti of Santnagar in Gadchiroli-Chamorshi road, in Gadchiroli city. An interview guide was prepared to conduct focused group interviews of male and female elders of the Kaikadi community, including the main key informants. Data was analyzed manually at is was qualitative in nature. The objectives of the study are as below:

Objectives of the Study

1. To study the living conditions of the Kaikadi on the encroached forest land.
2. To explore the positive and negative consequences of encroachment on the lines of the Kaikadi.
3. To unveil the social problems and development issues of Kaikadi youth.

Major Findings

(i) Native place

The elderly respondents of the Kaikadi community – residing on the encroached forest land in Kaikadi Vasti of Santnagar on Gadchiroli Chamorshi road in Gadchiroli district – said they came to Santnagar in 1996. The forest land on which they encroached is full of small shrubs and is on the outskirts of Gadchiroli City. They are a native of Tamil Nadu and Andhra Pradesh, said the respondents.

(ii) Dialect

The Kaikadi speak a dialect which is a mixture of Telgu, Tamil and Marathi.

(iii) Clans

The Kaikadi revealed that their original clan names are different from what they have adapted after settling down in Gadchiroli. These clan names are given below:

	Andhra Pradesh Clan	Maharashtrian Name
1.	Jagannath	Gaikwad
2.	Khandelvar	Khandelvar
3.	Ballari	Dasarvar, Jadhav
4.	Khedari	Kedari
5.	Kumbari	Kumbhare

Among themselves they give importance to their original Andhra Clans. While fixing marriages, they first consider their original Andhra clans. On enquiry, why they shifted to Maharashtrian surnames, they revealed that they wanted to be identified with Maharashtra.

(iv) Settlements in Gadchiroli

Besides Santnagar, the Kaikadi have also encroached on forest land in Gokulnagar, Chankai, and Langeda. Their approximate population in these four settlements is above 1500.

(a) Birth rituals

Traditionally Mantarsani (midwife) would conduct delivery. She was given a sari, blouse or coconut for her 3 days of service to the new mother and child. The Kaikadi burry the umbilical cord. On the third day after the birth the naming ceremony by the name "Purdu" is performed. The ritual of shaving the first hair of the new born called "barsa" is performed by a Mhali (Barber) after one month and a week. The barber is given Rs. 51/- or 101/- depending on the sex of the child. If the child is a male, the Mhali receives Rs. 101/- and if female he receives Rs. 51/-

(b) Puberty rites

There are no special puberty rites among the Kaikadis said the respondents.

(c) Wedding rituals

Monogamy is the most common form of marriage, among the Kaikadi. The practice of dowry is prevalent in this community. The dowry amount ranges from Rs. 5000/- to 20,000/-. The Kaikadis perform their weddings for three days.

1. **Mandav** or **Pandira** - On the first day a traditional pandol is fixed.
2. **Wedding or Penli** - On the second day the wedding rite is performed by the Peddamansi. The Peddamansi is a respected elder in the community.
3. **Wedding Procession or Mandya Phool** - On the third day the bride is taken to the groom's house is a procession called Mandya Phool.

The Kaikadi allow re-marriage of a widow as well as a widower.

(v) Death rituals

The dead are buried by the Kaikadis. On the ninth day after the death of a person, the "Navari Rite," of soul migration ritual is performed.

(vi) Traditional panchayat

The traditional panchayat of the Kaikadi is still prevalent and is active. It comprises of a council of village elders. If a girl or a boy marries outside the caste, they are fined Rs. 2000/- and asked to give a chicken feast and liquor to the pancyhayat members. If a pig of a family is stolen, the culprit is fined Rs. 200/- and the pig is taken back from him. The Kaikadis still follow the unwritten laws, of their community.

(vii) Deities

Duurgamata of Mewdaram village in Warangal district, in Andhra Pradesh, Sammaka and Sarraka are other goddesses are worshipped by them.

(viii) Traditional occupation

The Kaikadi elders stated that their traditional occupation was to rear pigs, transport clay and stones on donkey backs, make blankets from the fur of the sheep, work as daily wage labourers, stone workers etc.

(ix) From Nomadism to settled life

Traditionally the Kaikadis were nomads. Due to technological advancement, modernization, urbanization and globalization, they have stopped beginning, reduced the use of donkeys to transport clay and stones and even discontinued nomadic life. However, we do get to see Kaikadis in some districts following semi-nomadic life.

(x) Occupational shift

After settling down on the encroached land, the Kaikadis have taken up the following occupation:

(a) Construction and road daily wage labourers
(b) Agricultural labourers
(c) Goat rearing
(d) Piggery
(e) Broom making and selling
(f) Cleaning toilet safety tanks
(g) Rag picking
(h) Collection and sale of scrap
(i) Selling plastic toys
(j) Other types of daily wage labour.

Consequences of Encroachment

Some of the consequences of encroachment on forest land faced by the Kaikadi are both negative and positive as well.

(a) Negative consequences

The elderly folk revealed that encroaching on forest land has been a negative set back for us, the youth and our children. These negative consequences are as below:

(i) Temporary nature of houses

Since the land does not belong to us and that we can be driven by the Forest Department any time, we not build permanent houses.

(ii) The problem of roof blowing

Since most temporary houses have plastic roofs and temporary walls of sticks and plastic sheets. The roofs are blown off during rainy season.

(iii) Snakes, scorpions and insects

During the rainy season the problem of snakes, scorpions and insects is unavoidable. During the last six years two male adult died of snake bites in the camp. Since the settlement is 3 to 4 kms. away from Gadchiroli General Hospital, it becomes difficult for the Kaikadies to find a doctor after 6 p.m. and before 10 a.m. in the hospital.

(iv) Water in the tents

Heavy rains ultimately results into water logging in the house. During such times, the Kaikadis either sit on the cots or stools whole nigh or find shelter in the 8-9 permanent houses, in the camp.

(v) Lack of facilities and amenities

Since the Kaikadis have encroached on government forest land they are not entitled for following facilities and amenities namely:

- Public toilets and bathrooms
- Hand Pump, bore wells and tap water
- Samaj mandir
- Electricity
- Anganwadi/primary school
- Sub-centre
- Ration shop etc.

(vi) Deprived of purchasing economic assets

Due to the temporary nature of houses without locks, the Kaikadis cannot purchase economic assets.

(vii) Imprisonment

The elderly men and women were imprisioned for a month for encroaching on forest land.

(viii) Legal cases against them

The Forest Department has filed a case against the Kaikadis for ill-legal encroachment.

(ix) Life on the encroached land is insecured

Over all, the life of these Kaikadis on the encroached land is not secured.

(b) Positive consequences

Some of the positive consequences of encroachment and hanging in there have resulted into some positive aspects as well. These positive consequences are a ray of hope of survival for them. These are:

(i) Election cards

All the 70 families have received election cards and their names are in the electoral rolls. Directly or indirectly the politicians are supporting their stay on the encroached land as they are part of the vote bank. This political tie up has proved to be bon for the Kaikadis.

(ii) Economic ties

During the span of six years of stay on the encroached land, the Kaikadis developed economic ties with the local construction company owners, road repairing and building contractors of the Public Works Department, Pig meat dealers, broom sellers, goat meat dealers and traders.

Besides this one of the leaders in the camp has bought a truck that has a tanker. He takes up contracts of cleaning safety tanks of the toilets. The bungalow owners of Gadchiroli are aware of this. Since cleaning safety tanks is considered to be menial job, there is a support to these encroachers from the local residents as well.

Besides this, the Kaikadis work as agriculture and daily wage labourers for the local land lords and business people, is yet another advantage for them. These landlords and business people to support their stay on the encroached land.

(iii) Educational ties: A boon to children and youth

The aided Ashram Schools in Gadchiroli and Chandrapur take the children and youth of the Kaikadi people in their tribal Ashram Schools to show head counts as these schools do not get tribal students. They are also admitted in aided schools of the scheduled Ashram Schools. These children get lodging, boarding and educational facilities in the Ashram Schools.

(iv) Ration cards

Almost all the Kaikadi families have received ration cards. This is yet another source of support for them to stay on the encroached land.

(v) Scheduled caste certificate

The leader of the settlement, Shri Dasarvar, has received a Scheduled Caste Certificate of Kaikadi issued by the S.D.O. on the basis of this he can avail benefits meant for Scheduled Castes. This is yet another ray of hope of survival on the encroached land.

(vi) Support from Laxman Mane

The Kaikadis of Gadchiroli have received support from their state and national level leader Shri Laxman Mane. His unending support too is a ray of hope for survival.

(c) Religious ties

The local believers Churches have converted some of the Kaikadis, hence this religious tie is yet another source of support for them.

Problems of Kaikadi youth

It was observed that majority of the children and youth prefer to live in Aided Ashram Schools wherein their lodging, boarding, education, scholarship and other needs are taken care. Ashram Schools therefore a bon for the Kaikadi children and youth. In fact, the Kaikadis stated that one male teacher is given responsibility of 10-15 children every year. He sees to all the needs of our children – said the Kaikadis.

These ones who are in the encroached camp suffer from problems of permanent employment, food crisis, snake bites and scorpion stings, poor living conditions, lack of civic facilities and amenities.

Social identity of Kaikadi

As regards the social identity of the Kaikadi is concerned, different states have categorized them under different social categories. In Maharashtra they have been categorized as Scheduled Castes (Sr. No. 28), in Vidarbha and VJNT in other parts in Andhra Pradesh as Scheduled Tribe, in Karnataka as Scheduled Caste in Tamil Nadu as Scheduled Tribe.

According to Laxman Mane, the traditional occupation of all the Kaikadi in the country was making baskets, they speak a common dialect and have a common clan system. Then why the different categories he says.

Concluding Remarks

Encroachment of forest land has directly and indirectly influenced the life of Kaikadi youth positively as well as negatively. The encroached land and the togetherness of these families, who ones led a nomadic and in secured life has given rise to a strong sense of solidarity among the Kaikadi. Their economic, political and educational ties with the local landlords, business people, contractors and the politicians has been a ray of hope for survival on the encroached land. Similarly, illegal encroachment has also posed several threats for survival on that land.

Giving them land to stay, permanent houses to live in, employment for survival and a common social identity in the country is the need of the hour. The problems and welfare of the youth depends a lot on solving the above mentioned problems.

REFERENCES

Singh K.S. (1993), The Scheduled Castes, People of India Series, Vol. II, Oxford University Press, New Delhi.

Enthoven R.E. 1922, The Tribes and Castes of Bombay, Central Government Press, Bombay.

13

Social Issues of College Youth

– Ms. **Insha Khan**

A perpetual gap is on an increase between a student and the teacher in the current scenario where technology has driven this relationship to another stage altogether by connecting the two through various mediums. Earlier a student hardly got an opportunity to know a teacher beyond the boundaries of a subject. Evolving Technology in the field of education has undoubtedly worked in favour of a better student teacher relationship. It constantly keeps them connected via emails or mobiles constructing an out of class platform for interaction on general or syllabus related topics.

Well-equipped classes enhance class discussions through projectors or computers complimenting the teacher's explanation which makes the learning process simpler for students. Though student teacher relationship mainly depends on faith and dedication from both ends yet technology takes it to the next level. In this super consumed era of multitasking where both student and teacher is engaged in many other activities, technology reduces the distance and helps them stay in touch on a daily basis.

Generally, the youth today believes more in privacy and self-oriented style of living due to the lacking sense of belongingness with each other. In the process of participating for the rat race of career building, the class atmosphere is also treated in a professional manner followed by a sense of detachment and missing out on a chance to develop stronger relationships in the long run. They say that classrooms are a zone to learn and progress in life to emerge as better individuals but somewhere one has to compromise on the socializing front of gaining enough space and comfort to comprehend the value of human relations.

There has been an over- all change in the behavioural patterns of the youth gradually bringing in both positive and not so favourable approach towards society as a whole. Where on one hand they have become extremely independent from most of the restrictions or limitation coerced by the elders like earlier on the other hand the freedom has led to absolute negligence, no realization and arrogance in abundance. It will not be fair to put all into the same category but majority of the youth which is assumed to be the nation's backbone either pretends to be ignorant or actually lacks the sensitivity and sensibility to realize it.

We have since childhood instilled the courtesy and values of respecting elders even if they are not related to us but certain actions of some youngsters can be disappointing. An old couple in a city like Mumbai if attempts to correct a few boys in the theatre from passing snide and vulgar comments, they are asked to shut up or leave. Such individuals unknowingly on a day to day basis ripe apart all that Indian traditions and values consist as a legacy to be gracefully transferred from one generation to the other. Educational institutions can only be a medium of exposure but the change has to be in the person who imbibes maximum to benefit him and the society holistically.

It is rightly said that considering the present situation of education turning into a commercial sphere more than an entity to impart knowledge and learning, gone are the days of teachers holding the capacity of Dronacharya and students lacking the concentration and dedication that of Arjun from Mahabharata one of the brightest standards set ever for a student teacher relationship. Conduct in the class or in public of any human being depends highly on the background and the mannerism he/she picks up from educational institution which is the second home from childhood to adulthood till one joins the field. The final outcome is to be judged out there when people either look up to one's personality ingrained by positive outlook or looks down upon it due to inappropriate behavioural patterns developed in the long process of learning.

There are some students who suffer from severe inferiority complex in colleges which pushes them generally to the back seat of participation. There is a need to help the unwilling ones to be transformed into willingness to come forward though in this competitive era of speedy and anonymous life from one another, extending time to others is not a very convincing thought but as responsible citizens we have to be united. If a student is afraid of speaking in class due to language problem, the rest should encourage the person and turn him from an odd to an even instead of mocking his lacunae.

In this new age of Face books and twitters, the youth is suffering from an epidemic called disconnect from the immediate surroundings. Students physically present in the class prefer to be mentally available to others around the globe by either liking a picture of somebody relishing a chocolate fondue or commenting on some irrelevant status update. Being interactive is a way to experience and realize things better but going beyond a limit of absolute hibernation from the real world and total commitment to the virtual space can take an ugly shape. Generally, the youth is not very keen in actively eradicating issues in the vicinity but prefer to pass verdicts and statements on Indian corruption or polity. If there exist a problem then one as a group has to come out to challenge and question it rather than cursing every possible thing with half or no knowledge whatsoever on the topic.

The upcoming generation face role conflict to a large extent of dealing with peer pressure and family principles. There is a constant battle of values in the life of the youth who is perplexed and strangled between the inherent family bound culture and the so called 'in' trend culture which may have no concrete foundation . He/she suffers from trauma which at times takes an unpleasant turn and the person goes into a shell that is not easy to fight and rise above. If a student in college or classroom is constantly reminded of his loopholes of not wearing up to the mark outfits or mocked every-time he puts an effort to dilute the fear by coming forward to speak then it would only de-motivate the individual and be of no help.

Today, colleges as a platform of interaction and communication to various aspects of life have to work on the path of a student friendly atmosphere. It has to make every student feel equal in the eye of the institution by providing equal opportunity and encouragement to all the students for participating in college festivals or organizing it rather than reserving it for the few. It is a place where a person is expected to leave behind inhibition and act to develop skills even at the cost of making mistakes because that is how one learns for the real on field challenges. Over a period of time there has been a growth in the category system of virtual segregation between the good and bad student without giving enough time to the person to prove his/her ability. It varies from institutions to institutions, some function on a fair and accurate level and some follow favouritism where all are deprived of equal chance to test or prove his skills.

Currently, in colleges nobody has time for anybody, most of the time either the students are not interested enough or the professor fails to convey the information in the right or influencing manner. One cannot deny that the reducing concentration span of students has compelled the educational system to bring in force more rigorous courses for total engagement with hectic projects and field work. It has in a way worked in favour of the youth which is extended the space to go out and mix around with professional to get a hang of the reality in the field rather than just sticking to the books without application. The response from students belonging from various streams not just mass media is constructive as they get to practically test facts that are only elucidated in theory. They don't get restricted to one way communication of learning but it functions on a two way basis where even students contribute making it a comprehensive programme of total personality development.

Gradually technological advancement has also led to an increase in social alienation, depression and loneliness. Internet being constantly attached to the youth may help in exploring the globe better but is affecting social relationships. Impact of computers and smart phones have driven most of the youth away from the real world which requires total attention. There are some who actively participate in fixing or volunteering for causes concerning our society at the moment but that is not sufficient to deal with gigantic issues plaguing our nation. We find more individuals standing in a line outside an expensive lounge or pub abut very few youngster working or serving people in a blood donation camp or campaigns to fight social vices. If the youth feels that the society lacks enough inspiration to persuade them to follow social work then they are living with a misconception. Nobody can ever be spoon fed awareness or coerced to spread it as they can be trained in the field but can never be forced to inculcate the desire to work towards welfare of the deprived as it comes from within.

The Force that Drives us to the Garbage Bins
A Case Study of Rag Pickers

– Dr. **Robin D, Tribhuwan**
– Mr. **Rohit Sharma**
– Ms. **Avanti Patwardhan**

Introduction

It is a common sight in most Indian cities wherein one gets to see rag pickers with gunny bags, wandering in search of newspapers, plastic bags, bottles, tin sheets etc. Most of these rag pickers are women, young girls and children from slums, pavements or streets. They do not care for the scorching heat; the long distance walks, pavements or streets. They do not care for the scorching heat; the long distance walks; the abuses of security guards; the stigma associated with their occupation and other social problems they face as rag pickers. All that interests them is the stuff they have to collect. For, their daily bread depends on what quality and quantity stuff they collect.

This chapter highlights the socio-economic status, the problems and the developmental needs of rag pickers. The findings reported in this study are based on qualitative research conducted in two rag pickers' colonies in Pune city i.e. in the Parvati region and a slum located under the circuit house bridge. Data was collected using an interview guide, observation method and focused group discussion. Nearly 70 rag pickers were interviewed from both the slums. Besides conducting focused group interviews of 50 young women. Since the data was qualitative in nature it was analyzed manually. Some of the findings of this study are given below:

Who are Rag pickers ?

Our study has revealed that most of the rag pickers are from the lower caste groups and minorities. Besides being from the low strata of the caste hierarchy these rag pickers are economically very backward.

They have migrated from famine struck districts such as Beed, Ahemad Nagar, Osmanabad. Latur and Solapur of Maharashtra State. These districts have less industrial and other development resources as compared to cities like Bombay, Pune, Nasik and Thane. Hence rural inhabitants choose to migrate into these cities. The men folk work as daily wage labourers, while the women work as maid servants, construction workers, baby sitters, daily wage labourers or rag pickers.

Why do they prefer to take up this profession ?

Out of the total 70 rag pickers and other 50 who were interviewed in group discussion nearly 80 per cent preferred rag picking to other jobs because of following reasons:

(a) There is nobody to boss over you.

(b) One has the liberty to start and stop work anytime during the day.

(c) If one works as a daily wage labourer or maid servant her salary gets cut if she is absent for a day or two. But in this profession of rag picking nothing of that sort exists. If one works for longer time and throughout the week, she gets more money.

(d) Rag picker pickers get their income daily. But if they work as daily wage labourers they get paid either weekly or monthly.

(e) Finally, depending on one's collection their daily income ranges from Rs. 25-70, which is nearly 3-4 times more than the salary of maid servants or daily wage labourers.

Material Collected

Most rag pickers were found to collect bottles, scrap metal, plastic bags, card board, news papers, tin sheets, nails, plastic shoes and slippers, rags, tins and even glass pieces. These things are collected from the garbage bins, lane by lane, street by street etc., which is sold to the nearest scrap dealer. For instance, rag pickers from Lakshmi Nagar, Ghorpadi and the slum under the circuit house bridge sell the stuff to a Muslim scrap dealer, who has his shop under the bridge, whereas rag pickers from Dandekar bridge and Parvati region sell their scrap to dealers on Sinhagad road. Such scrap dealers have their shops within a vicinity of 10-15kms around which the rag pickers live.

Time Clock of the Rag Pickers

Their day begins at 6 in the morning. After they are through with bathing, they clean their houses, cook breakfast for the family, pack their husband's lunch, bathe the children, finish up other household work and set out in search of rags and other materials. The slum women from Yerawada, Ghorpadi and circuit house bridge region walk a distance of 6-8 kms, every day work for 7-8 hours. Some of these women also travel, without tickets, every day to Loni, Hadapsar, Uruli Kanchan and Kedgaon villages to collect scrap. These villages are 20-40 kms from their place of residence, which is a tiring job, People from circuit house slums eat food after they return in the evening.

It takes nearly 6-8 hours for these women to pick up the required material. Most of them have their lunch in the field itself, this was observed among the rag pickers of Parvati area. However, the rag pickers of circuit House Bridge come home at 3 or 4 pm and then have their lunch. They come back and sit in front of the scrap shop sought out the material collected and sell it to the owner. After having done this some women go to the grocery shops or vegetable markets to purchase food. Once they reach home a cup of tea may or may not be taken to get rid of their fatigue. The household activity starts after cooking dinner. While this activity is going on, some women have to simultaneously take the abuses and nonsense of their drunkard husbands. After the food is taken, these women have to clean the house, wash vessels, and make beds. By the time all these activities get over it is 10.30pm. This is how it works, so far as, their time clock is concerned.

Over 95 per cent of the respondents interviewed work full time, six days a week, during winters and summers. However the remaining 5 per cent work for all the seven days during summers and winters because their husbands do not give any money to run the house, are alcoholics, have mistresses on whom they spend money, or spend the money on smoking and gambling. Sunday's are off for most rag pickers. However, they do not rest on this day, in facts activities such as washing clothes of all the family members, cleaning the house, purchasing ration etc. is done on this day.

Are the Rag pickers Harassed ?

When this question was asked, there was 100 per cent "yes" as their response. Sure enough both women as well as children get harassed, ever teased and abused by people. The security mean of colonies, railway guards, police and even general public shout at the rag pickers, when they enter office, colony or home premises.

Perception about Self-image

Even though they stick on to this job, in their heart of hearts, they feel inferior and most of them prevent their children from taking up the same profession. However some poor rag pickers cannot help passing on this profession to the next generation. Some women opined that it was their bad luck or misfortune that they took up this job. The women would go to collect rags from Loni, Uruli, Hadapsar and Kedgaon villages and on their way back home sold the material have never revealed to their neighbours about their profession.

When asked, would you like your children to take up this job, most of them said no. They wish that their children should grow up to take up better jobs. Secondly, whenever they visit their native place, most of them do not tell their relatives about their real profession. Thirdly, college and school going children of the rag pickers feel lowly of themselves and never reveal it to their friends. This attitude was especially observed among the school and college going children of rag pickers from Parvati region. Although children, relatives and people around look down upon the profession of rag picking, the rag picker women have become used to this social stigma and do not care for all these societal views. They only know that this profession helps them to earn their daily bread, ranging from Rs. 15 to 50 daily depending on their luck.

Leadership Among Rag Pickers

It was observed that there is an understanding among the rag pickers as their territories of material collection are concerned. They do not eve fight among them, selves if a new person enters their territory. The concept of leadership to fight back injustice and harassment is by and large absent among the rag pickers, However one or two instances of ill treatment of women by the railway guards compelled them to take the matter to Baba Adhav, a social activist, who took up the case and saw to it that justice was given to the victim. The rag pickers have been given an identity card by Dr.Baba Adhav's organisation, and in case of problems they rush to him. Cas plan is yet another organisation which is helping the rag pickers. Thus, with regards to the idea of leadership to fight back injustice, is external or a borrowed one.

Their Views about Alternate Jobs

Most rag pickers expressed that they would not mind taking up small scale business such as vegetable, fruits dry fish selling or a permanent sort of jobs which would fetch them Rs. 1500-2000 per month, throughout the year. Some however felt that they would like to continue with the present job, but if jobs such as maid servants, baby sitters or daily wage labourers is offered to them in rainy season they would happily take it up.

Negligence of Children

Since these women are out the whole day for six to eight hours, they are neither able to supervise the studies of their children nor check on what they do throughout the day. It was observed that because of this negligence on the part of mothers children don't do well in their studies. Those ones who have dropped out from school or do not attend school get into quarrels, mischief and other problems. Those rag pickers having infants take them along or if there are grown up children, these infants are left with them. Small children left at home under the care of older children play along the road, get into trouble or accidents. In doing so these children get deprived of their mother's care and nursing for 6-8 hours.

What force drives them to the Garbage Bins?

Despite of the many problems associated with rag picking, why do they prefer to be what they are? What force drives them, to the garbage bins? The responses were as follows:

1. A background of utter poverty.
2. Women as wives and mothers are forced to take the economic responsibilities because:
   - their husbands are either alcoholics;
   - or gamblers;
   - or have mistresses on whom money is spent;
   - or unemployed;
   - or when the husbands desert them.
3. The size of the family is large and hence a woman has to come out to a helping hand to her husband to share the economic responsibility of the family.
4. This profession does not impose any obligation of time, discipline and job norms.
5. If their husbands are injured and cannot work or if they are widows.

Concluding Remarks

As revealed in the study the social and economic problems of the rag pickers are enormous, this paper has made an attempt to highlight few of them. Here again it is the woman who is forced to go to the garbage bins, lanes and by lanes in search of material which would fetch Rs.15-50 everyday. At times children automatically get pulled into this profession. Their lessons start first with sorting out the material collected by the mother, understanding its economic value, sometimes accompanying the mother to collect the material, visiting scrap shops where these things are sold and so on.

Knowing such an easy way of earning money, without being subordinate to anybody, they prefer to take up this profession. We have given a few suggestions, which would help the development agencies to upgrade the social and economic status of the rag pickers.

Suggestions

Towards this end, we would like to suggest following programmes for the families of rag pickers:

1. Establish crèches in the colonies of rag pickers for their children.
2. Start educational coaching classes for children who attend schools so that extra efforts are taken to upgrade their educational skills.
3. Efforts must be made to start some income generating programmes for these women during the rainy season, as rag picking becomes a problem then.

4. Mid-day meal programmes could be started for the children of rag pickers (especially those who stay at home).
5. Ashram schools should be established in urban areas so that the parents do not have to worry about education, food etc. of their children and they can take up some other profession and improve their socio-economic position.

Youth
Human Trafficking in India

– Dr. **Pranali Patil**

Introduction

Youth is generally the time of life between childhood and adulthood (maturity). Definitions of the specific age range that constitutes youth vary. An individual's actual maturity may not correspond to their chronological age, as immature individuals can exist at all ages. Youth is also defined as "the appearance, freshness, vigor, spirit, etc., characteristic of one who is young". Youth is a term used for people of both sexes, male and female, of a young age. The terms youth, adolescent, teenager, kid, and young person are interchanged, often meaning the same thing, occasionally differentiated. Youth generally refers to a time of life that is neither childhood nor adulthood, but rather somewhere in-between. Youth also identifies a particular mindset of attitude, as in "He is very youthful". The term youth is also related to being young. The term also refers to individuals between the ages of 16-24. Youth is an alternative word to the scientifically-oriented adolescent and the common terms of teen and teenager. Another common title for youth is young person or young people.

According to United Nations' definition of youth is people from 15 to 24 years of age Many countries also draw a line on youth at the age at which a person is given equal treatment under the law – often referred to as the "age of majority'. This age is often 18 in many countries, and once a person passes this age, they are considered an adult. However, the operational definition and nuances of the term 'youth' often vary from country to country, depending on the specific socio-cultural, institutional, economic and political factors.[*Source*: United Nations Division for Social Policy and Development]

Age Group of Youth as per National Youth Policy

The age group of set out in the National Youth Policy 2003 is 13-35 years. However, it needs to be recognised that all young people within this age group are unlikely to be a homogeneous group, sharing common concerns and needs and having different roles and responsibilities. It is, therefore, necessary to divide this age-bracket into three sub-groups:

- The first sub-group of 13-18 years should cover adolescents whose needs and areas of concern are substantially different from youth under the following age groups.
- The second sub-group of 18-25 years includes those youth who are in the process of completing their education and starting, getting a job or looking for a livelihood.
- The third sub-group of 25-30 years comprises young women and men who have completed their education.

Indian census 2011

India has the largest youth population in the world that is poised to increase further in the coming decade. 70 per cent of India's population is below the age of 35 years. This pool of youth population needs to be engaged in the mainstream development of India. According to the initial figures of the 2011 census, the youth population in the country including adolescents is around 550 million. This phenomenal rise in the youth population has made India the youngest nation with a demographic dividend appearing to be a reality. It is indeed vital to utilize this demographic dividend and channelize the youth and their creative energies for nation building. The UN General Assembly has declared 2011 as the International Year for Youth with the theme "Dialogue and Mutual Understanding" (Census 2011, Census Week, India Census 2011).

Youth is the stage of constructing the Self-concept. The self-concept of youth is influenced by several variables such as peers, lifestyle, gender and culture. It is this time of a person's life which they make choices which will affect their future. When we look at the human trafficking among youth we have to overview some case studies related to human trafficking in India.

Case Study One – Nagpur, Maharashtra

A baby girl was found abandoned near a garbage heap. She was picked up by some people and brought to a woman, apparently a widow, and in need of money. She was promised a handsome monthly allowance and asked to take care of the baby as if it was her own daughter, with enough to pay for her food, education and clothing. In fifteen years, the little girl grew with the woman, believing her to be the mother. The widow too developed a strong bond with the girl. The girl was a student of class X when a man came to the woman, told her that her "duties" with regard to the child were over, handed her some money and took the girl away. The story came to light when anti-trafficking activists subsequently rescued the girl.

Case Study Two – Mumbai, Maharashtra

After a rescue mission, a minor girl was being counseled by the group, which had done the rescue. The woman objected when the counselors addressed her as a female, insisting that "she" was a man. Non-pulsed at first, the counselor persisted, asking why the woman did not want to be addressed as one. The person narrated her story. "I was a youth living in a Mumbai suburb, commuting daily to work in the city. One day, in the local train, a fellow passenger gave me something to eat. I took it and lost consciousness. When I woke up, I was in a luxurious hospital suite, but in great pain. I discovered I had been castrated, and now had a vagina." Apparently a cosmetic surgeon had done the complicated surgery to create an artificial vagina. The victim was kept in the hospital for several weeks while the wounds healed. He was given hormone injections and began to develop breasts and other female characteristics. After a couple of months of stay in the hospital, he was discharged – now looking like a woman. He was subsequently passed onto a Mumbai brothel owner where he was forced to entertain clients like other inmates, and did so till he was rescued. The Child Welfare Committee before whom this youth, legally still a minor, was produced got extensive tests done which confirmed that "she" was a male. This remains the most bizarre case of human trafficking the rescue group has ever come across.

Case Study Three – also from Maharashtra

Minor girls rescued from brothels are usually put in the custody of government homes. The custody of the girls in the government homes meant for minors ends the day, the girl turn 18. On that day, the girl is set free from the "protection" of the shelter homes. Often the girls don't have a home to go to and are clueless about how to proceed once they are released. Often traffickers are in touch with the clerical staff of the government homes and know exactly when a particular girl is going to be turn 18 and will be released from the shelter home. On the appointed day, the trafficker's agent is waiting outside the gates of the shelter home in a car ready to pick up the homeless and clueless girl. The girl is picked up in a car, brought to a brothel readied to receive her and soon she is reintroduced into trafficking, now as an adult.

Theoretical Background

Human trafficking, world's third largest illegal activity after smuggling of drugs and weapons, continues to thrive despite adequate legal provisions. There are several arguments about when human trafficking could have started. Some say that the slave trade, in which Africans were captured by slave traders and shipped across the Atlantic to the Americas, was the first human trafficking. Although forms of slavery existed before the 1400, the 1400s marked the start of European slave trading in Africa with the Portuguese transporting people from Africa to Portugal and using them as slaves. Human trafficking and exploitation has been in existence across the globe for thousands of years. From the ancient Greek and Romans to the medieval times, and up until today, humans have been subject to various forms of physical and sexual slavery.

In 1562, the British joined in on the slave trade in Africa. The development of plantation colonies increased the volume of the slave trade. Later on throughout the 1600s, other countries became more involved in the European slave trade. These included Spain, North America, Holland, France, and Sweden. Others argue that the forced labour of children during the 1700s was the real beginning of what is now known as human trafficking.

The Fight against Sex Trafficking

The British were the first to make a law against slavery in 1807, when they passed a law that made the Transatlantic Slave Trade illegal. In 1820, the United States followed Great Britain's example by making the slave trade a crime that was punishable by death. In 1899 and 1902, international conferences to talk about white slavery were organized in Paris, France. Then in 1904, an international agreement against the 'white slave trade' was created, with a focus on migrant women and children. In 1910, 13 countries signed the International Convention for the Suppression of White Slave Trade to make this form of trafficking illegal. This International Convention led to the creation of national committees to work against the trafficking of white women. However, the First World War halted these efforts, and it was not until 1921 that the fight against trafficking continued. In June of 1921, the League of Nations held an international conference in Geneva, in which the term 'white slavery' was changed to 'traffic of women and children'. This was done to make sure that: the trafficking in all countries was dealt with, the victims of races other than those termed 'white' were recognized, and that male children were also recognized as victims. During this conference, 33 countries signed the International Convention for the Suppression of the Traffic in women and children.

In 1949, the United Nations Convention of the Traffic in Persons and the Exploitation of the Prostitution of Others was passed. This was the first convention about human trafficking that was legally binding to the countries that signed it and required the countries to make prostitution illegal. However, like all of the conventions before it, this convention still dealt only dealt with human trafficking that had a sexual purpose. In 2000, the United Nations Protocol against Trafficking in Persons was passed. It made all forms of human trafficking illegal.

Present Scenario of Human Trafficking

Human trafficking is internationally recognized and there have been many international laws passed against it, it is still a very serious issue around the world. According to a report given in 2004 by the US Department of State, 600,000 to 800,000 people are trafficked across international borders every year and more people are trafficked within their home countries (Cree, 2008). Human traffickers currently still use methods for obtaining their victims that are similar to the methods that were seen the League of Nations 1923 study. According to Linda Woolf, a professor of Psychology at Webster University, the methods include coercion, which includes promises of a job or marriage, kidnapping, and some girls are sold to traffickers by their own parents (Woolf).

Problems with the Concept

The concept of human trafficking refers to the criminal practice of exploiting human beings by treating them like commodities for profit. Even after being trafficked victims are subjected to long-term exploitation. According to some scholars, the very concept of human trafficking is murky and misleading. (Dumienski, Zbigniew, 2011) It has been argued that while human trafficking is commonly seen as a massive crime, in reality it is an act of illegal migration that involves various different actions: some of them may be criminal or abusive, but others often involve consent and are legal. Laura Agustin argues that not everything that might seem abusive or coercive is considered as such by the migrant. For instance, she states that: 'would-be travelers commonly seek help from intermediaries who sell information, services and documents. When travelers cannot afford to buy these outright, they go into debt'. One scholar says that while these debts might indeed be on very harsh conditions, they are usually incurred on a voluntary basis.

Trafficking in persons is a serious crime and a grave violation of human rights. Every year, thousands of men, women and children fall into the hands of traffickers, in their own countries and abroad. Almost every country in the world is affected by trafficking, whether as a country of origin, transit or destination for victims. UNODC, as guardian of the United Nations Convention against Transnational Organized Crime (UNTOC) and the Protocols thereto, assists States in their efforts to implement then Protocol to Prevent, Suppress and Punish Trafficking in Persons.

Meaning and Definition of Human Trafficking

General dictionary meaning and definition of Human Trafficking consists of three core elements:

1. The action of trafficking, which means the recruitment, transportation, transfer, harboring or receipt of persons.
2. The means of trafficking, which includes threat of or use of force, deception, coercion, abuse of power or position of vulnerability.

3. The purpose of trafficking, which is always exploitation. In the words of the Trafficking Protocol, article 3 "exploitation shall include, at a minimum, the exploitation of the prostitution of others or other forms of sexual exploitation, forced labour or services, slavery or practices similar to slavery, servitude or the removal of organs.

Human Trafficking is defined in the Trafficking Protocol as "the recruitment, transport, transfer, harbouring or receipt of a person by such means as threat or use of force or other forms of coercion, of abduction, of fraud or deception for the purpose of exploitation."The abuse of power or of a position of vulnerability or of the giving or receiving of payments or benefits to achieve the consent of a person having control over another person, for the purpose of exploitation. Exploitation shall include, at a minimum, the exploitation of the prostitution of others or other forms of sexual exploitation, forced labour or services, slavery or practices similar to slavery, servitude or the removal of organs.

Types of Human Trafficking

There are some broad categories of exploitation linked to human trafficking unlike most cases of human smuggling; victims of human trafficking are not permitted to leave upon arrival at their destination. They are held against their will through acts of coercion, and forced to work for or provide services to the trafficker or others. The work or services may include anything from bonded or forced labour to commercialized sexual exploitation. The arrangement may be structured as a work contract, but with no or low payment, or on terms which are highly exploitative. Sometimes the arrangement is structured as debt bondage, with the victim not being permitted or able to pay off the debt.

Bonded labour or debt bondage: is probably the least known form of labour trafficking today, and yet it is the most widely used method of enslaving people. Victims become "bonded" when their labour is demanded as a means of repayment for a loan or service in which its terms and conditions have not been defined or in which the value of the victims' services as reasonably assessed is not applied toward the liquidation of the debt. The value of their work is greater than the original sum of money "borrowed." (2009).

Forced labour: is a situation in which victims are forced to work against their own will, under the threat of violence or some other form of punishment, their freedom is restricted and a degree of ownership is exerted. Men are at risk of being trafficked for unskilled work, which globally generates $31bn according to the International Labour Organisation. Forms of forced labour can include domestic servitude; agricultural labour; sweatshop factory labour; food service and other service industry labour; and begging, (2009).The International Labour Organisation [ILO] has identified six elements, which individually or collectively can indicate forced labour these are:

- Threats or actual physical harm;
- Restriction of movement and confinement to the workplace or to a limited area;
- Debt-bondage;
- Withholding of wages or excessive wage reductions that violate previously made agreements;
- Retention of passports and identity documents (the workers can neither leave nor prove their identity status); and
- Threat of denunciation to the authorities where the worker is of illegal status.

Child labour: is a form of work that is likely to be hazardous to the physical, mental, spiritual, moral, or social development of children and can interfere with their education. They involved in debt bondage, forced recruitment for armed conflict, prostitution, pornography, the illegal drug trade, the illegal arms trade, and other illicit activities around the world.

Sexual trafficking: includes coercing a migrant into a sexual act as a condition of allowing or arranging the migration. Sexual trafficking uses physical or sexual coercion, deception, abuse of power and bondage incurred through forced debt. Trafficked women and children, for instance, are often promised work in the domestic or service industry, but instead are sometimes taken to brothels where their passports and other identification papers are confiscated. They may be beaten or locked up and promised their freedom only after earning through prostitution their purchase price, as well as their travel and visa costs (2011).

Sex trafficking: victims are generally found in dire circumstances and easily targeted by traffickers. Individuals, circumstances, and situations vulnerable to traffickers include homeless individuals, runaway teens, displaced homemakers, refugees, job seekers, tourists, kidnap victims and drug addicts. While it may seem like trafficked people are the most vulnerable and powerless minorities in a region (2007).

Domestic Servitude: Domestic servitude involves the victim being forced to work in private households. Their movement will often be restricted and they will be forced to perform household tasks such as child care and house-keeping over long hours and for little if any pay. Victims will lead very isolated lives and have little or no unsupervised freedom. Their own privacy and comfort will be minimal in rare circumstances where victims receive a wage it will be heavily reduced, ostensibly to pay for food and accommodation.

Organ Harvesting: Organ harvesting involves trafficking people in order to use their internal organs for transplant. The illegal trade is dominated by kidneys, which are in the greatest demand and are the only major organs that can be wholly transplanted with relatively few risks to the life of the donor.

Girl and Women Trafficking in India

According to a recent survey women are bought and sold with impunity and trafficked at will to other countries from different parts of India. These girls and women are sourced from Dindigal, Madurai, Tiruchirapalli, and Chengalpattu in TamilNadu, Gaya, Kishanganj, Patna, Katihar, Purnea, Araria and Madhubani from Bihar, Murshidabad and 24 Parganas in West Bengal, Maharajgunj from UP, Dholpur, Alwar, Tonk from Rajasthan, Mangalore, and Gulbarga and Raichur from Karnataka. These women and girls are supplied to Thailand, Kenya, South Africa and Middle East countries like Bahrin, Dubai, Oman, Britain, South Korea and Philippines. They are forced to work as sex workers undergoing severe exploitation and abuse. These women are the most vulnerable group in contracting HIV infection. Due to unrelenting poverty and lack of unemployment opportunities there is an increase in the voluntary entry of women into sex work.

Causes of Human Trafficking

Trafficking is caused by an entire range of different conditions and issues such as:

- **Lack of Awareness:** Many people who migrate for work within Indonesia or abroad are unaware of the dangers of trafficking and the ways in which migrant workers are deceived or pushed into abusive or slave-like labour.
- **Poverty**: Poverty has forced many households to devise survival strategies that have included migrating for work and bonded labour, i.e., renting out a person's labour to pay off a debt or a loan.
- **Material Expectations**: The desire for consumer products and higher standards of living fuel migration and render migrants vulnerable to trafficking.

The following cultural factors contribute to trafficking:

- **Women's Role in the Family**: Although cultural norms stress that a woman's place is at home as wife and mother, it is acknowledged that women may have to become supplementary wage earners in times of family need. A sense of duty and obligation drives many women to migrate for work in order to support their families.
- **Children's Role in the Family:** Obedience to parents and an obligation to support the family makes children vulnerable to trafficking. Child labour, child migration for work, and child bonded labour are deemed acceptable family financial strategies to survive.
- **Early Marriage:** Early marriage has serious implications for girls, including health hazards, the end of schooling, limited economic opportunities, disruption of personal development, and, often, early divorce. Divorced girls are legally seen as adults and are vulnerable to trafficking as a result of their economic vulnerability.

- **History of Bonded Labour**: The practice of renting out one's labour or that of a family member to pay off a loan is an accepted family survival strategy. People placed into bonded labour are especially vulnerable to abusive and slave-like work conditions.
- **Lack of Birth Registry:** People without proper identification fall prey to trafficking more easily, since their age and nationality cannot be documented.
- **Lack of Education:** People with limited education have fewer viable job skills and opportunities and are thus more prone to trafficking as they look to migrate for unskilled work.
- **Corruption and Weak Enforcement of Laws:** Traffickers can often bribe corrupt law enforcement and immigration officials to overlook criminal activities. Public administrators can also be bribed to falsify information on ID cards, birth certificates, and passports, making migrant workers more vulnerable to trafficking due to illegal migration. In addition, lack of state funds budgeted for counter trafficking efforts hampers law enforcers' ability to effectively deter and prosecute traffickers. A lack of effective anti-trafficking legislation, and if such legislation exists, a lack of effective enforcement;

Some Universal factors of human trafficking:

1. The expense of social charges that employers need to pay for the social protection of regularly employed workers.
2. Increasing demand for cheap and exploitable labourers in the construction, agricultural and industrial sectors.
3. Increasing demand for cheap and exploitable domestic labourers.
4. A rise in the demand for sex workers in a highly lucrative and globalising sex industry.
5. Ever more limits and obstacles to legal migration channels to countries with stronger economies and/or regions with better prospects.
6. The high profit potential for those engaged in the criminal activity;
7. The sophisticated organisation, resources and networking capacity of criminal networks.
8. Global economic policies that foster exclusion of marginalised people.
9. Disintegration of social protection networks

Consequences of Human Trafficking Victims

Obviously, human trafficking produces critical consequences in regards to the safety, welfare, and basic human rights of the victims, who are forced to live in the conditions of physical and mental imprisonment. Numerous mechanisms are used during the exploitation phase, commonly involving: repayment obligations; isolation – confiscation of identification documents; use of violence and intimidation; psychological imprisonment and torture.

Victims are often beaten, raped, limited in movement, denied food or water, tortured or drugged, in order to provide absolute obedience. These methods may be a form of punishment for disobedience, but may also serve as prevention to warn the victims of the potential repercussions in case of breaching the established rules of their enslavement.

Consequently, human trafficking victims suffer from chronic, long-term trauma. Traumatic events signify a significant threat to life or physical integrity. Most often, human response to danger causes increased blood flow of adrenalin, initiating a state of alert, after which individuals in such a crisis may choose to fight or flight, exhibiting strong emotions, such as fear or anger that can either mobilize or paralyze them. Normal human reactions to abnormal and traumatic events, like human trafficking, involve:

1. **Physical reactions:** headache and stomach pain; sudden sweating and heart disturbance; changes in sleep and appetite weakened immune system; alcohol or drug misuse.
2. **Psychological reactions:** shock and fear; disorientation and confusion; oversensitivity and distress; rumination of trauma; nightmares and flashbacks; minimization of the experience; isolation and detachment; problems with trust and/or feelings of betrayal; feelings of helplessness, panic and loss of control; decreased interest for daily activities; lack of sense of order or justice in the world; and fear of the future.

The intensity of the victim's reaction depends on the experienced trauma and emotional pain, and is often combined with maltreatment and abuse during childhood, which represents an important domain of clinical consequences caused by enslavement and physical abuse.

Community Consequences:

1. Growing influence of criminal organisations;
2. Other criminal activities, including money laundering, drug trafficking, weapons trade, etc;
3. Corruption among the government offices;
4. Increase in irregular migration;
5. Problems of national security;
6. Declining public confidence.

Needs of the Victims

In order to end the circle of violence and exploitation, victims must be identified and subsequently re-socialized/re-integrated through an institutionalized support system. Historically, prosecution-oriented approaches have been used; however, more and more organisations have begun to adopt a victim-oriented approach that views human trafficking primarily as an issue of human rights, consequently making it a procedural issue. Victim-oriented approaches entail the development of a programme scheme and performance of specific activities in each individual case of support. Comprehensive programmes that utilize process-orientation (emotional healing and overcoming trauma), effect-orientation (emotional stabilization and social inclusion), as well as the change of policies and measures-orientation (upgrading victims protection framework) have similarly been adapted in certain cases to help the victims of human trafficking.

The diversified needs of human trafficking victims may be satisfied only through coordinated actions of state institutions, non-governmental organisations, and international organisations. Once freed, victims require all the basic human needs, i.e. housing, food, clothing, materials for personal hygiene, etc. Furthermore, victims often need medical assistance for acute health issues, sexually transmitted diseases, and drug addiction. Parallel to these needs is the need for psychological support, which is essential to the full recovery of the victim.

Usually, legal aid through regulating civil status of the victim, provision of all pertinent documentation and adequate security measures is needed for access to health and social support, as well as administrative and court proceedings, where victims may appear as witnesses. In addition to all of the above, the need for education and employment is paramount in order for substantial re-integration of the victim. Some victims may even have specific personal needs to re-establish contact with family, whether the relationship is interpersonal or intimate. These needs can be satisfied through comprehensive and institutionalized programmes including: detection identification, rehabilitation, short-term re-integration, and sustainable social inclusion.

Methods and Strategies of Prevention

The UN's Protocol contains a number of provisions aimed at preventing trafficking. State parties are required to establish policies, programmes and other measures aimed at preventing trafficking and protecting trafficked persons from re-victimization. Strategies in all these areas have to be oriented towards the specific characteristics of the situation and the target groups.

1. The best method of prevention is its integration it with prosecution and protection. Prosecution includes several tasks like the identification of the traffickers bringing them to the book, confiscating their illegal assets. Protection of the trafficked victim includes all steps towards the redress of their grievances thus helping the victim survive, rehabilitate and establish herself/himself. Thus, prosecution and protection contribute to prevention.
2. The strategies should address the issues of livelihood options and opportunities by focusing on efforts to eradicate poverty, illiteracy etc. Education and other services should be oriented towards capacity building and the consequent empowerment of vulnerable groups.

3. Gender discrimination and patriarchal mindset are important constituents and catalysts of the vulnerability of women and girl children. This manifests itself in several serious violations of women's rights such as high incidence of female feticide and infanticide and the discrimination against women in healthcare, education and employment. Since these are vulnerability factors that trigger trafficking prevention, strategies need to be oriented accordingly.
4. Natural calamities and manmade disturbances do exacerbate the vulnerability situation. Therefore relief and aftercare programmes need to have specific components focused on the rights of women and children.
5. At the micro level, the prevention of trafficking in the source areas requires a working partnership between the police and NGOs. Public awareness campaigns and community participation are key to prevention programmes.
6. Political will is an essential requirement to combat trafficking.
7. Creating legal awareness is one of the most important functions of any social action programme because without legal awareness Legal awareness empowers people by making them aware of their rights, and can work towards strengthening them to develop zero tolerance towards abuse and exploitation.
8. Immigration officials at the borders need to be sensitized so that they can network with the police as well as with NGOs working on preventing trafficking.
9. Help lines and help booths are very important for providing timely help to any person in distress. NGOs working on child rights, missing person bureaus and police help lines are linked together as a alarming tool against trafficking.

Preventive Measures:

- Raise awareness: The trafficking trade thrives because it is kept in the darkness. The United Nations Office on Drugs and Crime, Prevent Human Trafficking, Human Trafficking.org and other groups are working to make sure people know what is occurring around the world. Not only do first-world citizens need to be educated, citizens of source countries need to make aware as well.
- Help create laws to prevent traffickers. Contact local lawmakers and show your support. Let them know that you are aware of the problem. Back up your support by voting for laws that aid in the prevention of human trafficking.
- Economic equality, stronger laws, and decreasing labour demand.
- Support strong enforcement of the laws. Do not support human trafficking in any way. Prostitution, mail order brides and sweatshops

are all forms of human trafficking to some degree. Prostitution is particularly vulnerable to trafficking.

- Join one of the many human rights organisations assisting trafficking victims. These groups work to raise the profile of human trafficking crimes around the world. By getting involved, you show that the issue matters. The more visible human trafficking is, the more people pay attention to it.
- Governments can also develop systems of co-operation between different nations' law enforcement agencies and with non-government organisations (NGOs). Another action governments can take is raising awareness of this issue. This can take three forms. First, in raising awareness amongst potential victims, particularly in countries where human traffickers are active. Second, raising awareness amongst police, social welfare workers and immigration officers to equip them to deal appropriately with the problem. And finally, in countries where prostitution is legal or semi-legal, raising awareness amongst the clients of prostitution to watch for signs of human trafficking victims, through films and Posters.

Countries are Affected by Human Trafficking

Human trafficking affects every country of the world, as countries of origin, transit or destination or even a combination of all. Trafficking often occurs from less developed countries to more developed countries, where people are rendered vulnerable to trafficking by virtue of poverty, conflict or other conditions. Most trafficking is national or regional, but there are also notable cases of long-distance trafficking. Europe is the destination for victims from the widest range of destinations, while victims from Asia are trafficked to the widest range of destinations. The Americas are prominent both as the origin and destination of victims of human trafficking.

The Victims and Culprits of Human Trafficking

Victims of trafficking can be any age, and any gender. However, a disproportionate number of women are involved in human trafficking both as victims and as culprits. Female offenders have a prominent role in human trafficking, particularly where former victims become perpetrators as a means of escaping their own victimization. Most trafficking is carried out by people whose nationality is the same as that of their victim.

Organisations are Tackle Human Trafficking

The Protocol to Prevent, Suppress and Punish Trafficking in Persons, especially Women and Children, was adopted by the United Nations General Assembly in 2000 and entered into force on 25 December 2003.The Trafficking Protocol, which supplements the United Nations Convention against Transnational Organized Crime, is the only international legal instrument addressing human trafficking as a crime and falls under the jurisdiction of the United Nations Office on Drugs and Crime (UNODC).

The purposes of the Trafficking Protocol are:

- To prevent and combat trafficking in persons
- To protect and assist victims of trafficking, and
- To promote cooperation among States Parties in order to meet these objectives.

The major challenges before the agencies:

1. One of the challenges relates to the gathering of accurate information in order that a true picture of the phenomenon can be guess. In this respect, some progress has been made but more needs to be done.
2. From UNODC's work across the criminal justice sector, we are fully aware that human trafficking is often only one activity of extensive and highly sophisticated international crime networks.
3. We need to consider the type of action that can be taken to raise awareness of the problem and take steps to prevent trafficking at source.
4. A major challenge is to ensure that action is taken to ratify and effectively implement the convention against transnational organized crime and the protocol to prevent, suppress and punish trafficking in persons, especially women and children.
5. Improving international cooperation and coordination, particularly in relation to developing information exchange and operational cooperation between law enforcement agencies needs to be strengthened.
6. There is a need to take a more holistic and partnership approach to tackling the problem. In this respect, the importance of mobilizing the support of NGOs, governments and the community at large.

REFERENCES

Global TV Campaign on Human Trafficking. UN Office on Drugs and Crime. 2003. Archived from the Original on 2007-10-06. http://web.archive.org/web/20071006161444/http://www.unodc.org/unodc/en/trafficking_tv_campaign_2002.html. Retrieved 2008-10-05 (archived from the original on 2007-10-0-6)

Cree, V.E. (2008).Confront Sex Trafficking: Lessons from History. International Social Work, 763-776.

Kangaspunta (n.d.)A Short History of Trafficking in Persons. Retrieved February 23,2010 from Freedom from Fear:http://www.freedomfromfearmagazine.org.

Woolf, L.M (n.d.) Sex Trafficking. Retrieved February 24, 2010 from Women and Global Human Rights:http://www.webster.edu/~woolfln/trafficking.htmld.

Dumienski, Zbigniew, 2011, 'Critical Reflections on Anti-human Trafficking: The Case of Timor-Leste', NTS Alert, May, Issue 2, Singapore: RSIS Centre for Non-Traditional Security (NTS) Studies for NTS-Asia.

"Difference Between Smuggling and Trafficking". Anti-trafficking.net. http://www.anti-trafficking.net/differencebetweensmugglingand.html. Retrieved 2012-12-30.

"UNODC on Human Trafficking and Migrant Smuggling". Unodc.org. 2011. http://www.unodc.org/unodc/en/human-trafficking/. Retrieved 2011-03-22.

"Amnesty International - People Smuggling". Amnesty.org.au. 2009-03-23. http://www.amnesty.org.au/refugees/comments/20601/. Retrieved 2011-03-22.

Labour Trafficking Fact Sheet, National Human Trafficking Resource Center.

Woman Stats Maps, Woman Stats Project.

Victims of Trafficking and Violence Protection Act of 2000". State.gov. http://www.state.gov/g/tip/laws/61124.htm. Retrieved 2011-03-22.

Definition of Trafficking - Save the Children Nepal (archived from the original on 2007-11-20)

Red Light: Black Life
A Study of Female Sex Workers

– Dr. **Robin D. Tribhuwan**
– Dr. **Jayshree V. Kharche**

Introduction

Prostitution is as old as human civilization. Women in all most all the parts of the world have been practicing prostitution. Studies have revealed that majority of these women are between the age range 1'5 to 45. Some of the major causes of why these young girls and women are forced into prostitution are:

1. Death of parents, husbands etc.
2. Poverty and destitution.
3. Ill-treatment or neglect by parents, husbands and relatives.
4. Kidnapping, deception, bad influence etc.
5. Sexual urge, illegitimate pregnancy etc.
6. Mental disposition or attitude such as ignorance, desire for easy life and low moral values.
7. Economic factors – The chief cause for young girls or women accepting this profession is poverty.
8. Social values against un-chastity – A girl who had illicit sex experience made feel that she has lost every thing and hence takes up this profession.
9. Mental deficiency or certain temperamental traits – This factor is also considered to be the cause of prostitution.

10. Ignorance - Vice rings operating in large urban areas frequently exploit girls by sweetly forcing them into this profession,
11. Unhappy marital relations – This is yet another factor,
12. Inordinate sex desire – Certain girls have inordinate desires and crave for sex stimulation for its own sake,
13. Desire for new experience and hence prostitution,
14. Vested interests – Highly profitable nature of business makes many girls, resort to prostitution,
15. Restrictions on widow re-marriages,
16. Devdasi system – (Madàn G.R.(1980:203)

Sex workers are of two types namely:

1. **Brothel based:** Those sex workers practicing in the houses and buildings,
2. **Street based:** Those waiting on the roads, near bus stops, railway stations and on the streets.

This chapter throws light on the darker side of their life, as female sex workers, keeping in view the following objectives:

1. To understand the socio-economic and educational background of female sex workers.
2. To study the problems faced by them as sex workers.
3. To unveil the basic facilities and amenities at the brothel centers.
4. To analyse their perception about the darker side of their life.

Methodology

The sample comprised of 200 female sex workers from Latur district. Out of 2000 female sex workers in the district, the authors selected 10 per cent. An NGO working with the sex workers was selected to carry out the survey. Confidentiality and anonymity of the interviews was maintained. The interview schedule was anonymous (though linked), and the data was stored in a secured and sealed location. Precautions were taken not to document the names of female sex workers interviewed. Their consent was taken as well. The data was analyzed by using Excel software. Focused group interviews of pimps, social workers, sex workers above 45 years of age was taken.

Major Findings

1. Caste and ethnic status

Out of the total 200 respondents selected, it was observed that they belonged to 22 different caste groups, and two ethnic groups.

2. Marital status

The data revealed that 21 per cent were unmarried; 16 per cent married; 22 per cent divorced; 16 per cent widows; 22 per cent separated and 3 per cent included other categories. Interestingly the divorced, separated and widows constituted to 60 per cent of the total number of respondents. There was significant co-relation of single status of a young girl or a woman with practice of sex work. The unmarried sex workers said no husband, no fear of practicing sex work.

3. Age range of sex workers

It was observed that 28 per cent of the respondents were between 15 to 25 years of age, 68 per cent between 26 to 35 years, and 4 per cent above 35 years. Clients prefer young girls said the pimps.

4. Mother tongue

84 per cent of the respondents spoke Marathi; 15 per cent Hindi and 1 per cent Telugu.

5. Educational status

The data revealed that 36 per cent of the respondents were illiterate, 23 per cent studied up to primary, 41 per cent up to high school and none above tenth grade.

6. Base of practice

79 per cent of them had brothels as their base of practice, while 5 per cent were street while 15 per cent did not reveal their base of practice.

7. Age at the beginning of the profession

It was observed that 47 per cent of the respondents began their career as female sex workers between the age range 21 to 25 years of age, 30 per cent between 31 to 35 years, and 2 per cent above 35 years of age.

8. Family planning operations

22 per cent of the respondents had under gone tubectomy, 13 per cent laparoscopy, 42 per cent none of the above and 23 per cent did not responded.

9. Use of contraceptives

67 per cent of the respondents used condoms, 33 per cent oral pills, and only 1 per cent copper-T. It was however, observed that their regular partners, those who frequently visited them and showed some affection did not use condoms.

10. Abortions

It was found out that 23 per cent of the respondents had undergone abortions at least once, 24 per cent did not and 53 per cent did not respond.

11. Pregnancy status

24 per cent of the total number of respondents was found to be pregnant. It was observed that the female sex workers preferred a female child. When the Sex worker attains 45 years of age, her daughter starts earning as a sex workers and takes care of her mother.

12. Monthly income

The data revealed that 4.5 per cent earned Rs.501 to 1500 per month; 49 per cent between 1501/- to 2500/-; 31 per cent between 2501 to 3500/-, 4 per cent between 3501 to 4500/- and 12 per cent above 4501/- rupees. This amount was their net income after deduction of the rent, food, alcohol, pan and tobacco expenses, including the income of pimps, police and goons.

13. Loan

79 per cent of the female sex workers stated that banks did not give them loan, 7 per cent received loan from money lenders and pimps, while 15 per cent did not respond.

14. Number of hours incurred in the profession

8 per cent said that they work for 1-3 hours a day; 24 per cent said 3 to 6 hours; 24 per cent for 6-9 hours; 38 per cent for 9 to 12 hours and 2 per cent above 12 hours; while, 4 per cent did not respond. The number of hours incurred for the profession includes, waiting for a client, having drinks, pan, tea, cold drink, food including sex with him.

15. Visits to native place

20 per cent visited once a year, 23 per cent twice, 6 per cent thrice, while 51 per cent did not respond.

16. Type of sex preferred

The respondents revealed that majority of clients prefer vaginal sex, while few prefer anal and oral sex. Some stated that some clients like masturbation.

17. Who harasses sex workers?

39 per cent revealed that police harass them; 8 per cent said that the brothel owners; 32 per cent said the goons; 13 per cent stated the middlemen/ agents; 4 per cent said the clients; 5 per cent their regular partners; and, 0.4 per cent said inmates harass them.

18. Who takes care of medical expenses ?

One of the significant questions asked to the respondents. 48 per cent stated that it is self managed; 18 per cent said brothel owner takes care; 7 per cent said the agent; 5 per cent the client; 18 per cent said their regular partner takes care of it; 3 per cent family members; and, 1 per cent the NGOs.

19. Availability of First Aid Box

81 per cent stated that first aid box was not available at the place of practicing sex; 2 per cent said it was available; while, 17 per cent did not respond.

20. Toilet facilities

47 per cent of the respondents stated that toilet facility was available at the place of their professions; 39 per cent said it was not there; while, 14 per cent did not respond.

21. Addiction among female sex workers

Interestingly 8 per cent of the respondents were addicted to alcohol; 29 per cent chewed betel leaf (*pan*); 27 per cent consumed ghutka; 28 per cent chewed tobacco; 3 per cent were smokers; 17 per cent took intravenous drugs and 3 per cent applied *mishery* (a kind of tobacco) on their gums.

22. Personnel preparing food for sex workers

It was observed that 54 per cent of the respondents prepared their own food; 19 per cent said it was prepared by inmates; 7 per cent by the brothel owners; 16 per cent ordered from restaurants; 1 per cent received from caterers; and, 3 per cent received tiffins.

23. Sex work, personal and social image

During the course of informal interviews all the female sex workers unanimously said that as prostitutes they were socially stigmatized. That they had no status in the society. That they are only sex machines satisfying their clients. That, they have to work hard between the age ranges 15 to 35, to earn more, by taking more clients. That, harder they work the more money they get. They have to consistently please the brothel owners, goons, police, pimps, agents and middlemen. They take alcohol and intoxicating substances to forget that they are women. They are also deprived of love, emotions, interaction with family members and relatives. Life after 45 is futile and of no use, they said. It was observed unless they themselves become pimps, agents or middle personnel.

Concluding Remarks

Life in the red light zones is certainly black and dark for the female sex workers, who are pushed into these zones. They have to be extra strong to face problems created by the brothel owners, the police, the goons, the middle men and agents, the clients, their regular partners, family members and relatives and at times their inmates. A female sex worker aged, 47 said that I am a living corpse. That I pray to God not to make me a prostitute in the next birth. I am fed-up of this black/dark life. An international NGO based in Pune revealed that 67 per cent of the sex workers examined by them were infected.

REFERENCES

Madan, G.R.1966, Indian Social Problems, Allied Publishers, New Delhi

Punekar, S.D. and Rao, Kamla, 1962, A Study of Prostitutes in Bombay, pp. 90-95.

Part – III

Educational Issues of Youth

Distractions and Hurdles in Learning Process Among College Youth *Parent's Perspective*

– Dr. **Robin D. Tribhuwan**
– Dr. **K.S. Patil**

Introduction

The concept of Guru-Shishya Parampara is very popular in the traditional education system in India. Despite of being strict, teachers were respected and looked upon as great sources of knowledge. The traditions of showing gratitude to the teachers is still reflected in the celebration rituals of "Guru Pornima". Popular musicians, singers, dances and other artists, learn the respective art so as to master the same, from their teachers.

The teachers then developed several techniques of teaching their students. For example a tabla teacher would instruct his students to practice 'trital' (16 beats rhythm) for 3 to 6 hours a day for 4 to 6 months. The students would reciprocate by sincerely and respectfully following the instructions of his Guru. That, kind of devotion, sincerity, passion and interest to learn, is not found in the present younger generation.

The technological advancement, modernization, urbanization, impact of mass media, globalization, planned development, awareness and empowerment, is changing the attitude of students towards their devotion and sincerity to learn and educate themselves. The process of learning in formal educational institutions is getting disturbed due to several forces and factors. The present chapter unveils the perceptions of the parents of college youth, regarding the distractions and hurdles in learning, keeping in view the following objectives.

Objectives of the Study

1. To study the perceptions of parents of college youth, regarding the various distractions and hurdles that hinder their learning.
2. To understand the consequences of these forces, on the career of the students and on the expectations of parents.
3. To suggest measures to control these temptations among college youth so as to promote self-learning, and interest in studies.

Methodology

The present study was carried out in ten colleges situated in Pune and Nagpur. The group discussions were held with 200 parents of college students. 20 focused group discussions were conducted with ten parents, both in Pune and Nagpur at various intervals within a span of ten months. An interview guide was prepared to get the responses of the parents. Efforts were made by the researchers to see that every focused group interview consisted of equal number of mothers and fathers. Parents were interviewed by framing question on two issues namely distraction and hurdles that hinder the process of learning among college youth. Since the documented data was qualitative in nature, it was analyzed manually. The perceptions of the parents of the college youth regarding the distractions and hurdles in their studies is as below:

1. Mobile cell phones
2. Television with cable connection
3. Computers with internet facilities
4. Fad for readymade notes.
5. Kitty parties.
6. Liquor/beer parties.
7. Visits to theatres.
8. Craze & demand for two wheelers.
9. Time pass in college canteens, restaurants, gardens & malls.
10. Demand for pocket money.
11. Fashion.
12. Attraction of opposite sex.

1. Mobile cell phones

The parents opined that although mobile cells are very useful, they are one of the major obstacles in learning process. These days several brands of cell phones are available in the market with several facilities such as:

(i) S.M.S.
(ii) Songs

(iii) E-mails
(iv) Internet
(v) Games
(vi) Movies
(vii) Camera
(viii) Photos
(ix) Face book
(x) Conversation/chatting etc.

The college youth get involved into the above facilities in the cell phones and are hence distracted from their studies.

2. Televisions with cable connections

Televisions with cable connections have hundreds of channels as options. The youth get attracted to these. This in turn has negative impact on their studies.

3. Computer with internet

Youngster often visits cyber-cafe for using internet. If these facilities are at home, with friends and in the offices it is much more convenient. They are most happy to use them to play games, see videos, mail friends, and chat with relatives and friends and so on. This is yet another hurdle in the learning process of the college youth.

4. Fad far ready-made notes

College youth demand money from parents to photo copy ready-made notes. This prevents them from reading books, latest journals, and encyclopedias to prepare their own notes. Thus, fad for readymade notes is yet another distraction.

5. Kitty parties

Organizing kitty parities in K.F.C., MC-Donald, and Pizza hut, restaurants or at home is yet another craze among college youth. This too has an adverse impact on their studies.

6. Liquor/beer parties

Adventurous youth, especially the males, love to organized liquor/ beer parties in the hostels, homes, bars or other places to enjoys themselves. This is one of the biggest worries of the parents. It is an obstacle in the studies of college youth.

7. Visits to theatres

Visits to theatres either in a group or with a girl friend are yet another craze among the college youth that hinders their studies.

8. Craze & demand for two wheelers

Most of the college students demand two wheelers from their parents. A male feels proud, when a girl sits behind him covering her head and face with a scarf. These bikes are used more, to visit theaters, malls gardens, restaurants etc. This craze of possessing a mobile does hinder studies.

9. Time pass in college canteens, restaurants, gardens and malls

Chatting with friends & passing time in canteens, restaurants, gardens & malls is yet another hurdle in their studies.

10. Demand for pocket money

Students demand for pocket money & spend the same on tea, snacks, ice creams & cold drinks etc. This is yet another worry for the parents who are not economically well off.

11. Fashion

The craze from wearing branded shoes, using good bags, glasses, caps, sun coats etc certainly burdens the parents financially. This behaviour also triggers their mind to attract and impress the opposite sex. This too, disturbs their learning process. They pay more attention to fashion than studies.

12. Attraction of opposite sex

Use of good cloths, cosmetics, bags, shoes, body lotions, deodorants etc. Demand for two wheelers, pocket money and money to go to good parlors etc are naturally linked with impressing & attracting friends. Once the youth get involved into romantic affairs, they spend more time in theatres, parks, canteens, restaurants, writing love letters, sending emails, SMS etc. This in turn distracts their attention from studies.

Consequences

It was observed that every obstacle is intertwined with the other. The above-mentioned distractions certainly have the following impacts on the parents and the college youth as well.

(a) Impact on parents

Parents of the children, who are victims of one or more of the above-mentioned distractions directly or indirectly suffer from:

- Stress;
- Worries regarding grades or failure of their children.
- Worries about fast driving, addiction, bad company.
- Worries about paying money for Xerox, pocket money, mobile phone bills, internet bill etc.

(b) Impact on the students

The students who scoreless grades, fail and repeat the same class. They get addicted to alcoholism, smoking, chewing Kharra or Ghutka. In case they get into serious love affairs, the question that troubles them in how to lead a married life without a job?

The parents of the college youth also opined that it is the students who need to understand that their educational career is a top priority. That, the above-mentioned distractions should not tempt them & hinder their studies. That, parents & teachers must teach the significance of educational career.

Suggestions

On the basis of the focused group discussions with parents, a few teachers and few college youth, we suggest following methods to create awareness among the college youth to prevent from falling prey to the distractions and hurdles that hinders their studies.

Counselling

Counselling in the college, in community halls, at religious centers by educationists, philosophers, teachers, religious leaders and successful people to college youth will certainly contribute in overcoming this problem.

Role of Parents

Parents must socialize their children in a friendly and loving way to give priority to their studies, request the expectations of parents & teachers and not prey to distractions that will hinder their studies.

Role of Teachers

A teachers' role is equally important in molding the habits of the students. They should make the college youth understand their responsibility.

Role of College Administration

College administration must see to it that the students abide by the rules & discipline. Lectures by educational experts & psychologists, doctors, artists etc should be organized in the college to educate the youth on adverse impact of distractions. Efforts must be made to strictly implement rules that will prevent students from using mobiles & internet in the class rooms and during lectures. Notice boards & poster to create awareness regarding the misbehaviour, use of cell phones, etc should be put up in the college premises.

College Youth

The college youth themselves should realize that learning and educational career is more important for them than temptations.

Socio-economic Status of Women Lecturers in Pune University's Jurisdiction
A Survey

– Dr. **Jyoti Suhas Gagangras**

Introduction

It is always been fascinating to write about the status and roles of women, both in the society family, and at their place of work.

While writing about the status of women with in the family, U. Lalitha Devi (1982: 44) stated that, family in the area in which the role of women is traditionally the most prominent. Indeed, women had practically no role outside the home in traditional middle and upper class families and their whole life had been spent in the family.

The forces of social and cultural change have turned the tables. Educated, employed, modern and empowered women, no longer hang around in their homes. It is generally accepted fact that the participation of women in employment outside home has greatly changed their family and social lives. Perhaps the most far – reaching effect has been the economic independence attended by working women. Another possible effect is the redistribution of the work within the family so that the employed women can still participate in their work, while continuing many of their traditional family obligations. The modern families tend to preserve a satisfactory division of labour.

The tasks previously assigned to the wife are being shared by the husband and wife jointly or partially by the in-laws, so that the wife can have near equal responsibility for earning the family living. Where the husband/male members do not share the house-hold work, alternate help of a relative or servant is often sought. Thus, employment of women may be viewed as a cause of decrease in the differentiation of sex roles.

In the tradition-bound society man is the head of the house hold and he makes most of the decision. But this predominance of the male has been considerably undermined due to employment of women. The employment and education of women have given them resources which their unemployed counter parts do not have. The salary income of a working woman is substantial contribution to the family income which would be expected to give her greater interest in financial decisions and greater respect from her husband and other members of the family. Secondly, the participation of the women in the activities outside world through her job gives her contacts with fellow-workers, which increases the knowledge and skill she brings to decision making, such factors have made working women resourceful and competent decision makers.

Do families with working women agree to the changed status of a male-dominated decisions towards mere egalitarian joint decisions ? Has the social, economic, educational and political status of a working woman really changed? Do the family members, colleagues at work, community members still expect a working woman to perform her traditional roles? What is the rural and urban scenario in terms of status and roles of women? Well, these and other research question haunt the mind of a researcher. Keeping this, back ground in mind. The present study aims to unveil the status, role and the expectation of the family members, colleagues at work and the society of women lecturers in Pune University's Jurisdiction.

Objectives of the Study

1. To study the socio-economic background women lecturers.
2. To analyze the expectations of their spouses, in-laws, children and the colleagues at work place.
3. To assess the change that has taken place in their personal, familial and social life.

Research Methodology

The present study was carried out in 52 colleges of Pune Universities Jurisdiction. These colleges were from Nashik, Ahemednagar and Pune Districts. The researcher selected 284 female lecturers as respondents. Table 18.1 presents rural-urban respondents from 3 districts.

Table 18.1: District Wise Rural-Urban Respondents Selected

Sr. No.	District	Rural	Urban	Total
1.	Nashik	34	47	81
2.	Pune	45	59	104
3.	Ahemednagar	45	54	99
	Total	**124**	**160**	**284**

A questionnaire was prepared, pre-tested and finally administered to gather data from the respondents. Observation and case study methods were used too. The quantitative data was analyzed using excel software, while quantitative data was analyzed manually. Simple random sampling method was used to select the sample. The data analyzed is presented as below.

Major Findings

1. Nature of employment

Out of the total 284 women lecturers 56 were employed on clock hour basis, while 104 were on non-grant basis and the rest 114 were granted posts. As evident, from table 18.2 majority of the posts fall under the category of clock hour and non-grant basis.

Table 18.2: Nature of Employment

Sr. No.	Type of Posts	Rural	Urban	Total
1.	Clock Hour Basis	30	26	56
2.	Non-granted posts	52	52	104
3.	Granted posts	42	72	114
	Total	**124**	**160**	**284**

2. Age range of the respondents

Out of the 284 respondents 126 were between the age range 23 to 35, 80 were between 36 to 50 and 78 were above 50 years of age.

3. Marital status

The table given below presents marital status of the respondents studied.

Table 18.3: Marital Status

Sr. No.	District	Rural	Urban	Total
1.	Unmarried	24	18	42
2.	Married	90	122	212
3.	Divorced	02	07	09
4.	Widows	03	04	07
5.	Did Not Respond	05	09	14
	Total	**124**	**160**	**284**

4. Administrative posts held

The data revealed that out of the total 284 number of respondents are six were principals, 17 were vice principals and 87 were Head of the Departments. These figures reveal that the percentage of administrative representation among women lecturers is less. It was observed that not a single female lecturer was an academic dean, registrar, pro-vice chancellor or vice-chancellor of Pune University during the survey.

5. Membership of academic organisations

Out of the 284 respondents only 125 women lecturers had membership of academic organisation Majority of them i.e. 82 were from urban areas and 43 were from rural areas.

6. Preference of children

One of the questions in the questionnaire aimed to find out the choice of preference of children the table below depicts their choice of number of children preferred.

Table 18.4: Choice of Number of Children Preferred

Sr. No.	No. of Children Preferred	Rural	Urban	Total
1.	None	11	24	35
2.	One Child	21	52	73
3.	2 to 3	68	39	107
4.	Above 3	–	–	–
5.	Did Not respond	24	45	69
	Total	**124**	**160**	**284**

It is evident from the above table that out the 284 respondents 35 preferred not to have a child, 73 wanted one, 107, 2 to 3 and no one wanted more than 3 children. 69 respondents did not respond. The table further reveals that women lecturers from the urban areas preferred less or no children.

7. Caste/tribe composition

Interestingly majority of the respondents did not wish to reveal their caste/tribe identity. They said they do not believe in revealing the same. Table number 18.5 depicts caste/tribe status of the respondents.

As evident from table number 18.5, the representation of the Brahmins, Marathas and scheduled castes seems to be more among the respondents studied, followed by the O.B.C.'s Interestingly, Out of the 284 respondents only 3 belonged to the tribal communities.

Table 18.5: Caste/Tribe Status of Respondents

Sr. No.	Caste/Tribe	Rural	Urban	Total
1.	Brahmins	03	21	24
2.	Maratha	20	10	30
3.	Scheduled Castes	12	15	27
4.	Scheduled Tribes	01	02	03
5.	Other Backward Class	07	08	15
6.	Minorities	02	03	05
7.	Did Not Respond	56	124	180
	Total	**101**	**183**	**284**

8. Religious status of the respondents

As evident from the data out of the 284 respondents, 224 were Hindus, 3 were Jains, 4 Christians, 5 Muslims, 42 Neo-Buddhists, 2 skills and 4 did not respond.

9. Family types

Out of the 284 respondents 74, lived in joint families, 140 in nuclear families, 4 where singles while 66 did not respond. The preference of living in nuclear families was observed to be high, among women lecturers both in rural and urban areas. Prevalence of nuclear families among the respondents from urban areas was high.

10. Educational status

Out of the 284 respondents majority i.e. 146 completed their masters, 86 completed M.Phil and only 32 were Ph.D. It was observed that women lecturers who completed Ph.D. were at a higher advantage when it came to status and respect in their families, among relatives, friends and colleagues, followed by these who completed M.Phil and Masters.

11. SET/NET clearance

It was observed that out of the 284 respondents. 121 cleared the state Educational Test. Cleared/National Educational Test, while 70 did not clear the same. 93 were exempted from both.

12. Socio-economic status reflections

Informal interviews with women lecturers studied revealed following facts regarding their socio-economic status.

(a) **Traditional tasks:** The house hold child rearing responsibilities traditionally assigned to a women are shared by the husband and the in-laws are jointly shared now.

(b) **Status:** The spouse, in-laws, parents as well as family members of the respondents studied were proud of her social status as a lecturer/Associate professor, vice-principal or principal as it were.

(c) **Status conscious:** All the respondents were conscious and their status as lecturers and felt psychologically elevated of the same.

(d) **Freedom of participating in decision making:** Their status as lecturers and income earners certainly contributed in getting freedom to participate in decision making.

13. Expectations from the family members

Qualitative data depicted through case studies revealed that:

(a) Expectations from the Respondents:

The children, in-laws as well as the husbands expected the respondents (married ones) to cook food for them. They did not enjoy the food corked by the Maid servants (in few cases). The family members expected the mothers (respondents) to look after their children. Being with the family at home, on holidays, festivals, weddings, and other family and community celebration was yet another expectation of the spouse, in-laws, children and other family members.

14. Expectation from colleagues

The colleagues at work place expected the women lecturers to perform the duties assigned to them by the principals, vice-principals as well as the Heads of the Departments. It was observed that, the female lecturers on clock hour basis and non-granted posts were burdened with extra-curricular and academic activities by the principals, vice-principals and the Heads of the Departments, as compared to the lecturers of granted posts.

Women lecturers who were on temporary posts were burdened with work more, as compared to the permanent ones. The male colleagues were mere aspirant candidates for posts of principal, vice-principal, heads of the departments as compared to the female lecturers.

It was observed that the representation of male lecturers and Associate professors in the academic bodies of the universities and in the power structures was higher as compared to female lecturers.

15. Expectations from the society

Although, women lecturers are respected in the society due to their occupational status, the society at large expects them to perform their household, child rearing, traditional culturally assigned duties including work in the colleges. This expectation was on a higher degree among the communities of women lecturers in the rural areas, as compared to these in the urban areas.

16. Changes in socio-economic life

Both quantitative and qualitative data revealed following facts about the socio-economic changes in the lives of women lecturers studied.

(a) Finance support to the family

The monthly salary of the respondents was certainly a boon to their families. The women lecturers, especially these on granted posts were able to accumulate both movable and immovable property, due to their hand some salary.

(b) Status

As mentioned earlier, the working women's status as lecturers, Associate professors, heads of the departments, vice-principal, principal, certainly elevated their families and the communities they belonged to.

(c) Decision making

In most cases, especially in the nuclear families, the women lecturers enjoyed the freedom of taking joint and/or own decisions, with regards to several aspects of family, personal and social life.

(d) Links with outside world

As a result of being a lecturer and/or associate professor or an academic administrator the links and social interactions of the respondents, with students, their parents, with colleagues, academicians, administrators etc. was on the rise. The horizon of their social and academic net work widened.

Tours to other districts, states and countries were also possible due to their occupational status. Field work to villages, NGOs or corporates was yet another advantage.

(e) Decreasing sex roles

Employment of women lecturers certain decreased their sex roles and division of labour such as child-rearing, washing clothes, clearing the house, cooking etc. The in-laws, the spouses and even relatives shared the house hold responsibilities of the women lecturers.

(f) Operating Bank Accounts

All the respondents had their own salary account, which was operated by them. Net working with bank was yet another advantage.

Concluding Remarks

The achieved status of lecturer or associate professor, including the administrative roles held by the respondents, certainly elevated their social image among their family members, relatives their colleagues and in their respective communities. Their social network with outside world increased due to their occupational status. The respondents were proud that they could earn money and contribute to the family. The household responsibility was shared by their in laws, spouses and relatives. However, it was observed that their spouses, in-laws and relatives expected them to cook-food and rear children.

Representation of scheduled Tribe Women lectures was far too less. The women lecturers were kept away from power structures in academics, this is perhaps due to male dominance in university power structures.

REFERENCES

U. Lalitha Devi, 1982, Status and Employment of Women in India, B.R. Publishing Corporation, New Delhi.

Manohar, Murali K. (ed) 1983, Socio-economic Status of Indian Women, Seema Publications, New Delhi.

Social and Educational Problems of the Pardhi Youth

– Mr. **Girish Sarode**
– Ms. **Anjali Gawande**

Introduction

Maharashtra ranks second in the country as regards tribal population size is concerned. The total population of tribal's in Maharashtra is 85.77 lakhs. There are 45 tribes in the state. Out of these 45 tribes, some of the Progressive tribes are Koli Mahadev, Kokna, Andh, Bhil, Mavchi, Koli Malhar, Warli etc. It is also pertinent to note that some of vulnerable groups are Katkaris, Dhorkoli, Dubla, Dhodia, Madia, Kolam and the Pardhi. The present paper aims to unravel the social and educational problems of Pardhi youth keeping in view the following objectives.

1. To unravel the cultural profile of the Pardhis.
2. To unveil the social problems of Pardhi youth.
3. To study the educational problems of Pardhi youth.

Methodology

The researchers studied 10 hamlets and 100 Pardhi families in Nagpur district. An interview guide was prepared to document data on the cultural issues of the Pardhi. Focused group discussion with Pardhi youth, their parents and teachers, were held.

Brief Profile of Pardhi Culture

An analysis of the literature on Pardhi tribe, revealed, following aspects of their culture.

1. **Geographical distribution:** The Pardhis are geographically distributed in Maharashtra, Gujarat, Madhya Pradesh, Chhattisgarh & Andhra Pradesh. In the State of Maharashtra, they found in Dhule, Jalgaon, Solapur, Satara, Kolhapur, Pune, Ahemadnagar, Yavatmal, Nanded, Wardha, Gadchiroli and other districts of Vidharbha.
2. **Origin:** Singh K.S. (1993) has stated that the Pardhi trace their origin to Rajputana, where they used to be appointed as watchmen by the Rajput rulers. Russel and Hiralal (1916) are of the opinion that the Pardhi are a mixed group made up of Bawaria or other Rajput out castes. Enthoven R.E. (1925) states that the word, Pardhi is derived from "Paradh", meaning hunting. The phase Pardhi are known for their hunting traps.
3. **Language:** K.S. Singh (1993) states that the mother tongue of Pardhis is Gujarati and they use Marathi language for inter-group communication. Russel and Heeralal (1916) state that Pardhis perhaps belong to Maratha country, as they are numerous in Khandesh and many of them talk a dialect of Gujarati. In the northern districts their speech in a mixture of "Marwari" and "Hindi", while they often know Marathi and Urdu as well.
4. **Sub-divisions of the Pardhi Tribe:** Like other wandering groups, the Pardhis have a large number of endogamous groups (Russell & Heeralal, 1916).

   These groups are:

   (i) **Shikari or Bhil Pardhis:** Who use fire arms;

   (ii) **The Phase Pardhis:** Who hunt with traps and snares;

   (iii) **The Langoti Pardhis:** So called, because, they wear only a narrow strip of cloth round the lions;

   (iv) **The Takankars:** Who make stone artifacts. The langoti Pardhis and Takankars have strong criminal tendencies.

   (v) **The Chitewale Pardhi:** Who hunt with a tame leopards;

   (vi) **The Gayake Pardhi:** Who stalk their prey behind a bullock;

   (vii) **The Gosain Pardhis:** Who dress like religious mendicants in ochre coloured clothes and do not kill deer, but only hares, jackals and foxes.

   (viii) **The Shishi ke Telwale:** who sell crocodile oil;

   (ix) **The Bandar wale:** Who go about with monkeys;

   (x) **The Hareen Pardhis:** Who kill deer;

   (xi) **The Bahelias:** Who kill only birds of black colour. Their exogamens groups are nearly all those of Rajput tribes, as Sisodia, Pawar, Solanki, Chauhan, Rathore and so on.

(xii) **Goan Pardhis:** Those who live in the villages and seldom wander around.

5. **Occupation:** There are diverse opinions regarding the occupations of the Pardhis.Singh K.S. (1993) is of the opinion that the traditional occupation of the Pardhis was to collect stone slabs, which they often sold to builders. Some times they make grinding stones of those stone slabs and sell them. At present they are mainly engaged in agricultural jobs. Some of them are employed as well.

   Tribhuwan Robin & Ragnahild (2004) have revealed that the Pardhis living on the pavements of Pune ,sell balloons, statues & scrap. Russell & Heeralal (1916) have stated that hunting animals, birds and crocodiles using traps, nets, tamed leopards, stags, hawks and cows is yet another feature of the traditional occupation of the Pardhis. Varous techniques of hunting birds, animals & repitiles have been highlighted by the authors.

6. **Clans:** The Pardhi are divided into a number of exogamous clans (kuls) such as Adhav, Sonawane, Solanki, Pawar, Chauhan, Shinde, Suryavashi, Dabhade, Sesodia etc.

   Enthoven R.E. (1925) has stated that the bulk of the tribe is however, divided into, totemistic divisions worshipping different devaks, of which the principal are:

   (i) Thorns of ariaishrub (Mimosa Jubricaulis)
   (ii) Thorns of bor tree (Zizyphus juyuba)
   (iii) Leaves of the Sami tree (Prosopis spi cigera)
   (iv) Mango tree (Mangifera Indica).
   (v) Jambhul (Eugenia jambolina)
   (vi) Umber (Ficus glomerata)

   Sameness of devak is a bar to inter marriage:

7. **Religion:** Enthoven, R. E. (1925) has stated that the Pardhi belong to the Hindu religion, though a few (30) were recorded at the 1901 census as musalmans. He further stated that those residing in Belgaum district chiefly worship Laxmi, Durgava and Dayamaya. In kutch they worship "Gatrad mata". The goddess of the chavan clan is the devi of the famous pavagad hill in Gujrat.

   The other deities worshipped by the Pardhis are Amba, Bhavani, Jarimari, Khandoba, Chatarshingi and Saptashringi.

   Singh K.S. (1993) has stated that the principal deities of the Pardhi are Kuriarimata and her seven sisters. Every clan has a sacred specialist called gokaria. Junagad and pawagad are the main religious centres of the Pardhis. Animism is one of the main features of Pardhi religion.

8. **Family Types:** Both nuclear and joint family types are found among the Pardhis. Patriarchy, patriliny and patrilocal residence is the norm of lineage among the Pardhis.
9. **Marriage:** Polygyny among the Pardhis is allowed, though its incidence is not high. Marriage to one's mother's brother's daughters is allowed. Junior levirate and junior sororate are practiced. Bride price is bein greplaced to a great extent by "hunda" (dowry). A necklace (Mangalsutra) is the marriage symbol for their women. Divorce is allowed, but not encouraged. Widow remarriage is practiced. Extended families were prefered earlier,but these are now breaking up. The property of a deceased person is shared equally by his sons.

   Enthoven (1925) has stated that polygyny and widow remarriage are allowed among the Pardhis, but polyandry is unknown. Tribhuwan Robin (2008) observed that the wives of Pardhi men who are in th jail get married, if the period of stay in the jail in for overten years. The practice of throwing. "akshata" (red rice) is prevalent among the Pardhis.
10. **Festivals:** Enthoven R.E. (1925) has stated that the chief festivals (Holidays) of the Pardhi are Shimga & Dasara. They sacrifice animals.
11. **Puberty rites:** Sing K. S. (1993) stated that "pehli navan" is the ritual the Pardhis observe when a girl attains puberty.
12. **Dress Pattern:** The men wear a shirt and a dhoti or a loin cloth. A woman wears a sari. These days' men have started wearing shirt and pant.

   Russel and Heeralal (1916) have stated that in dress and appearance the Pardhis are disreputable and dirty. Their features are dark and their hair matted and unkept. They never wear shoes and say that they are protected by a special promise of the devi (goddess) to their first ancestor that no insect, or reptile in the forest should injure them.
13. **Traditional Panchayat:** The Pardhis still preserve their traditional method of trial by ordeal. Russell & Heeralal (1916) state that if a woman is suspected of mis conduct she is made to pick one paise coin, out of boiling oil, or a pipal leaf (Ficus religiosa) is placed on her hand and a red-net axe laid over it, and if her hand is burn or she refuses to stand the test, she is pronounced guilty.

   In the case of a man, accused is made to dive into water; and as he dives, an arrow is shot from a bow. A swift runner fetches and brings back the arrow, and if the diver can remain inside the water until the runner has returned, he is held to be innocent. If an unmarried girl becomes pregnant, two cakes of dough are prepared, a piece of silver being placed in one and a lump of charcoal in the other. The girl takes one of the cakes, and if it is found to contain the coal, she is expelled from the community, while if she chooses the piece of silver, she is pardoned.

Enthoven R.E. (1925) has stated that the Pardhis have social organisation with a head-man called, 'naik' or leader, and settles disputes at the community level. Tribhuwan Robin (2008) has revelealed that the Pardhis have Maha Panchayat as well. These are attended by many Pardhis.

14. **Diet:** The Pardhis eat flesh of goat, sheep, deer, fowls, hogs, peacocks, partridges, quails and almost all feathered game and fish. They are also fond of liquor. The Pardhis of Kutch do not eat flesh of partridges.
15. **Settlement Patterns:** Traditionally, most Pardhis lived outside the villages in temporary huts. Their huts were made up of bamboo poles, with cloth or stick walls. Most of them would live under shades of trees, while on the move. They lived in bands of 10 to 25 families. These days, they are living better houses. Some of them are living in houses made up of brick walls and tiled roofs.
16. **Social Status:** Pardhis are looked down upon by the non-tribal, tribal and even other nomadic groups, because of their criminal tendencies. Infact the Britishers classified them as Ex-criminal Tribes. During the British rule and even little later, the Pardhis had to report to a police station to enter a new village or leave their settlements.

    There were times, if thefts took place in a village, the police would pick up the Pardhis first. This harassment continues, in several Pardhi hamlets. There is an urgent need to remove this social stigma of ex-criminal tribe among the Pardhis. Their nomadic and semi nomadic nature keeps them on the move.
17. **Dance Forms:** Vaishnav T.K. (1998- 810) has pointed out that the Pardhis of Chhattisgarh have varieties of folk dances such as karma dance, Bihave, Rahas, dudaria etc. He further stated that the musical instruments played by the Pardhi are Dhol, Dafada, Manjira, Mohari etc.
18. **Folk Songs:** Some of the folk songs sung by pardhis are wedding songs, romantic songs and those, sung rituals etc (vaishnav T.K. 1998: 810).
19. **Beliefs Regarding Supernatural World:** Russell and Heeralal (1916) have stated that the in Hoshangabad the Pardhis sacrifice a fowl to the ropes of their tents during Dashera & Diwali Festivals. They clean their hunting implements, gadgets, traps & nets on Dashera and make offerings of turmeric and rice.

    They are reported to believe that sun and moon die and are reborn daily. The hunter is calling is one largely dependent on luck or chance, and as might be expected. The Pardhis are firm believers in omens and observe various rules by which they think their fortune is affected. A favorite omen is the simple device of taking some rice or jawar in the hand and counting grains. Even numbers are considered lucky, while odd ones are unlucky.

The bellowing of cows, the mewing of a cat, the howling of a jackal and sneezing are considered unlucky. If a snake passes from left to right, it is a bad omen, and if it is right to left, it is good omen. A man must not sleep with his head in the doorway of the tent. It is believed to be unlucky.

A Pardhi will never kill or see a dog and they will not hunt wild dogs, even if money is offered to them. This is probably, because they look upon the wild dog as a fellow hunter, and consider that to do him injury would bring ill- luck upon them. When he has caught a number of birds in his trap, he will let a pair of them loose, so that they may go breeding.

Women are permitted to take part in the work of hunting, but are confirmed strictly to their household duties. A Pardhi may not swear by a dog, a cat or a squirrel. Their most solemn oath is in the name of their deity "Guraiya". It is believed that anyone who falsely takes the oath will become a leper.

A woman must never step across a rope or peg of a tent, nor upon the place where the blood of a deer has flowed on the ground. During her menstruation a woman must not cross a river nor sit in a boat. Mr. Sewell notes that their women eat at the same time as the men, instead after them, as among most Hindus.

20. **Hunting Techniques:** As mentioned earlier, Pardhis are skillful and too good in hunting techniques. They tame dogs, leopards and hawks to hunt birds and animals. Given below are some of the techniques of hunting.

    (a) **Hunting with Leopards:** The manner in which the cheetah Pardhis use hunting leopard (Felis jubata) for catching a deer is described by Jordon in the district gazetteer of Chhindwada district as follows.

    - The leopard is caught full-grown by a noose. Its neck is first clasped in a wooden vice until it is half-strangled, and its feet are then bound with ropes and a cap slipped over its head. It is partially starved for time being. Being always fed by the same man, after a month or so it becomes tame and learns to know its master. It is then led through villages held by ropes on each side to accustom it to the Presence of human beings.
    - On a hunting Party, it is carried on a cart. The deer and the blackbuck regard the country carts without suspicion. The leopard then springs forward to get the prey. It holds the prey by the neck and brings it to the keeper.

    (b) **Use of Hawks:** Hawks are also used in a very indigenous fashion to prevent duck from flying away, when they are put on water.

The Pardhis tame hawks to catch ducks, green pigeons, and other birds.

(c) **Crocodile hunting:** Crocodiles are hunted only in the months of PUS (December), Magh (January), and chait (March), when they are generally fat and yield plenty of oil. The Pardhis sell this oil in bottles. The crocodile oil is good for joint pain.

(d) **Bird hunting:** Pardhis are expect & skilled bird trappers. They make traps & nets to hunt birds. Quails, patridges, green pigeons, peacocks, water ducks are sold by them to villagers.

(21) Death Rituals: The Pardhis bury their dead, with the head of the corpse pointing to the south. Women who die in child-birth and persons who have visited the shrines of their goddesses are cremated. The bones and the ashes are consigned to water. On the tenth day after the death of a person, rice balls are offered to the deceased, and caste-men.

Tribhuwan Robin & Gambhir R.D. (2012) in their research study on Tribal Identity have revealed that hard core or non-material cultural traits do not change early or take long time to change. Tribhuwan Robin (2010) provided examples of hard-core cultural traits of the Thakur Tribe. He stated that hard-core cultural traits are the essence of Thakur culture. The Pardhis have sustained their hard-core cultural traits which is the essence of their identity.

Social Problems of Pardhi Youth

Some of the social problems faced by the Pardhi youth are as below:

1. Un-employment.
2. Educational dropouts
3. Social stigma as ex-criminal groups.
4. Harassment by the police.
5. Early age at marriage, especially among females.
6. Semi-nomadic life style.
7. Poverty.
8. Harassment from forest department officials.

Educational Problems of Pardhi Youth: A Case Study

The researchers took Nagpur Integrated Tribal Development Project, to study the enrollment of Pardhi youth & children in Ashrams Schools.

Government Ashram Schools

Nagpur I.T.D.P. has 14 Government Ashram Schools. The total number of tribal students in the Government Ashram Schools are 2561, with 1261 males and 1300 females.

Aided Ashram Schools

In all there are 27 Aided Ashram Schools having a total strength of 10,749 tribal students with 5934 males and 4813 females.

Thus, out of the total 13,710 tribal students in Nagpur I.T.D.P., both in Government and Aided Ashram Schools, the total number of male students are 7207 and female students are 6113. The researchers made efforts to gather enrollment of Pardhi boys and girls in Nagpur I.T.D.P. Ashram Schools. Given below is the table that throws light on the enrollment of Pardhi Students for the year 2012-2013.

Table 19.1: Ashram School wise Number of Male and Female Pardhi Students during 2012-2013

Name of the Ashram School	Male	Female	Total
Tas	04	02	06
Udasa	05	04	09
Dahegaon	00	01	01
Wadgaon Jn.	02	05	07
Ukhali	07	02	09
Savali Mohgaon	00	02	02
Ladgaon	03	01	04
Shirpur (Bh.)	08	05	13
Deoli Pendhri	25	29	51
Total	**54**	**51**	**105**

From the above table it is evident that out of the total 54 Pardhi males 11 are in Government Ashram Schools and 43 are in Aided Ashram Schools. Similarly out of the total 51 girls, 6 are in Government Ashram Schools and 45 are Aided schools. This means out of the 105 Pardhi students only 17 are in Government Ashram Schools. The percentage of enrollment of Pardhi students in Aided Ashram Schools is high. Secondly, out of the total 13,710 students in Nagpur I.T.D.P. only 105 students are Pardhi. Out of the total number (7207) males only 54 are Pardhis & out of the total number (6113) of girls any 51 are Pardhis.

This clearly indicates that enrollment of Pardhi students is far too less in Nagpur I.T.D.P. There is a need to explore the total number of Pardhi males, females & total tribal students in Maharashtra.

According to the Tribal sub-plan 2012-13, there are 552 Government and 556 Aided Ashram Schools in the state of Maharashtra. The total number of trial students in Government Ashram Schools are 2,10,244, with 1,10,922 males and 99,322 females. The total number of tribal students in Aided Ashram Schools are 2,49,028, with 1,47,297 males and 1,01,751 females.

This means there is a need to expose the total number of Pardhi students, the males & females in the state. There is a need to also explose the number of Pardhi male & female students in the 471 tribal hostels in the state.

Reasons for Dropouts

Focused group discussions with Zilla Parishad School teachers, Ashram School teachers and Pardhi Parents revealed that the Pardhi students' dropout from schools for following reasons:

- Household responsibility.
- For taking care of the young ones at home, while the parents are at work.
- Early age at marriage.
- Nomadic and semi-nomadic life style of the tribe.
- Dis-interest in studies.
- For taking care of goats, chicks and the hunted birds.
- Daily wage labour responsibility at the tender teen age.
- Illiteracy of parents.
- Poor socio-economic background of the family.

Facilities in Ashram Schools

The Students in the Tribal Ashram Schools receive following facilities and amenties free of cost for studying right from first up the twelfth grade. There facilities are:

- Free lodging and boarding:
- Two pains of uniforms, books, note books and other stationary free of cost.
- Soap and hair oil.
- Boxes for clothes & books.
- Sports equipments for various sports such as cricket, volley ball, foot ball, base ball, etc.
- Breakfast, lunch and dinner in given free of charge.
- Computer facilities in the school.
- Sports competitions and cultural programmes are organized to search & promote sports & cultural talent.
- Television is compulsorily provided in the recreation hall.
- Play ground is provided for students to play.
- Day scholars from non-tribal communities are admitted so as to promote inter-community interaction and communal harmony.

It was observed that facilities in Eklavya Residential Schools are the best in the state, followed by Aided Ashram Schools and laxity in the Government Ashram Schools out of the several tribal development programmes implemented for tribal, Ashram schools and tribal hostels have proved to be a boon to the tribal's. In fact, majority of the tribal's are aware of their two programmes.

Concluding Remarks

Pardhi community is one of the vulnerable groups in Maharashtra. Majority of them do not have land and are economically, socially an educationally very backward. The poor background of the Parents, temporary & poor housing, nomadic & semi nomadic life style, social stigma as excremental group has had an adverse impact on the social & educational aspects of their life.

Role of IGNOU in Andaman & Nicobar Islands

– Dr. **Kasturi Pesala**

Introduction

Indira Gandhi National Open University (IGNOU) is a Central University established by an Act of Parliament in 1985. It is the apex Distance Education Institution in the country providing education & training to millions of untrained/under-trained population through Open & Distance Mode, using multi-media approach. It has tried to increase the Gross Enrollment Ratio (GER) by offering high-quality teaching through the Open and Distance Learning (ODL) mode. It caters over 4 million students in India and 36 other countries through 21 Schools of Studies and a network of 67 regional centres, around 3,000 learner support centres. IGNOU is the largest university of the World, in terms of enrolment strength & student support network.

The mandate of the University is to:

- Provide access to higher education to all segments of the society;
- Offer high-quality, innovative and need-based programmes at different levels, to all those who require them;
- Reach out to the disadvantaged by offering programmes in all parts of the country at affordable costs; and
- Promote, coordinate and regulate the standards of education offered through open and distance learning in the country.

- To achieve the twin objectives of widening access for all sections of society and providing continual professional development and training to all sectors of the economy, the University uses a variety of media and latest technology in imparting education. (www.ignou.ac.in)

The University has made a significant mark in the areas of higher education, community education and continual professional development. The University has been networking with reputed public institutions and private enterprises for enhancing the educational opportunities being offered by it. As a world leader in distance education, it has been conferred with awards of excellence by the Commonwealth of Learning (COL), Canada, several times. In January 2010, it was listed 12th in the webometric ranking of Indian universities, based on the calibre of its presence on the Internet.

Over the years, IGNOU has lived up to the country's expectations of providing education to the marginalised sections of society. Free of cost education is being provided to all jail inmates across the country. A large number of SC/ST students have been admitted to various programmes of the University.

Regional Centres

Regional Centres are established normally with cooperation and support of the respective State Governments. The perspective plan is to provide one Regional Centre for every state in the country.

The Regional Centre has been defined under Section 2(J) of the IGNOU Act as under: "Regional Centre" means a Centre established or maintained by the University for the purpose of coordinating and supervising the work of the Study Centres in any region and for performing such other functions as may be conferred on such Centre by the Board of Management (BoM).

Further, under Section 5(1) (XXII) of the Act, the University is empowered to confer autonomous status to a Regional Centre have been established by IGNOU to coordinate and supervise the work of the Study Centres.

There are 67 Regional Centres out of which (56) are the Regional Centres, IGNOU-Army Recognised Regional Centres (6), IGNOU-Navy Recognised Regional Centres (4) and IGNOU-Assam Rifles Recognised Regional Centre (1). All these are responsible for the promotion of the Open University system; development, maintenance and monitoring of Study Centres and Student Support Services; and organisation of staff development programmes in the region.(www.ignou.ac.in)

Regional Centre, Port Blair

IGNOU Regional Centre Port Blair was established on 27th March 2006 as a Post Tsunami Rehabilitation policy initiative & decision taken by Hon'ble Prime Minister Dr. Manmohan Singh during his visit to Islands. The IGNOU aimed at holistic development of the place with a need based approach in development of the region.

The Regional Centre of IGNOU Port Blair was established to cater the needs of 3 districts of Andaman & Nicobar Islands. The Regional Centre has been making efforts to activate all the relevant and need based Programmes of the University in this Region by keeping its goal of "Reaching the Unreached" so that people need not travel long distances in quest of education.

Facilities for Learners at Regional Centre, Port Blair:

- Study Materials (Self learning materials) is also available on the website of IGNOU and can be freely downloaded through (eGyankosh). In order to enrich the study material, extensive use of audio/video programmes were developed by Electronic Media Production Centre (EMPC) at IGNOU headquarters. To further supplement the educational programme , the study lessons are broadcast/ telecast on Gyanvani FM channels and Gyandarshan TV channels.
- Library
- EDUSAT facility (a satellite dedicated only to education)
- Induction Programmes
- Workshops/Seminars
- Regular conduct of examinations every six months (June & December)
- 7 Examination centre including one for jail inmates at Potharapur.
- Convocations

Establishment of Learner Support Centres

IGNOU Regional Centre, Port Blair has established 11 Study Centre in these islands. By keeping its goal to "Reach the unreached" the study centres were opened in the distinct remote islands including 3 in Nicobar group of Islands (Campbell Bay, Kamorta, CarNicobar), one in South Andaman(Hut bay). The study centre is also opened for the deprived group of the society by providing free education to jail inmates at District Jail, Pothrapur.

Academic Activities by Regional Centre (Workshops,Orientation & Trainings):

1. Academic counselors training.
2. Coordinators meet.
3. Every year Conducting Orientation Programmes for training of Study Centre staff for initiating them into Open & Distance Learning Systems.
4. Initiated the process of identification of new need based academic programmes like Certificate/Diploma programmes for Tourist Guides.
5. General Orientation Programme about Indira Gandhi National Open University and its academic initiatives in islands was carried out alongwith Press Information Bureau, Port Blair for Media Persons in A&N region.
6. Organized Two Day State Level Seminar cum Orientation Programme on Social Work Response to HIV/AIDS.

Admission Data of RC Port Blair:

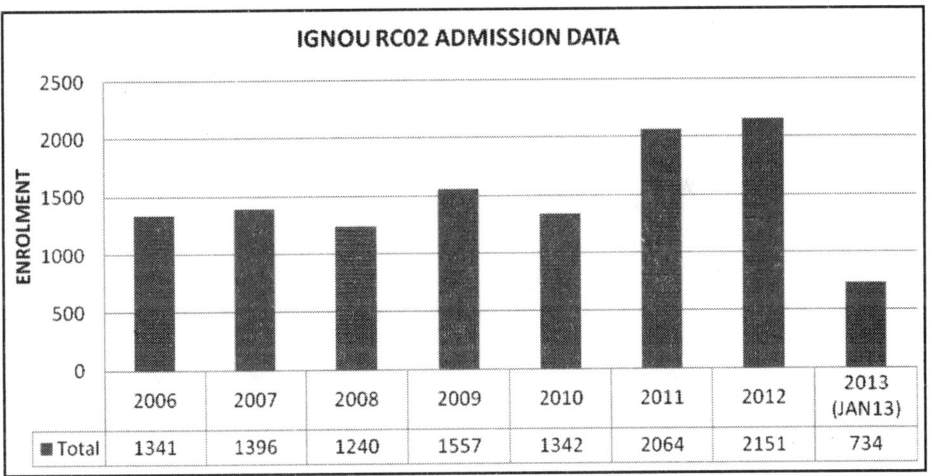

	2006	2007	2008	2009	2010	2011	2012	2013 (JAN13)
Total	1341	1396	1240	1557	1342	2064	2151	734

(A) From Year 2007 To 2013 (January Session)

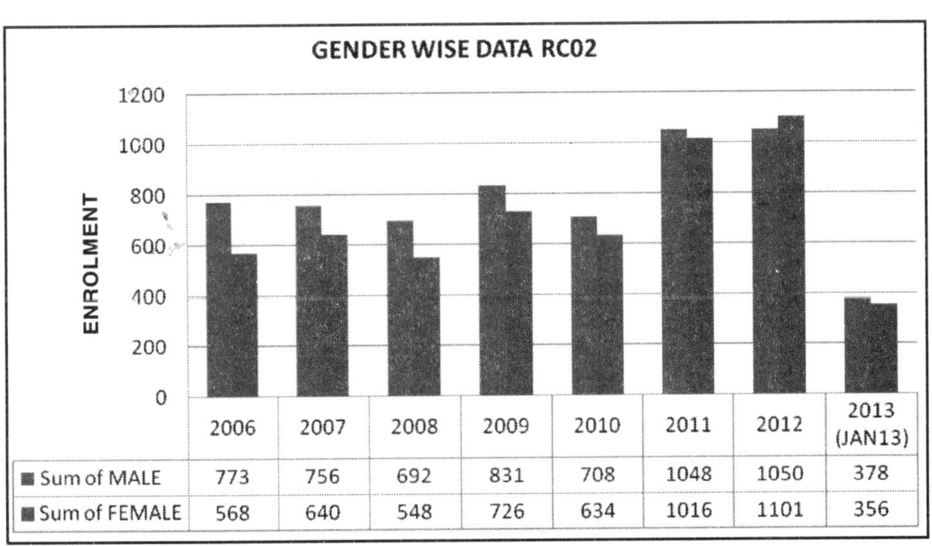

	2006	2007	2008	2009	2010	2011	2012	2013 (JAN13)
Sum of MALE	773	756	692	831	708	1048	1050	378
Sum of FEMALE	568	640	548	726	634	1016	1101	356

(B) Gender wise Admission Data (From year 2007 to 2013 January Session)

7. Two seminars on: *(i)* NREGA *(ii)* Substance Abuse & de-addiction amongst youth in A&N at Car Nicobar.
8. Training to immigration staff of Police Department on Soft Skills.
9. Training for Nursing Staff & Senior staff Nurses on "Management Technique".

Future Plans

The Regional Centre is also planning to start few study centre in the remote islands of these islands. There by opening up new vistas of higher education for the people of remotely located isles in Andaman & Nicobar region. The focus will be to strengthen student support services and usage of ICT to deliver its services.

REFERENCES

Website(www.ignou.ac.in)

IGNOU Profile 2012

IGNOU Regional Centre , Port Blair (Learners Data base)

White paper on Student Support Services, Regional Service Division, IGNOU

Part – IV

Alcoholism and Drug Addiction

The Problem of Drug Abuse in the World, in South Asia and A Microcosm

– Dr. Joy C. Kurian

Introduction

Drug and alcohol abuse touches all Indians and most of the people around the world in one form or the other. This enormous problem of drug abuse has affected all categories of people, rich and poor, literate and illiterate, urban and rural, young and old, male and female and it has broken through the barriers of caste, creed and race. However, a closer look at this social evil shows us that it is our children who are most vulnerable to its influence. As parents, teachers, administrators and conscious citizens, we need to educate ourselves about the dangers of drugs so that we can teach our children about "this trip without a return ticket". Yes, we must go further still by convincing them that drugs are morally wrong.

As more and more individuals and groups are speaking out, young people are finding it easy to say no to drugs. Encouraged by a growing public outcry and their own strength of conviction, students are forming peer support groups in opposition to drug use. It has been encouraging to see how willingly young people take healthy attitudes and ideas to heart when they are exposed to an environment that fosters those values.

Outside the home, the school is the most influential environment for our children. This means that the schools must protect children from the presence of drugs, and nurture values that help them reject drugs.

This report presents the world scene, the south Asia scene and it also covers a microcosm of individuals living in the Pune District in the state of Maharashtra in India. I hope the report will provide the kind of practical knowledge parents, educators, students and communities can use to keep their schools drug-free. Only when this happens can we protect our children and insure that they can get on with a safe learning environment.

The World Scene

The United Nations World Drug Report of 2011 states, "Globally, some 210 million people use illicit drugs each year, and almost 200,000 of them die from drugs. There continues to be an enormous unmet need for drug use prevention, treatment, care and support, particularly in developing countries. Drug use affects not only individual users, but also their families, friends, co-workers and communities. Children whose parents take drugs are themselves at greater risk of drug use and other risky behaviors. Drugs generate crime, street violence and other social problems that harm communities. In some regions, illicit drug use is contributing to the rapid spread of infectious diseases like HIV and hepatitis."

On the supply side, illicit cultivation of opium poppy and coca bush is now limited to a few countries, but heroin and cocaine production levels remain high. Although 2010 saw a significant decrease in opium production, this was largely due to a plant disease that affected opium poppies in the major growing regions of Afghanistan. Yet between 1998 and 2009, global production of opium rose almost 80 per cent, which makes the 2010 production decline less significant over the last decade. Meanwhile, the market for cocaine has not shrunk substantially; it has simply experienced geographical shifts in supply and demand. Just a decade ago, the North American market for cocaine was four times larger than that of Europe, but now we are witnessing a complete rebalancing. Today the estimated value of the European cocaine market which is $33 billion is almost equivalent to that of the North American market which is $37 billion.

Drug trafficking, the critical link between supply and demand, is fuelling a global criminal enterprise valued in the hundreds of billions of dollars that poses a growing challenge to stability and security. Drug traffickers and organised criminals are forming transnational networks, sourcing drugs on one continent, trafficking them across another, and marketing them in a third. In some countries and regions, the value of the illicit drug trade far exceeds the size of the legitimate economy. Given the enormous amounts of money controlled by drug traffickers, they have the capacity to corrupt officials.

Globally, UNODC estimates that, in 2009, between 149 and 272 million people, or 3.3 per cent to 6.1 per cent of the population aged 15-64, used illicit substances at least once in the previous year. About half that number is estimated to have been current drug users, that is, having used illicit drugs at least once during the past month prior to the date of assessment. While the total number of illicit drug users has increased since the late 1990s, the prevalence rates have remained largely stable, as has the number of problem drug users, which is estimated at between 15 and 39 million.

Cannabis or Ganja is by far the most widely used illicit drug type, consumed by between 125 and 203 million people worldwide in 2009. This corresponds to an annual prevalence rate of 2.8 per cent - 4.5 per cent. In terms of annual prevalence, cannabis is followed by ATS (amphetamine-type stimulants; mainly methamphetamine, amphetamine and ecstasy), opioids (including opium, heroin and prescription opioids) and cocaine. Lack of information regarding use of illicit drugs – particularly ATS - in populous countries such as China and India, as well as in emerging regions of consumption such as Africa, generate uncertainty when estimating the global number of users. This is reflected in the wide ranges of the estimates.

The figure below gives more recentstatistics on the consumption of drugs.

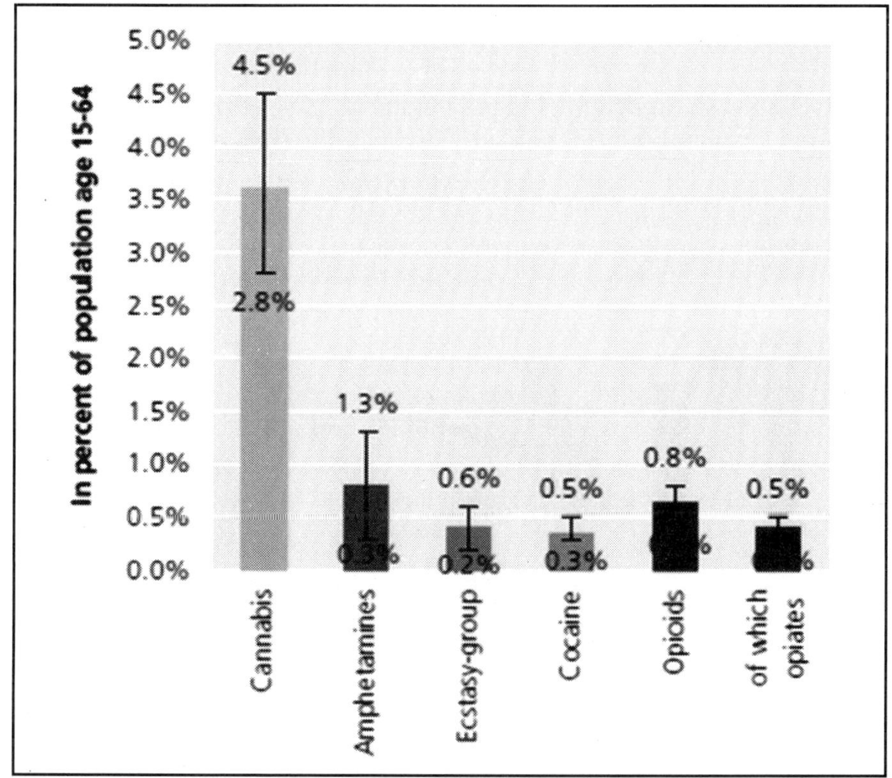

Annual Prevalence of Drug use at the Global Level, by Illicit Drug Category, 2009-2010

Source: **UNODC Estimates Based on ARQ Data and Other Official Sources**

Global opium poppy cultivation amounted to some 195,700 ha in 2010, a small increase from 2009. The vast bulk - some 123,000 hectares were cultivated in Afghanistan, where the cultivation trend remained stable. The global trend was mainly driven by increases in Myanmar, where cultivation rose by some 20 per cent from 2009. There was a significant reduction in global opium pro-production in 2010, however, as a result of disease in opium poppy plants in Afghanistan. The global area under coca cultivation continued to shrink to 149,1002 ha in 2010, falling by 18 per cent from 2007 to 2010. There was also a significant decline in potential cocaine manufacture, reflecting falling cocaine production in Colombia which offset increases identified in both Peru and the Plurinational State of Bolivia. While it is difficult to estimate total global amphetamine-type stimulants manufacture, it has spread, and more than 60 Member States from all regions of the world have reported such activity to date. The manufacture of amphetamines-group substances is larger than that of ecstasy. Methamphetamine - which belongs to the amphetamines-group - is the most widely manufactured ATS, with the United States of America reporting a large number of detected illicit laboratories. Cannabis herb cultivation occurs in most countries worldwide. Although there was insufficient data available to update the global cultivation stimate, the relatively stable seizure trend suggests a stable level of production. Indoor cultivation of cannabis herb is still largely limited to the developed countries of North America, Europe and Oceania. Cannabis resin production estimates were not updated this year, but based on ARQ replies to UNODC, Afghanistan and Morocco were major producers. The tables below give the statistics for the cultivation and production of Opium poppy and Coca.

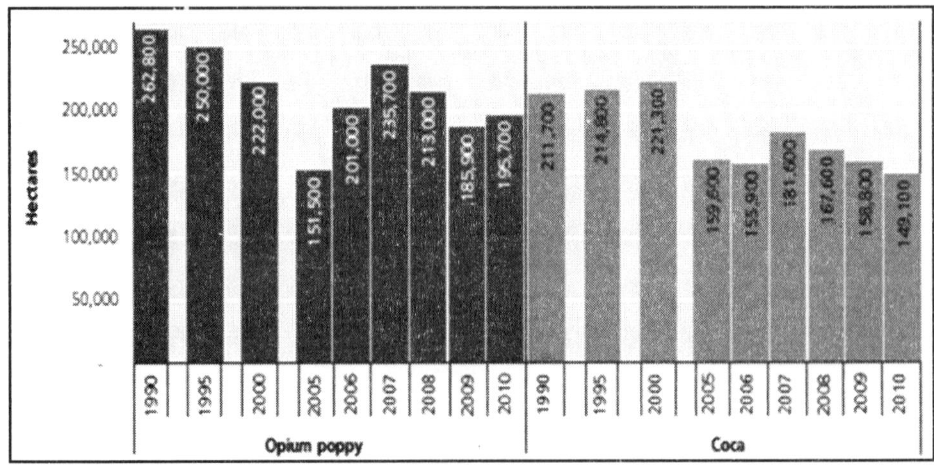

Global Opium Poppy and Coca Cultivation (ha), 1990-2010*

* For Mexico (Opium, Poppy) and the Plurinational State of Bolivia (Coca), in the Absence of data for 2010, the estimates for 2009 were imputed to 2010

Source: UNODC.

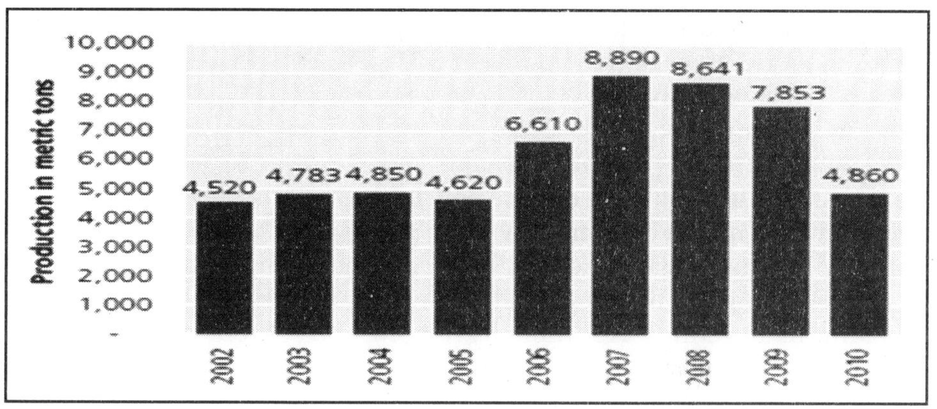

Global Opium Production (mt), 2002-2010

Source: UNODC, illicit Crop Monitoring Programme (ICMP)

The South Asia Scene

Asian opiate prevalence estimates range between 0.2 and 0.5 per cent of the population aged 15-64, or an estimated 6.5 to 13.2 million people. Most of the opiate users in Asia reportedly use heroin or opium which is sometimes adulterated and called Brown Sugar, and more than half of the world's estimated opiate users live in Asia. Although recent prevalence estimates are not available for most countries in Asia, less than half (46%) of the countries that responded to the ARQ perceived an increase in opioid use. However, 38 per cent of the responding countries, mostly in South-East Asia, perceived a decrease in 2009. Countries in South-West Asia continue to have high prevalence rates for opiate use. Together, these countries account for nearly one third of opiate users in Asia. In Afghanistan, around 60 per cent of the estimated opiate users use opium. In the Islamic Republic of Iran, 40 per cent of the estimated opiate users consume opium, and the rest mainly consume heroin. In the Islamic Republic of Iran, 83 per cent of treatment admissions in 2009 were for opiate use, in Pakistan, the share was 41 per cent in 2006/2007. Opiates are also the most common cause of drug-related deaths reported in these countries. In the Islamic Republic of Iran, the rate of drug-related deaths was 91 per 1 million people aged 15-64; the majority of these related to opiate use. Moreover, overall opiate use in Afghanistan increased from 1.4 per cent in 2005 to 2.7 per cent of the population aged 15-64 in 2009. Heroin remains the most problematic illicit drug in Central Asia and the Caucasus which is the region between Europe and Asia. Experts in Central Asia perceived a stabilizing trend of opioid use, but the proportion of officially registered heroin users continued to increase, with 47 per cent of registered drug users in Kyrgyzstan identifying themselves as heroin users, and 82 per cent in Tajikistan in 2009. Injecting drug use is also common, with shares ranging from 46 per cent of drug users in Uzbekistan to around 70 per cent in Kyrgyzstan and Kazakhstan. Opiate prevalence in the Caucasus is lower than the world average, ranging from 0.31 per cent in Georgia to 0.22 per cent in Armenia. With the exception of Azerbaijan, opioids is also the main substance group reported in drug-related death cases in the region, with rates ranging from 7 per million people aged 15-64 in Uzbekistan to 115 in Kazakhstan. Although most of the countries in South Asia lack recent opiate use estimates, use levels seem to vary in the region. A 2006 study of drugs and HIV in South Asia found that 90 per cent of the drug users interviewed in Bangladesh and 2 per cent in Bhutan were currently using heroin (either smoking or injecting). Additionally, among the respondents, the use of prescription opioids ranged from 1 per cent in Bhutan and Sri Lanka to 20 per cent in India. Heroin injection was most common among drug users in Nepal, followed closely by those in India. In East and South-East Asia, opiates continue to be used at high rates. In 2009, heroin ranked as the main drug used in China, Malaysia, Myanmar, Singapore and Viet Nam. Most countries in the region have reported stable or decreasing trends in opiate use, except the Lao People's Democratic Republic, Singapore and Viet Nam. Opiate prevalence increased from 0.6 per cent in 2008 to 0.8 per cent in Myanmar in 2010. As in previous years, the prevalence of opium use in the opium-growing villages in Myanmar (1.7%) was higher than in the non-opium growing villages (0.6%). With an estimated prevalence of 0.18 per cent of the population aged 15 and above, heroin use in Myanmar is less widespread than opium use. Treatment demand for heroin dependence remains high across East and South-East Asia, ranging from 50 per cent of all treatment demand in Singapore to around 80 per cent in China and 98 per cent in Viet Nam.

The Microcosm

According to the Press Trust of India report presented on May 3, 2006 it is estimated that there are about 6.25 *crore alcoholics, 90 lakh cannabis and 2.5 lakhs opiates and nearly 10 lakh illicit drug users in India.

The Scheme for Prevention of Alcoholism and Substance (Drugs) Abuse is being implemented through 350 NGOs for running 387 De-addiction Centers and 52 Counseling Centers all over India for providing facilities like treatment, rehabilitation services and conducting awareness programmes for victims of substance addiction.

It is indeed an open secret that addiction to drugs is on the increase in educational institutions as well, the incidence being particularly high (60%) among students of schools and colleges located in big cities. Not only is drug addiction harmful to the individual, but it also affects the addict's family and society at large. Here is a supportive statementfrom the W.H.O expert committee.Drug addiction is *"a state of periodic or chronic intoxication, detrimental to the individual and the society, produced by repeated consumption of a drug either natural or synthetic"*. (Dupont 1984)

Table 21.1: South Asia: Use of Opioids Among Drug Users, 2006

	Opium	Heroin Smoked	Heroin Injected	Propoxyphene	Buprenorphine
Bhutan (n=200)					
Ever used	0	37	3	32	28
Current users	0	4	3	3	2
% of current users	0	2	1.5	1.5	1
Bangladesh (n=1073)					
Ever used	140	989	46	3	295
Current users	7	961	6	1	154
% of current users	0.7	89.6	0.6	0.1	14.4
India (n=5732)					
Ever used	1535	3017	1623	1713	1466
Current users	858	2123	1228	1103	1115
% of current users	15	37	21.4	19.2	19.5
Nepal (n=1322)					
Ever used	181	1159	606	149	1013
Current users	117	880	456	97	858
% of current users	8.9	66.6	34.5	7.3	64.9
Sri Lanka (n=1016)					
Ever used	107	558	23	39	6
Current users	36	520	4	14	0
% of current users	3.5	51.2	0.4	1.4	0

Source: UNODC Rapid Solution and Response Assessment of Drugs and HIV in Bangladesh, Bhutan, India, Nepal and Sri Lanka

Yes, like a shadowy octopus, the problem of drug abuse has reached even the school rooms in Pune, and it is high time thatpreventive measures and awareness programmes be launched in our schools so that our students will recognize the enemy before it strikes.

*1 crore = 100,000 lakhs

What greater shock can the parents experience than to find that their own child is experimenting with or has become addicted to that which is capable of making life a living hell! (Ray 1972)

As part of the educational programme, in all our schools in Pune, a regular audio-visual awareness programme projecting the effects of drugs being pushed today by peddlers must be urgently undertaken to safeguard the innocent minds and thus in return ensure a cleaner, dynamic and vibrant India.

The economic costs of drug abuse are high in terms of man-days lost at work, the health hazards posed on the user and the cost of treatment. It also leads to the diversion of a lot of money to criminals and to the consequent corruption of law enforcement agencies. Additionally, many addicts take to crime in order to be able to support the habit. Some steal while others get involved in the drug trade. (Tobias 1986)

More important than the economic costs is the "human cost" in terms of misery, self-destruction and suffering not only of the addict, but also of those close to him, such as his family, his friends and co-workers. The tremendous suffering caused by drug abuse cannot be quantified, but far outweighs the economic damage. (Hawley 1984)

Research shows that current treatment techniques used with heroin abusers are not very effective and even with years of treatment the relapse rates as high as 90 per cent are common. Studies have shown that over a period of years a number of herion addicts "mature" and stop the habit themselves. It has been observed that they stop a number of times, either in treatment or by themselves, before finally giving up the drug. (Rubel 1984)

Therefore, from a "public health" point of view, given the large number of addicts and the paucity of treatment facilities let alone effective therapy, providing effective detoxification is by itself a useful strategy. Detoxification is the first step in the rehabilitation of the addict during which period the addict is helped to abstain from the drug so that his body can adjust to a drug free state. (N I D A 1981)

Often addicts use detoxification to keep the cost of their habit down. Most of them know that once they have developed a tolerance to heroin, following detoxification, they would require a smaller amount of heroin to obtain the same effect. So even if the addict's motivation is not to give up the drug or to enter into long treatment, one should not deny him detoxification, since it helps him to keep his expenditure on the drug down. Often this helps keep the addict from having to resort to criminal activity in order to support the habit. It also helps keep down the total quantity of the drug ingested and reduces the health hazards. (N I D A 1985)

Many addicts resort to self-detoxification using medication haphazardly or using other unscientific methods which by themselves pose a danger to the health and life of the addict. It is therefore important to provide a cheap, painless, easily accessible technique of detoxification which would be acceptable to the addict. A frequent criticism of this approach has been that if painless detoxification were made easily available toan addict, there would be little motivation for him to stay off the drug once detoxified, because he knows that he can easily give up the drug whenever he would like to. Many psychiatrists believe that an addict should be allowed to suffer the withdrawal symptoms, as this would act as deterrent to his resuming the habit. However, since 80 per cent or more addicts relapse after detoxification, the thought of undergoing painful and expensive detoxification process frequently makes them keep on postponing repeat detoxification. This prevents them from seeking treatment. Also, many doctors feel that is is not ethical on humanitarian grounds, to make a patient suffer, especially when there is no scientific evidence to show that it helps. (NID A 1981)

The Researched Findings of Two Microcosm

Methodology

Area and Tools of Study

Data for this study was collected from two centers:

1. A general survey to assess the problem of drugs from a population in a high-school in Pune was selected.
2. For the collection of in depth information from addicts, the total population comprising of addicts from a rehabilitation center in Pune was selected.

The techniques or tools used are as follows:

1. Brief questionnaire was used to screen the population in the high school.
2. Assessment of the addicts files at the rehabilitation center.
3. Personal interviews with the recovering addicts for the collection of case histories.

In order to collect vital information about the drug addicts, admitted to the rehabilitationcentre, the patients were called one at a time to the Social Worker's office, where they were interviewed personally. Forty five addicts who were under treatment at the Centre were thus interviewed.

Hypothesis

Drug addiction among the youth is on the increase and is reported to be present in all the major cities and Educational Institutions in the country. This exploratory study is conducted with a view of studying the problem and finding ways and means ofbuilding awareness programmes to help those who may otherwise fall a prey to this multidimensional problem.

Aims and Objectives

The project aims to uncover the creeping madness of drug abuse in our schools at Pune with the following objectives:

1. To examine the vital evidence presented by recognized authorities on drug abuse.
2. To collate reliable facts and information about the nature and effect of the great variety of drugs in use today and its supply centers.
3. To give helpful insights into the many factors giving rise to the dependence and addiction problems.
4. To provide reasonable measures for controlling the growth and impact of drug abuse.
5. To outline information regarding the role of homes and institutions in countering the menace of drug abuse.
6. To develop a realistic understanding of why students use drugs.
7. To suggest ways and means of detoxification and rehabilitation of users.
8. To organise, with the help of ex-drug addicts, well structured anti-narcotic drug campaigns.
9. To study the effects of the intake of drugs and its impact on the students scholastic programme.
10. To explore the physical, psychological and socio-culture effects of the drugs being consumed.

Major Components Studied in the Case Histories

The main components of the Case histories are:

1. History of patients
   (a) Types of drugs taken by patients
   (b) Assessing the reason for taking drugs
   (c) Time and frequency of taking drugs
   (d) Amount of money spent on drugs
   (e) Place for procuring or purchasing drugs
   (f) Desire to quit drug addiction

Before choosing the population for study, factors like:

1. The Socio-Economic status of addicts
2. Religion of addicts
3. Educational status of addicts
4. The major reasons for falling into the drug habit were discussed with non-users to find out the general belief to build a proper hypothesis for the ultimate construction of an awareness programme for students.

According to a certain Superintendent of a Hospital, the Rehabilitation Center had till the commencement of this study addicts, each of whom was treated for a period of 45-60 days (in some cases 90 days). Less than half of them had to be re-admitted and over 50 per cent of them are reported to be doing fine.

Economic Status

The rehabilitation center comprises of addicts under treatment who are at various levels. Out of the 45 addicts, many were previously working in factories, shops and in Government services. These patients came to the Rehabilitation Center for detoxification. Many of them lost their jobs, because the drug habit resulted in many days of absenteeism from work. For example, if a patient worked in a particular factory after getting the month's pay, they would not report for work for one or two weeks and since the owner or manager could not function, they were ultimately asked to resign from their jobs.

Education

With reference to the people who admitted themselves as drug addicts and their educational standards, it was observed that some of them fell in the following categories:

- Primary School
- SSC
- Graduate Degree holders
- Post Graduate Degree holders

Many of them had to drop out of their educational programme because they were hooked to the drug habit and could not cope with their class assignments and attendance.

Religion

At the rehabilitation center patients came from different religious backgrounds, such as: Hindus, Sikhs, Muslims, Jains and Christians. However, the majority of the patients were Hindus. This is not a surprise, since the majority of the population in the country and the State are Hindus.

Limitations

This project had the following limitations:

1. To meet the patients when the researcher was free was not always possible, because they had their own programme going on at the rehab center.
2. Some of the patients were not willing to disclose their complete personal case history.
3. As a researcher it was difficult to take part in group therapy, a participant observation method, due to lack of training in the field of psychology and psychiatry.

Analysis of Data from the School

Analysis of the data collected from the school are presented below:

Total Enrolment	270
Males	170
Females	100

With the above sample it was decided to take 10 per cent of the male (17 males) and 10 per cent of the females (10 females) from each class, using the stratified random sampling technique. This was done in the following manner.

For each standard, i.e. 8th to 11th the male and female students were listed separately in alphabetical order and every second student from the sequential alphabetical list among the males and females were chosen to answer the questionnaire. As the total number of students in standard 12 were only 30, and of these 3 were absent, from this standard, the total sample of students were incorporated in the sample under study. Given below is the standard-wise breakdown:

Standard	Total	Male	Female
8	80	17	10
9	68	17	10
10	52	17	10
11	40	17	10
12	30	17	10
Total	**270**	**85**	**50**

Of the 85 males and 50 females selected, the features observed are as follows:

The number of students who used drugs	47 (35%)
The number of students who did not use drugs	88 (65%)
Total sample under study	135

Of the response received through the questionnaire, it was observed that a few respondents answered the questionnaire partially. It may be that they had the fear that they would be punished or dismissed if they revealed the problem of drugs they got into.

However, of the responses received, the following salient features were clearly observed:

Initiation into Drugs

With reference to the 47 students who were initiated into drugs/alcohol, the responses are as follows:

Sr. No.	Introduced to Drugs by	No.	%
1.	My own choice	2	4
2.	Friends	18	38
3.	Relations	1	2
4.	Parents	2	4
5.	No response	24	5

The above table clearly shows that the greatest number of students (38% were initiated to drugs through their friends.

Frequency of the Drug Intake

The following table depicts the frequency showing the drugs or beverages that were used by the students.

Sr. No	Name of Drug	No	%
1.	L.S.D.	2	4
2.	Heroin	2	4
3.	Marijuana (Ganja)	6	13
4.	Bhang	6	13
5.	Charas	5	11
6.	Brown sugar	7	15
7.	Opium	1	2
8.	Cigarettes	23	49
9.	Bidi	6	13
10.	Tobacco (Tambacu)	7	15
11.	Mandrax	3	6
12.	Compose	3	6
13.	Alcoholic beverages	12	26
14.	Beetle leaf (Pan supari)	31	66

Please note: the total number of addicts in this project is only 47 and they will not match the above numbers, as many of the addicts were poly-drug users.

A closer look at the above table shows that Sr. No. 2, 6 and 7 are derived from one common source, namely the *Papaver somniferum* plant (poppy). Hence combined effect in the categories gives us 21 per cent

Similarly we could bring together Sr. No. 3, 4 & 5 which are derived from the *Cannabis sativa* plant (Marijuana) and the combined effect in the category gives us 37 per cent.

The third group of categories which could be combined are Sr. No. 8, 9 & 10 since they are derived from *Necotiana tobacum* plant (Tobacco), and the combined effect in this category gives the highest rate of 77 per cent.

The fourth category comprising of Sr. No. 1, 11 & 12 could be placed under the synthetic or artificially prepared drugs in the laboratory and the combined effect of the category gives a rather low profile of only 16 per cent.

Although alcoholic beverages stand above on a separate category, it presents a high percentage of 26 per cent.

The last but the highest 66 per cent independent category namely Beetle leaf and Beetle nut (*Pan & Supari*) is the most frequently used, mild stimulant by the student population.

Place of Procurement

With reference to the place from where the students got the drugs, there are four categories as shown in the table below:

Sr. No.	Drug obtained from	No.	%
1.	A shop	8	17
2.	A friend	9	19
3.	A regular peddler	4	9
4.	Did not disclose	26	55
	Total	**47**	

As observed in the above table and in Analysis No 1, it is primarily the addict's friends who introduced him/her to drugs and again it is mostly his friends who are the main suppliers of the dreaded drugs.

Home Situation

With regards to the home situation before the addict got into the habit, it is interesting to note the following:

Sr. No.	Home Situation	No.	%
1.	Stable home	27	57
2.	Broken divided home	5	11
3.	No comments	15	32
	Total	**47**	

As normally predicted, we would expect more drug addicts in the broken divided home, but to my surprise, I found that 57 per cent of the addicts came from stable homes.

Reason for intake of Drugs

The reason for taking drugs was many and varied. The common classified reasons given by the addicts are as follows:

Sr. No.	Classified Reasons	No.	%
1.	My friends are taking it	9	19
2.	I like the feeling it brings	6	13
3.	There are too many problems at home	2	4
4.	I cannot cope up with my studies	3	6
5.	I am fed up of life	6	13
6.	It gives me strength and vigor	3	6
7.	It drowns all my worries	6	13
8.	I took it as an experiment	4	9
9.	I feel there is nothing wrong	2	4
10.	I felt like doing it	2	4
11.	I have no particular reason	2	4
12.	I took it like a medicine	2	4

Unique Features

The above table shows that the four major reasons given by the addicts are as follows:

1. My friends are taking it 19%
2. I like the feeling it brings 13%
3. I am fed up of life 13%
4. It drowns all my worries 13%

The other unique feature that emerges from the project is as follows:

1. Many of the addicts started with cigarettes and alcohol and thus it was easy to get into the use of other drugs.
2. The amount spent by the addicts to purchase drugs ranged from Rs 100/- to 500/- per day.
3. Once they got into the habit, many of them said they had to take the drugs frequently, others regularly, and still others occasionally.
4. Quite a few of them said they had to steal money or articles which were not their own, sell it and make the cash to keep on with the habit.
5. Most of them reported that they were fed-up of drugs and was ready to do anything to get rid of the habit.

The Rehabilitation Center

The analysis of the data collected from the addicts admitted in the Rehabilitation Centre is tabulated below to bring out the salient features.

All the patients were from the State of Maharashtra in India, but majority were from Nashik, Mumbai and Pune districts. As the patients were interviewed the patients said that Nashik is a growing city and there is a direct communication between Bombay and Nashik. Those who sell the drugs were ladies and belonged to the muslim community in Nashik town. All the patients spoke Marathi. However, there were a few who spoke Hindi and understood English. Most of them worked in factories, Government Services, and a few had their own business.

Salary Earned by Addicts

The salary of the addicts varied from Rs. 800-2500/- per month. However, few of them did not have any work.

Basic evaluation was done in these areas:

(a) Type of drugs that were used
(b) Frequency of taking drugs
(c) Amount spent on drugs
(d) Procurement or purchase of drugs
(e) Source of funds to maintain the drug addiction
(f) The desire to quit the habit

Types of Drugs Consumed

On the types of drugs taken by the patients, the evaluation proved the following:

1. 88 per cent started with the use of cigarettes
2. 71 per cent take Brown sugar (an adulterated form of Heroin)
3. 26.7 per cent take cigarettes with other drugs
4. 44 per cent take alcoholic beverages
5. 11.11 per cent take tobacco
6. 20.9 per cent take charas

Introduction to the Drug Habit

1. With reference to the drug habit the following facts emerged: only 4.4 per cent got into the habit because their parents also used them at home.
2. 88.9 per cent were introduced to drugs by their friends.
3. Only 6.7 per cent were introduced to drugs by their relatives.

Reasons of taking Drugs

The response as to the reason for taking drugs is as follows:

1. 35.6 per cent stated that it gave them a good feeling.
2. 33.3 per cent stated that they took it because their friends were taking it.
3. Only 4.4 per cent stated that they took drugs because they could not study.
4. 8.9 per cent stated that they were fed up of life and they started on drugs.
5. 17.8 per cent stated that they started on drugs because of home problems.
   Frequency of Drug Intake

With reference to the frequency of taking drugs, the following information was collected:

1. 77.8 per cent had to take the drugs regularly.
2. 8.9 per cent had to take the drugs occasionally.
3. 13.3 per cent had to take drugs rarely.

Amount Spent on Drugs per Day

On the amount of money spent on drugs per day, the study indicated the following:

1. About 4.4 per cent spent Rs. 100/- and above.
2. About 15.6 per cent spent Rs. 200/- and above.
3. About 26.7 per cent spent Rs. 300/- and above.
4. About 53.3 per cent spent Rs. 500/- and above.

Procurement of Drugs

With reference to the place of obtaining the drugs, the following information was collected:

1. About 15.6 per cent buy from shops.
2. Those who buy from friends formed 18.8 per cent of the population.
3. About 62.2 per cent buy from peddlers.
4. Only 4.4 per cent stole it from their parents cupboard.

Source of Funds

The response received about the means of getting money to purchase the drugs was as follows:

1. 48.9 per cent of them stole from different places.
2. 22.2 per cent borrowed money from people.
3. 17.8 per cent of them worked and earned the money.
4. 11.1 per cent gambled to get the money.

Desire to Quit the Habit

By assessing the desire to quit the drug habit, the study indicated the following:

1. 82.2 per cent have a desire to quit.
2. 17.8 per cent had not decided as yet.

Meeting attendance record indicated that almost every time all the patients were present for interview and counseling. However, one hindrance was there that there was no specific time scheduled and there was laxity on the part of some patients to attend.

Meetings at the Rehab Centre and Suggestions

Meetings at the Centre were conducted only during the day and the attendance ranged between 30-35. For the first few days not all attended due to the therapies like Yoga and Meditation that were in session at the same time.

Much could have been done to increase the attendance. Many would have attended the meeting if:

1. Movies could have been screened.

2. Mixed programmes could have been devised – like short plays, quizzes, participation for musical programmes etc.

3. There could have been skits or demonstrations by the researcher.

4. All of them could have understood the programme even if it was in English.

At the end of the treatment period, most of the addicts were highly motivated and were ready to give up the habit. Infact, they said, "they have nothing to lose now, they have lost much by being addicts", they promised to open new chapters in their lives.

Tabulation of Analysed Data

Rehabilitation Centre

Types of Drugs taken by the Patients before Admission	No. of Patients	Percentage
Marijuana	40	71.1%
Brown Sugar	32	20.7%
Cigarettes	12	20.7%
Alcoholic Beverages	20	44%
Tobacco	5	11.11%
Charas	13	28.9%

Who Introduced Patients to Drugs	No. of Patients	Percentage
Parents and home environment	2	4.4%
Relatives	3	6.7%
Friends	40	88.9%

Reasons for taking Drugs	No. of Patients	Percentage
Good feelings	16	35.6%
Friends taking	15	33.3%
Can't study	2	4.4%
Fed up with life	4	8.9%
Problem at home	8	17.8%

Frequency of Drug intake	No. of Patients	Percentage
Regularly	35	77.8%
Occasionally	4	8.9%
Rarely	6	13.3%

Amount Spent per day on Drugs	No. of Patients	Percentage
Rs. 100 +	2	4.4%
Rs. 200 +	7	15.6%
Rs. 300 +	12	26.7%
Rs. 500 +	24	53.3%

Place of Obtaining Drugs	No. of Patients	Percentage
Shop	7	15.6%
Friends	8	17.8%
Peddler	28	62.2%
Parents cupboard	2	4.4%

Means of getting Money to buy Drugs	No. of Patients	Percentage
Steal	22	48.9%
Borrow	10	22.2%
Work	8	17.8%
Gamble	5	11.1%

Desire to Quit	No. of Patients	Percentage
Yes	37	82.2%
Undecided	8	17.8%

Ready to be Assisted	No. of Patients	Percentage
Yes	34	75.6%
No	–	–
Undecided	11	24.4

To summarize and to bring out the salient features of the above tables, we might say that of the total samples studied at the Rehabilitation Centre, 88 per cent used Marijuana as the main drug, 88.9 per cent said that they were introduced to drugs by their friends, 33.6 per cent said that they took to drugs because it gave them a good feeling, 77.8 per cent said they had to use drugs on a regular basis, 53.3 per cent said that they spent over Rs 500/

- per day on drugs, 62.2 per cent said that they procured the drugs from a regular peddler, 48.9 per cent said that they had to rob and steal to maintain their drug habit, 82.2 per cent sincerely felt that they were on the wrong path and wanted to quit the habit and 75.6 per cent of the addicts were ready to be assisted by the doctor and social workers to get rid of the overpowering desire to take drugs.

Conclusion

The usual reaction of a parent who discovers that his child is on heroin is resentment, hurt and anger. A slap is the instinctive remedy that many a parent try. Most often, he is forced to a doctor, who hospitalizes him promptly. What most parents do not realize is that immediate hospitalization without motivation or usage of force (emotional or physical) is of no use. In fact it may, at times, catalyze disaster.

The four keys to help an addict are: Love, Patience, Understanding, and Prayer. Parents should tread carefully when talking to a child who is abusing any drug.

Satish, for example was suspected of using heroin since a month. When his father was informed, he locked Satish in his bed room for about a week. When they finally opened the door, Satish pretended to have realized how bad drug addiction was. At 3 a.m., the next morning, he ran away from home. His parents discovered him after two weeks at Shuklaji street in Bombay, the drug addict's paradise literally in rags.

He was, then, under instruction of his father, beaten up by some goondas. This method worked for another fortnight before Satish slipped away once again.

On reflection, Satish's parents realized that locking him up only made matters worse. In fact Satish had graduated from smoking hash to chasing Brown sugar, in that period.

People who are the most affected are the parents, husband or wife, sister, brother and child. These people should realize that the more distorted their emotions get, the less effective their help becomes. A few parents get to believe that they are SOLELY responsible for their child's drug habit.

If we follow logic, then we would shift the parents behaviors onto the grandparents etc. in short, all would blame Adam and Eve our first parents as recorded in the Bible.

No one is fully responsible for another's actions

Most addicts generally are victims of curiosity or experimentation. It is only after they get 'hooked' that they start probing for faults in those around them. Sometimes the emotions of parents are even dictated by the Drug Addicts. Instead of explaining the consequences of addictions; parents scream; beg, cry; plead or practice the silent treatment. Some parents, for fear of society even cover up for their child's habit. This further worsens the matter.

The parents cry is: "I don't know what to do with my son. If I throw him out or do not give him the money to procure his drug, he asks my relatives, and neighbors. And our well-earned'izzat' (esteem) will be lost in society".

What will people think? Says the mother of a high school child who had resigned to the fact that her son was an addict and that there was no hope. Seema a recovering drug addict, says – actually, I used to evoke anger in my mother. She was very easy to 'con'. Most times, she would hit me. That was good for me because I would feel justified in smoking. Believe me, when things were okay at home, I would feel guilty when I smoked."

All parents should realize that when they get very emotionally disturbed, at that point in time all chances of helping are lost. Drug addicts excel in precipitating crisis by arousing anxiety in those who love them, particularly parents. Generally, in such cases, the user and the parents reach a stage where neither can cope with reality.

Many a times, the parents emotionally blackmail the addict to give up. They infuse guilt into the addict. This excessive charge of guilt may be enough to give up the drugs. But such a method can never ensure permanent sobriety.

One thing parents should realize is that they cannot 'con' the addict. At least not for long. Sapna's parents conned her to meet a therapist saying that she didn't have to stop using the drug. The doctor, a senior psychiatrist, talked to her for five minutes and pronounced 'Detoxification'. She was forcefully injected a high dose of 'Serenace'. When she woke up, she found herself crucified to the hospital bed with bandages. Futility of escape dawned on Sapna after a couple of hours. But then, she was even more sure of starting again, once she was discharged. She did.

On the other hand, Harmit's mother approached the problem in a rational way. She says,I tried to gain knowledge about drug addiction first. When I learnt, what would be my role, I was shocked. I was advised to be calm and composed and to show 'love'. Thank God, I got the courage to apply what I learnt. But that was not enough. Every time Harmit wanted to stop, he would get the withdrawal symptoms, I knew he needed help and so I consulted a doctor who had cured his friend.

Parents usually feel that merely keeping an individual away from drugs, for a certain period is enough. And that the addict must give up the same day.

Here is yet another testimony: My son, Aslam, was kept at this clinic in Bandra, Bombay, fourteen times. Every time it was the same. I spent about Rs. 20,000/- each time and Aslam does not smoke in the clinic, but from the day he is discharged he goes back to the drug within a few weeks, Says the father who had spent more than Rs. 2,00,000 on his son's treatment. He was surprised to learn later that giving up drugs was easy. (in fact the detoxification was done at home without even any 'cold turkey'). Aslam is now sober for more than nine months and has realized that giving up was very easy. That the psychological dependence was more important to get rid off.

Parents usually look for short cuts, but there aren't any. The most common sentence I've heard is 'Doctor, please give him the medication. He won't start again'.

They approach the doctor because they learn through sources that patients do not get the cold turkey. And they think treatment of drug addiction is over after seven to ten days.

They must realize that hospitalization is not enough. Detoxification is not the answer-it is just the first step.

Points to Remember

1. No addict can be forced to give up the drug.
2. When you discover your child is on drugs, start with yourself. Gain knowledge about heroin addiction and have the courage to apply it with determination.
3. Do not treat your son or daughter on your own. Reach out to a person who is competent in the treatment for addiction.
4. Accept the reality – no matter how harsh it is.
5. Do not let the addict control your behavior. At no cost be ambivalent. Don't ever panic.
6. Do not infuse guilt via moralizing, or lose your temper.
7. Understand him, make him feel wanted and show that you care.
8. Be patient. Do not look for shortcuts. Recovery takes about 4 to 6 months.
9. Pray to God. It works.
10. Do something. To do nothing is the second worst choice you can make.

To forcibly hospitalize him, without motivation is the worst choice you can make, though it may afford temporary relief.

Given below are twelve important suggestions for parents, schools, students and communities:

A Plan for Achieving Schools without Drugs

Parents:

1. Teach standards of the right and wrong, and demonstrate those standards through personal example.
2. Help children to resist pressure and the use of drugs by supervising their activities, knowing who their friends are, and talking with them about their interests and problems.
3. Be knowledgeable about the drugs and signs of drug use. When symptoms are observed, respond promptly.

Schools:

4. Determine the extent and the character of drug use and establish a means of monitoring that use regularly.
5. Establish clear and specific rules regarding drug use that include strong corrective actions.
6. Enforce established policies against drug use fairly and consistently. Implement security measures to eliminate drugs on school premises and at school functions.
7. Implement a comprehensive drug prevention curriculum for kindergarten through standard 12, teaching that drug use is wrong and harmful and supporting and strengthening resistance to drugs.
8. Reach out to the community for support and assistance in making the school's antidrug policy and programme work. Develop collaborative arrangements in which school personnel, parents, school boards, law enforcement officers, treatment organisations and private groups can work together to provide necessary resources.

Students:

9. Learn about the effects of drug abuse, the reasons why drugs are harmful, and ways to resist pressures to try drugs.
10. Use an understanding of the danger posed by drugs to help other students avoid them. Encourage other students to resist drugs, persuade those using drugs to seek help from parents and the school principal.

Communities:

11. Help schools fight drugs by providing them with the expertise and financial resources of community groups and agencies.
12. Involve local law enforcement agencies in all aspects of drug prevention: assessment, enforcement and education. The police and courts should have well established and mutually supportive relationships with the schools.

REFERENCES

Blum, H. Richard and Bovil, Daniel. (1974). *Controlling Drugs among Indian Youth*. Delhi: Mittal Publishers.

Cockett, R. (1971). Drug Abuse and Personality in Young Offenders, London, Butterworths.

Dennison, Darwin & Thomas Prevet. (1980). *Alcohol and behaviour and Active Education Approach*. London: The C.V, Mosby Company.

Doyle, C. (1980). The Dangers of Tranquility. Observer Living, Sunday 24 February, No. 45.

DuPond, Robert L. *Getting Tough on Gateway Drugs*, Washington, DC. American Psychiatric Press, 1984.

Fazey, C. (1977). The Aetiology of Psychoactive Substance use, Paris, UNESCO.

Ghodse, H. (1976). Drug Problems dealt with by 62 London Causality Departments. British Journal of Preventive and Social Medicine, 30, 4, 251-6.

Goode, E. (1970). The Marijuana Smokers, New York, Basics Books.

Goode, E. (1973). The Drug Phenomenon: Social Aspects of Drugtakling. New York, Boobs-Merril Co. Inc.

Gopal, Ashok. (June 1987). *Brown Sugar in Pune: Poona Digest*, 3(9), 33.

Goshen, Charles Edward. (1973). *Drinks Drugs and Do-Gooders*. New York: The Free Press.

Hawley, R. *A School Answers Back: Responding to Student Drug Use*. Rockville, MD: American Council for Drug Education, 1984.

Huxley, A. (1972). The Doors of Perception and Heaven and Hell, Harmondsworth, Penguin.

Johnson, B.D. (1973). Marijuana Users and Drug Subcultures, London, Wiley.

Judson, H.F. (1973). Heroin Addiction in Britain London Harcourt Brace Jovanovich.

Kandel, D.B. (ed) (1978). Longitudinal Research on Drug Use, London, Halstead (Wiley).

Kapur, Tribhuwan. (1985). *Drug Epidemic Among Indian Youth*. New Delhi: Joshi Publishers.

Laurie, P. (1972) Drugs: Medical Psychological and Social Facts, Harmondsworth, Pelican.

Manatt, Marsha. *Parents, Peers, and Pot II. Rockville, MD: National Institute on Drug Abuse*, 1983.

Mann, Peggy. *Marijuana Alert*. New York, NY: McGraw Hill, 1985.

Miller, Judith D., Ira H. Cisin, and Herbert I. Abelson. *National Survey on Drug Abuse: Main Findings*, 1982.

Mirchandani, Dayal. Outpatient Detoxification fo Substance Abusers. Conference Report, 1988.

Rockville, MD: *National Institute of Drug Abuse*. 1981 (ADM 84-1152).

Rockville, MD: *National Institute on Drug Abuse. Cocaine Addiction*: It Costs Too Much.National Institute of Drug Abuse, 1985.

Rockville, MD: *National Institute on Drug Abuse. Drugs and the Family*. National Institute of Drug Abuse, 1981 (ADM 83-1151).

Rockville, MD: *National Institute on Drug Abuse. Handbook for Prevention Evaluation*. National Institute on Drug Abuse, 1981.

Plant, A Martin and Peck, F. David. (9185). *Alcohol, Drugs and School Leaves*. New York: Tavirlock Publication.

Polich, J. Michael. (1980). The Curse of Alcoholism. New York: Interscience Publication.

Ray, Oakley, S. (1972). Drugs Society and Human Behavior. Saint Louis: The C.V. Mosby Company.

Reenes, D. Alexander. (1980). *Disorder of the Nervous System*. Chicago: Year Book Publication.

Rubel, Robert J. *A Comprehensive Approach to Drug Prevention. Astion*. National Alliance for safe School, 1984.

Schofield, M. (1971). The Strange Case of Pot, Harmondsworth, Pelican.

Southland, V.C. (1970). A Synopsis of Pharmacology. London: W.B. Saunders Company.

Stimson, G.V. (1973). Heroin and Behaviour, London Irish University Press.

Tobias, Joyce M. Kids and Drugs. Annandale, VA: Panda Press, 1986).

West, D.J. (ed) (1978). Problems of Drug Abuse in Britain, Cambridge, Institute of Criminology.

Weiner, R. S. P. (1970). Drugs and School Children. London, Longmans.

Young, J. (1971). The Drugtakers, London, Paladin. Tobacco in Britain, London, Heinemann.

Alcoholism Among Youth in India

– Dr. K.S. Patil

Introduction

Men and women since the inception of human civilization, to celebrate joyful events such as marriage, childbirth, a new job, promotion or any other social success have used alcohol. No festival is complete without the consumption of mood elevating substances, be it Christmas, where wine flows like water, or the Hindu festival of Holi, in which the use of Bhang is considered a traditional drink. Of course, this does not mean that alcohol is restricted only to joyful occasions. People who want to escape from reality freely use these; for example, labourers drown their fatigue after hard work in country liquor, a disappointed lover, marries the bottle, people especially the youth, try to relive the stress of modern life by turning to alcoholism. There are countless reasons why people take drugs or alcohol (Khan, 1985). Alcoholism, compulsive craving for drinks is an oldest phenomenon because the societies, in all parts of the world, have been using alcohol to enjoy the pleasurable sensation or to alter mood.

Theoretical Background

The history of alcoholic drinks appears to be as old as the history of humanity is itself. Man has always felt a desire to eat, drink, or otherwise consume substances that made him feel elated or euphoric. The earliest historical records indicate familiarity with psychoactive drugs, the family and society; alcoholism has emerged as a vital issue of the quality of life and the welfare of the people (Hirasingh, 1992). In the last few decades and particularly since 1980 a sinister pattern of alcohol used has developed, predominantly among the youth. This pattern of using alcohol is not easily controlled and results in a high proportion of users who often ruin their lives and careers before they have really began. The main groups who fall prey to the alcohol are the educated young people, the college students. The leaders of the population so effected may not be very large, but youth is a very special section of society with right to the protection and guardianships of the elders and leaders of our country (Tool, 1987).

The ancient populations of the Far and Middle East had a number of substances at their disposal capable of producing fermented drink. It seems that honey furnished the first drinkable ethanol: all the nations of the West and the Old World came to be familiar with mead. In the prehistoric period, the western Mediterranean had at its disposal dates, cereals, grapes and many other fruits. Egyptian papyri provide evidence of several alcoholic drinks, and the frescos in the tombs show drunken people. Inscriptions from Ugarit and Sumer also carry allusions to intemperance." The law code of Hammurabi (1700 BC): the Ancient Greek world was a society where wine played a considerable role. The Greeks drank mead from the earliest times and probably developed the cultivation of Caucasian vines around 1000 BC. Legend would have it was Dionysus who taught them how to make wine. This is well considered by some to be the son of Zeus and a Theban princess, and by others to be of Thracian origin, he is said to have fled to Egypt to escape the fury of the jealous Hera. It was there that he learnt to make wine. The cult of Dionysus was also called the cult of Bacchus. The public ceremonies that it inspired were often linked to 'phallopheries', rustic fertility rites featuring choirs, dances and parades, out of which were born poetry, comedy and drama. Initially, the Greeks resisted these foreign rites, which pushed men and women to the worst excesses, but they rapidly became part of daily life.

The socio-cultural dominance of the section of a population and the external impact on the day-to-day life of the people seem to influence alcohol abuse. According to Malinowski, (1958) the term culture is too comprehensive and refers, to that complex quantity which any other activities or potentials acquired by an individual as a member of society. The comparative distinction of the constituents of life style identified culture with religions. Hence, different religion apparently reduces various cultures patterns. The existence of Hindu way of life as compared with other culture has no more predominant. It is because of its historical values of cultural tradition, multiplicity of religious beliefs, caste system, the structure of family and its striking rural character over a period of time, these traditions had responded to different social situations and needs including alcohol use. These traditions have undergone substantive changes under modernization might have imbued social norms with certain form of group behaviour. In Indian condition, alcoholism was never a social problem. The ancient Indian teachings of four stages of life, Brahmacharya, Grihastha, Vamprastha and Sanyasa had the built in social system of handing over powers to the younger generations. It was presumed that after 50 years, one should not get involved in the worldly affairs. Every society, the world over, has a social structure, which can broadly be divided into three social classes namely the high, middle and low. Research studies have revealed that socio-economic status is a significant determinant for understanding any particular society. Research evidence on the significant impact of class on human development inspired the researchers to study the social structure of any given society.

Concept of Alcohol

Alcohol is made when grains, fruits, or vegetables are fermented. Fermentation is a process that uses yeast or bacteria to change the sugars in the food into alcohol. Fermentation is used to produce many necessary items-everything from cheese to medications. Alcohol has different forms and can be used as a cleaner, an antiseptic, or a sedative. So if alcohol is a natural product, why do teens need to be concerned about drinking it? When people drink alcohol, it is absorbed into their bloodstream. From there, it affects the central nervous system (the brain and spinal cord), which controls virtually all body functions. Because experts now know that the human brain is still developing during our teens, scientists are researching the effects drinking alcohol can have on the teen brain.

Effects of Alcohol

Alcohol is a depressant, which means it slows the function of the central nervous system. Alcohol actually blocks some of the messages trying to get to the brain. This alters a person's perceptions, emotions, movement, vision, and hearing. In very small amounts, alcohol can help a person feel more relaxed or less anxious. More alcohol causes greater changes in the brain, resulting in intoxication. The youth who have overused alcohol may stumble, lose their coordination, and stain their speech. They will probably be confused and disoriented. This can make someone very friendly and talkative or very aggressive and angry. When large amounts of alcohol consumed in a short period, alcohol poisoning can result. Violent vomiting is usually the first symptom of alcohol poisoning. Extreme sleepiness, unconsciousness, difficulty breathing, dangerously low blood sugar, seizures, and even death may result.

Alcohol is the number one drug of choice among youth and adolescents. In 2002, about 2 million youth ages 12 through 20 drank 5 or more drinks on an occasion, 5 or more times a month (SAMHSA, 2003). Alcohol use by youth under age 21 poses both acute and long-term risks. In 2002, 1.5 million youth ages 12 through 17 met criteria for admission to alcohol treatment. Alcohol is the leading contributor to the leading causes of death each year for young people under age 21, including 7,000 deaths from alcohol-related injuries 1,500 homicides 300 suicides (NHTSA, 2003); (CDC, 2004); Smith et al, 1999; Levy, Miller, Cox, 1999; Hingson and Kenkel, 2004. Studies show 40 per cent of those who start drinking before the age of 15 meet criteria for alcohol dependence at some point in their lives. Early exposure to alcohol may have long-lasting effects on intellectual capabilities and may increase the likelihood of alcohol addiction. Half of all persons who die in traffic crashes involving drinking drivers under age 21 are persons other than the drinking driver (NHTSA, 2003).

Reasons for Attracting Youth Towards Alcohol

Biological changes and physical development are matter of evolution; consider many scientists, whereas the development of mind and its behaviour may be term as higher evolution. The attitudes, behaviour, response and the activities of a person are governed by the personality of a person says (Skinner). This personality is the self in a person Esysenck,(1953). Each self is associated with various types of energies (Piaget). These energies are the source of feeling and sentiment Adler, (1943). The self functions as a response to the communication between mind and external world, giving free access to one type of self and suppressing the other, amounts to manipulation of feelings and sentiments. It is at this stage when a person struggles with the suppressed behaviour whereby the inner self becomes more dominant, Jung, (1939). This inner self therefore tries to search a medium to overcome its suppression by way of consolidating the remaining self has to derive some sort of pleasure. It is at this stage a person opting for alcohol. This first encounter with alcohol becomes a pleasurable moment even if it produces certain types of measuring for a person and thereby he is tempted to establish a link for easy access. He, therefore, gets addiction to the alcohol n the process of attaining pleasure.

There are also certain psychotic persons who can achieve reasonably satisfactory relations with others only through the aid of alcohol: though his difficulties may be imaginary, they are very real and compelling to the person who has them. The heredity has been suggested as a predisposing factor. R. J. Williams who believes that individuals may inherit metabolic pattern which result in nutritional deficiencies that a in a turn give rise to a craving for alcohol. These kinds of persons have requires more vitamins, and when these need are not satisfied they revert to alcoholism. However, the focused group discussions with youth, parents, teachers, doctors and social workers following could be the reasons to attract the youth towards alcohol:

1. Peer pressure
2. Alleviation of mood

3. More pocket money
4. Failed in love
5. Celebration of joyful events
6. Deviant behaviour
7. Personality disorders
8. Pleasure
9. Adverse impact of Indian cinema
10. Stress
11. Fashion
12. Business meetings

Stages of Alcohol Consumption

It is an established fact that nobody wants to become alcoholic. The youth who drink alcohol never know that they will be addicted to alcohol in near future. It does not mean that all who drink alcohol become alcoholic but there are some youth with the problem of personality disorders fall prey to such kind of deadly disease that is alcoholism or alcoholic dependence. There are three stages of drinking alcohol as follows:

1. Social level of dinking
2. Psychological level of dinking
3. Physical level of drinking

Social Level of Drinking

In this state of mind the people initially start drinking alcohol due to peer pressure and social obligations such as celebration of joyful events, even to overcome the sorrowful happenings, stress due to changing pattern of life style, failure in the achieving success, social conflicts, family disputes and so on. This kind of social level of drinking is occurs occasionally and youth enjoying the euphoria and mood alleviating substance to feel the social status and recognitions from the surroundings. They usually drink one or two pegs of alcohol i.e. 60 ml. To 90 ml. of alcoholic drink at one seating on the occasion of social functions which could come seldom during a period of one year. They have been called as social drinkers. The frequency of drinking alcohol is controlled and such kind of youth does not get urge or the craving for the alcohol. In this segment of the population do not have any kind of problems neither it effects their family nor social life.

Psychological Level of Drinking

This is the second stage of the drinking level in which the frequency of the drinking has been increasing day by day with the excuse of various reasons that may not be the relevant or justifiable but people do try to find out some or the other ways to go for alcoholic drink. In first stage, the state of mind the youth do not get urge or craving for the alcohol drink whereas in this stage they develop the feeling, urge and craving especially in the evening to go to take alcohol. The quantity, which is mentioned in previous stage, can be seen increased. This is very dangerous and even the abuser will never know that when they are become alcoholic, it means that they will cross second stage and reach in third stage of physical dependency.

Physical Level of Drinking

The physical level of drinking is the third stage where the abuser is surrender or dependent on alcohol. The youth who crossed social and psychological level of drinking alcohol and reached into physical level of dependency is called the Alcoholic. It is very difficult to live without alcohol, as the abuser suffers from sever withdrawal symptoms such as insomnia, body-ache, abdominal pain, and loss of appetite, unable to carry out any kind of work or assignments, strong craving, hallucinations, suspiciousness and so on. In this stage, there is no more enjoyment or the euphoria but it is the physical need of the abuser and therefore, he has to drink alcohol to overcome with the withdrawal symptoms. However, majority of the alcoholics manage to get money for the alcohol some or the other way. They have usually been neglected by the family and discarded by the society. Due to the problem of alcoholism, not only the person who is alcoholic suffer from various elements but also the entire family is living under tremendous stress, humiliation, economic loss and disturbance. It is very difficult to get back to pre-morbid stage and required specialized mode of treatment such as chemotherapy, psychotherapy, relaxation therapy, counseling, meditation, yoga. The duration of the treatment is depends upon the severity of the illness. However, the frequency of relapses is very high and majority of alcoholics die due to failure of lever.

Kind of Problems Faced due to Alcoholism

The family environment and genetics can perpetuate a cruel and destruction in the life. There are so many problems accrued such as marriages break up of marriages, domestic violence. The habit of alcohol interfere with youth's bodies and minds leads to serious emotional and development problems by masking the stress and anxiety. Researchers estimate that youth who begin drinking before the age of 15 are four times more likely to develop a serious alcohol problem later in life than those who wait until they are 21. The following problems faced by youth who are having the habit of drinking as alcohol.

1. Emotional problems

Alcohol abuse can cause or mask emotional problems such as anxiety or depression. It can also increase the severity of these emotional problems. Studies show that eighth-grade girls who drink heavily are three times more likely to attempt suicide than girls in their grade who do not drink, and teenage girls aged 12-16 who drink are four times more likely than their non-drinking peers to suffer from the problem of depression.

2. **Behavioural problems**

Youth drinkers have an increased risk of social problems, depression, suicidal thoughts and violence. According to the Substance Abuse and Mental Health Services Administration, 39 per cent of teenage drinkers exhibit serious behavioural problems and 31 per cent suffer extreme levels of psychological distress. Regular alcohol consumption is also associated with higher levels of attention-deficit disorder, hyperactivity and aggressiveness.

3. **Dependency**

Studies prove that the youth who start drinking at early age the greater the chances to develop a problem with alcohol. In fact, youth who reported drinking before the age of 15 are four times more likely to become dependent on alcohol than those who started drinking later in life.

4. **Unsafe sex**

The youth that drink are more likely to have unprotected sex, with a stranger, or engage in various forms of sexual activity. This leads to higher risks of STDs, teen pregnancy and sexual assault.

5. **Learning disabilities**

Youth that indulge in drinking found to be performing worse in school, are more likely to fall behind, and have higher dropout rates. Research shows that youth drinkers score worse than their non-drinking youth on vocabulary, visual-spatial and memory tests.

6. **Brain damage**

Heavy drinking among youth over many years can result in serious mental disorders or permanent, irreversible damage to the brain or nervous system. According to the American Medical Association, scientific evidence suggests that even modest alcohol consumption in adolescence can result in permanent brain damage.

7. **Road accidents**

Alcohol-related traffic accidents are a major cause of death among youth. A recent study showed that 28 per cent of 15 to 20 year old drivers who were killed in car crashes had the problem of drinking.

8. **Narcotic drugs**

Alcohol is often a gateway drug to other illicit substances. Youth those drinks are more likely than non-drinking youth to use other drugs like marijuana, cocaine, and heroin. In addition to this the following problems the youth can develop:

1. Stealing habits
2. Theft
3. Illegal activities
4. Suspicious

5. Paranoid
6. Delusion

Treatment for Alcoholism

Consumption of alcohol gives to kick to the user. This state is described activating the senses and the users wish to remain in the same state of mind. The state of mind is associated with psychological dependency to the alcohol. The addict can't adjust to non-availability of alcohol and hence the psychological dependency drags the addict to the state craving the treatment generally given by psychological strengthens the will power of a alcohol addict to counter the withdrawal symptoms and sustain the craving state. Because of the fact that psychological dependency and state of mind, at times, can dominate the detoxification and will power of a person and may revert, back him to his previous alcohol habits. Hence, it becomes necessary to think of yet another type of treatment, which would keep the mind more, concentrated and awakened. Raising the level of alertness can also be a solution to the problem of alcohol addiction. This can be achieved by practicing of Yogasan, psychological exercise, etc. There are varied individuals with diverse backgrounds and treatment needs. The individual in treatment is a unique person who is a product of all his life experiences. The foremost concern is, therefore, a diverse one employing different stokes for different folks. In this case, factor such as readiness, level of alcohol use, his individual and community resources as well as his significant relationship are to be considered in the planning of treatment needs. The following treatment services are helpful to overcome the problem of alcoholism.

1. Chemotherapy
2. Narcotic Anonymous meetings
3. Psychotherapy
4. Recreation therapy
5. Meditation
6. Physiotherapy
7. Religious therapy
8. Yoga therapy
9. Motivational Speeches

Relapse Prevention

The youth, who is undergoing treatment in the center for a required period, he has to be discharged from the center. It is compulsory for the addicts to continue with medication even while at home. In addition, he is expected to report at the hospital once in a week at the beginning and later once in a forth night to check to progress and modify the course of treatment. However, this process cannot effectively carry out by the client alone; he is in need of an intensive pursuance by self-motivation in controlling the withdrawal and craving effects. He often lacked will power to overcome the attack psychological organism, and hence the family members must be conscious enough to realize the importance of treatment by encouraging client to go to rehabilitation center for the follow-up.

Rehabilitation of the Alcoholic Dependents

The philosophical assumption normally adopted in the treatment centers is that alcohol dependent himself is the key factor for his own rehabilitation. He must play an active role, as he, himself, would have to play this part in his life outside Abdullah, (1985). An individual in treatment cannot be isolated from his family and community. The problem of alcoholism does not merely resides in him and cannot be solved by reference to him isolation with involving those close to him. The involvement in the rehabilitation process is of individual, group, and community. Community in a wider sense could be treatment centers dedicated to a particular cause. The behaviour pattern of an individual, group and community is a stepping-stone to rehabilitation. It is, therefore, a process of committed life. It is a life commitment, first to the ideal of becoming a normal and acceptable person in the society. This means, that one has to adapt to all those practices and methods, which conduce, in one way or the other to the fulfillment of commitment. In other words, it is a commitment to what we can also call the process or the path of evolution of a man does his betterment. It is not difficult to commit oneself, at least to limited extent, but it is no means to remain faithful to that commitment over a considerable period. There are so many obstacles, distractions, weakness imperfection with oneself, constantly getting in a way, that backsliding or recession from one's original commitment only easily occurs. Continual reminders of that commitment are therefore necessary.

An individual in the full sense of individual is one who is prepared to change; who accepts the necessity of change and who is overcome all odd by surpassing the craving miseries. He is one who has unified all his selves and the whole force of his being to the higher evolution. Moreover, he is one who regards norms and morals of rehabilitation as means to an end, not as ends in them, and treats him accordingly. In more contemporary terms, the individual is firstly one who is self conscious, in the sense that he is aware of what he is dining, and why. He is aware of his own motion and thoughts, and of the extent to which his particular skills and association have conditioned him, and so on. He is aware of his own basic motivations, of what is happening between him and other people or aware of his relationship. Above all, he has to be aware of his own irreplaceable uniqueness as one of an infinite number of foci of universal consciousness.

Secondly, the individual can be independent. He may not be the victim of his own unconscious urges, not emotionally dependent on other people or on a group. He does not mind differing from other people. In addition, independence does not mean refusing one's objective physical limitations. Thus, self-consciousness and independence are the principal characteristics of the individual from a more contemporary point of view. Groups are, as one knows, of many different kinds, both large and small. There are family groups, both nuclear and extended. There are groups of alcohol addicts also groups of social workers.

The rehabilitation centers works on the assumption that an alcohol dependent has become what he is because of a complex of psychological and social factors and that the alcoholism is only a symptom of the underlying psychological and social maladjustment. The approach is, therefore, an individual cum group approach with individual and group counseling techniques, together with meaningful occupational, vocational, spiritual and recreational activities, D. Mohan, et al (1986).

Motivation by setting a goal for his life, the recovering alcoholic can be motivated to make the extra effort with the training and studies. University counseling centers have been in use on some campus in India, offering prevention and rehabilitation facilities with some success Khurana, (1974). Recovering alcohol often require time and gentle guidance to relate to, and interact with others in a healthy manner. Special counseling may be needed usually in a protected environment before the alcoholics are ready to enter in general society. Family and friends have a special role to play in rehabilitation and the re-integration of the person back into the family and the local community by empathetic and supportive attitudes at home and outside.

Many researchers see Mint, (1985) are in view that after a month's stay in the detoxification center, selected cases may be sent to rehabilitation centers where vocational training, physical exercise, and psychotherapy may be given to the alcoholic. The skills required in the prevention, care, treatment and rehabilitation of the alcoholic are so many highly specialized Khorana, (1974). The rehabilitation services should include group therapy, vocational training, individual and family counseling Gondevia, (1992).

The family is the main source of providing the education and values to the youth who become alcoholic. Therefore, re-education of the family members needs to be taken care by the counseling center. Re-education does not mean that the alcoholic addict required to e give the formal education. Nevertheless, he must provide the information, which is concerned about alcohol addiction and its effects on human body. The following main topics have to be taken into consideration during the course re-educating the family members:

1. Family counseling
2. The values and perspective of the family
3. The home environment

4. How to improve interactions among family members
5. How to change the attitude and behaviour of the family
6. How to focus the attention of the family members towards the problem of alcoholism
7. How to get open discussion about the addiction in the family
8. Family environment scale relapse education
9. Family therapy
10. Aftercare
11. Follow-up
12. Family intervention

Conclusion

Alcohol is a depressant, which means it slows the function of the central nervous system. Alcohol actually blocks some of the messages trying to get to the brain. This alters a youth perceptions, emotions, movement, vision, and hearing. In very small amounts, alcohol can help a person feel more relaxed or less anxious. More alcohol causes greater changes in the brain, resulting in intoxication. Alcohol abuse is emerging as a major public health problem in the country. The increasing production, distribution, and promotion of alcohol have already seen drink-related problems emerging as a major public health concern in India. There has been a rapid change in patterns and trends of alcohol use in India. According to a study (WHO, 2004) most of the violence took place during intoxication. The Indian constitution includes the prohibition of alcohol among its directive principles; alcohol policy is devolved to individual states. The youth who have hackneyed alcohol may stagger, lose their coordination, and slight their speech. They will probably be confused and disoriented depending on the degree of intoxication.

In view of the above, it can be suggested that the young generation should keep them away from such kind of deadly habit of drinking in an early age so that they can concentrate more on their studies and career. The young age of the youth is confusing state of mind, they are not able to take proper decisions in the life, and hence the responsibilities of the parents and the family members have been increased to keep watch on activities of the children.

REFERENCES

Ahuja, Ram, (1997). Social Problems in India, Jaipur: Rawat Publication,

Abdulla, A.P. (1983) Alcohol and Alcoholism, New York: Vol. 18. No. 4.

Aderson, S.L. et al (1983), Family Therapy in the Treatment of Alcoholism, Social Work in Health Care.

Asher, Ramona and Brissett, Dennis (1988), Codependency: A Review from Women Married to Alcoholics, International Journal of the Addiction, Vol. 23 (4).

Berger, A. (1986), Family Involvement and Alcoholic's Completion of a Multiphase Treatment Programme, Journal of Studies on Alcohol.

Chitnis, S., (1994) Drug on College Campus, Bombay: Tata Institute of Social Sciences.

Chopra, G.S., and Chopra, P.S. (1965). Studies on 300 Indian Drug Addicts with special reference to Psycho-sociological Aspects – Etiology and Treatment Bulletin on Narcot. XVII, 2, 1.

Desai, N.G. (1986). Treatment Outcome of Alcohol Dependence, In. Ray. S.

Dube, K.S. and Handa, S.K. (1969) Drug Habit in Health and Mental Disorder, Indian Journal of Psychiatry, 11-23.

Patil, K.S., (1993) Drug Addiction Among Youth in Goa with Special Emphasis on Treatment and Rehabilitation.

Hunt, l. (1983). Alcohol Problems are Social Problems: A Challenge to Social Worker, Paper given at the 29th International Institute on the Prevention and Treatment of Alcoholism, Zagreb (Unpublished).

Jackson, J.K. (1962). Alcoholism and Family, In D.J. Pitman and C.R. Synder (eds.), Society, Culture and Drinking Patterns, New York, John Wiley and Sons.

Joan, E.; Chankappura (1986). Alcoholism – Psychosocial Variables, A Doctoral Dissertation, University of Delhi.

Khan, M. Z., (1985) Drug Use Amongst the College Youth, Bombay: Somaiya.

Mishra, H. and Kumaraiah, V. (1989). Behavioural Intervention in Alcoholism and Drug Addiction, in. R. Ray and R.W. Pickens (Eds.), Proceedings of the Indo-US Symposium on Alcohol and Drug Abuse, NIMHANS, Bangalore.

Patterson and Kaufman (1982). The Alcoholism Syndrome: Definition and Models, In. Encyclopedic Handbook of Alcoholism, New York, Garder Press.

Sathyanarayana Rao and Kuruvilla (1992). Study on the Coping Behaviour of Wives of Alcoholics, Indian Journal of Psychiatry.

Singh, G. (1986). Epidemiology of Alcohol Abuse in India, In Ray, R., Pickens, W.R. (Eds.), Proceedings in the Indo-US Symposium on Alcohol and Drug Abuse, Bangalore: NIMHANS.

Suman, L.N. and Nagalaxmi, S. V. (1995). Family Interaction Patterns in Alcoholic Families, NIMHANS Journal, Jan. 13 (1).

Varma, Vijay. K., (1980) Extent and Pattern of Alcohol Related Problems in North India, Indian Journal of Psychiatry, 22-18.

Vaillant, G. (1983). The National History of Alcoholism, Cambridge Mass, Harvard University Press.

WHO, (1974). Organisation of Mental Health Services in Developing Countries, Sixteen Technical Report No. 564, Geneva, World Health Organisation.

WHO, (1986). Drug Dependence and Alcohol Related Problems - A Manual for Community Health Workers with Guidelines for Trainers, Geneva, World Health Organisation.

Kharra Chewing Habit Among the Youth in Vidharba

– Dr. **Robin D. Tribhuwan**
– Dr. **Pandit R. Fulzele**

Introduction

The World Health Organisation defines drug addiction as a state of periodic or chronic intoxications, and detrimental to the individual and the society, produced by repeated consumption of a drug either natural or synthetic.

It is estimated that there are over 20 to 48 million drug addicts in the world. In India, there are over 7,00,000 (7 lakhs)brown sugar addicts, with one lakh alone in Mumbai (Kurian J.C., 2013)

Kurian J.C. (2013) further, states that, it is an open secret that addiction to drug is on the increase in educational institutes as well, the incidence being particularly high (60%) among student of schools and colleges Drug addiction is not only harmful to the individual, but also affects his family and society at large.

The Vidharba region in the state of Maharastra consists of eleven districts and is popularly known for chewing kharra- an abusive substance. Besides chewing Kharra, the use of tobacco, ghutka, pan, betel nut etc. is very common among people. Spitting, after chewing kharra, tobacco, ghutaka or betel nut is common too.

This chapter throws light on the practice of kharra consumption among the youth in Vidharba, keeping in view following aims.

Aims of the Paper

1. To study the social, cultural & psychological aspects inter twinned with kharra consumption.
2. To explore the expenditure pattern, among youth associated with kharra consumption.
3. To analyzed the impact of kharra consumption on the economic life of youth.
4. To unviel the sale of kharra through "pan thelas" (stalls)

Hypothesis

Based on the pilot study conducted by the authors among 100 youth & by carrying out focused group discussions with youth, parents, teachers, pan stall owners, dentists and health educators following hypothesis were developed.

1. Friend circle & social get gatherings of adolescent & youth are the main determinants that hook the youth into kharra consumption.
2. The habit of chewing kharra is high among the males than females.
3. Consumption of kharra leads to dental carries throat & digestive disorders.
4. A kharra addict spends a considerable amount on buying kharra.
5. The habits of chewing kharra ultimately gives rise to yet another habit namely spitting anywhere & everywhere.

Research Methodology

(a) **Locale of the study**

The present study was carried out in Gadchiroli district, in the Vidharba region of the State of Maharastra ,India.

(b) **Target population**

The target population of the study are youth ie students labourers , Government & Private sector workers and pan stall owners ranging from 18 to 35 years of age.

(c) **Research tools**

An interview scheduled was designed, pre-tested and finalized after carrying out a pilot study. Focused group discussions were held with key informants such as parents, teachers, pan stall owners, dentist, health educators & social workers. Observation was used to cross check the data.

Given below are the types of respondents interviewed

1. College youth – 100
2. Young labourers – 100
3. Workers belonging to private & Government sector – 100
4. Pan stall owners – 100

Total – 400

Thus, a total of 400 respondents were interviewed to understand the concept of kharra consumption among the youth of Vidharba.

(d) **Sampling:** Random sampling technique was used to select the sample.

(e) **Analysis:** Quantitative data was analyzed using excel soft ware where as qualitative data was analyzed manually.

What is kharra?

Kharra is a mixture of crushed betel nut, combined with calcium carbonate (lime) and tobacco, Earlier, people would mix kharra on one palm by rubbing with the thumb of another hand.

However in the late nineties, people started using plastic paper to mix the above mentioned substance and then rub the plastic paper on a wooden stool (pat) for a period of 10 to 20 minutes.

Some of the tobacco brands in which the betel nut crush is mixed & rubbed are Mazza, Baba-120,Baba -160, kimam, balck jarda etc, The betel nut crush can be raw or fried(bhunji). Some Shops in Vidharba have khara mixing machines because of its demand.

Price of Kharra

The price of kharra depends on the quantity and brand of tobacco used. Given Below are rates for 10 gms of kharra ,mixed with different brands of tobacco right from 1995to 2013.

Table 23.1: Price of Kharra

Sr.No.	Year	Tobacco Brands					
		Nagpur thavkar	Rabul	Mazza	Black Jarda	Baba 120	Baba 160
1.	1995 to 1998	Rs. 1.50	Rs. 1.50	–	–	Rs. 2.00	Rs. 3.00
2.	1998 to 2001	Rs. 2.00	Rs. 2.00	–	–	3.00	4.00
3.	2001 to 2003	Rs. 2.50	Rs. 2.50	–	–	5.00	7.00
4.	2004 to 2006	Rs. 3.00	Rs. 3.00	–	–	5.00	7.00
5.	2006 to 2008	Rs. 3.50	Rs. 3.50	–	–	6.00	10.00
6.	2008 to 2011	Rs. 5.00	Rs. 5.00	5.00	5.00	7.00	12.00
7.	2011 to 2012	Rs. 8.00	Rs. 8.00	8.00	8.00	12.00	15.00
8.	2012 to till date.	–	–	10.00	10.00	15.00 17.00	25.00 30.00

Table 23.1 reflects the increasing price rates of kharra mixed in different brands of tobaccos from 1998 till date. The respondents stated that the kharra rates depend on the quantity of kharra & quality or brand of tobacco used . Although the table highlights rates for 10 gram of kharra, it was observed that there are addicts who consume 50 to 100 gms per day.

Why youth are attracted to kharra consumption ?

It was observed that the habit of chewing kharra starts at the age of 9 to 14 and more particularly from 15 to 18 and is continued till death. During the youth and adult hood its consumption is high though. Some of the reason or causes of kharra consumption are as below:

1. Friends instigate or force to consume kharra.
2. Curiosity of an experience of getting a kick.
3. Another reason or consuming kharra is to pass time
4. They find it difficult go to the toilet without chewing it.
5. Consumption of kharra helps people to work vibrantly, speedily & effectively, said the youth.
6. Social gatherings, meetings with friends, gossiping, tea meeting etc. calls for chewing kharra as well.

Major Findings

The quantitative & qualitative data gathered from 400 youth revealed following facts.

1. Age range of consumption

It was observed that 33 per cent of the respondents started chewing kharra between the age range 10 to 15; 37 per cent between the age range 15 to 18 and 31 per cent above the age of 18 to 35.

2. Educational status

Statistical data revealed that 24 per cent of the respondents were ill-literate; 18 per cent studied up to primary; 28 per cent up to high school; 30 per cent were graduates & post graduates. It was observed that educational status and kharra consumption had no significant co-relation, among the four categories of respondents studied.

3. Annual income

It was observed that 27 per cent of the respondents earned an annual income of less than Rs. 20000/- 23 per cent did not earn any thing. 24 per cent earned between Rs. 21000/- to 50000/- 27 per cent of the respondents earned between Rs. 51000/- to 400000/- College youth spend money for kharra from their pocket money and demanded more from parents. It was observed that the labourers spend 15 to 20 per cent of their annual income on chewing kharra it higher the income better the quality of tobacco used in the kharra.

4. Number of pudis per day

A pudi contains 10 grams of kharra. Statistical data revealed following facts. 15 per cent of the respondents consumed one pudi (10 gms) per day; 35 per cent two pudis (20gms); 40 per cent consumed 3 pudies (30gms); 10 per cent (40 & above gms); ie 4 & above pudis.

5. Type of tobacco consumed

The data revealed that 7 per cent of the respondents consumed kharra mixed with urja (Nagpur)the costly tobacco; 70 per cent consumed kharra mixed with mazza tobacco; 20 per cent used Jarda 120; and only 3 per cent used the costliest tobacco namely Baba 160.

6. Prevalence of high consumption

Focused group discussions revealed that kharra is consumed in high quantity in Nagpur, followed by Bhandara, Gadchiroli, Gondiya, Chandrapur etc. Secondly, most respondents opined, that those who chew 40 to 50 grams of kharra every day are psychologically dependent on the substance. They get mentally disturbed if they do not chew kharra.

They are addicted to the same. The researchers also came across respondents, who consume 70 to 100 grams of kharra a day, and annually spend Rs. 25000/- to Rs. 40000/- on the same.

Out of the 400 youth interviewed 65 per cent stated that they feel uneasy when they do not consume kharra, 15 per cent said they get angry & upset over minute issues; 10 per cent said that it has impact on their digestive system and the rest 10 per cent said it has impact on their mental & physical well being.

7. Impact on Health: An Emic-view

On Analyzing the insider's views regarding the impact of kharra on their health following facts were unveiled. 40 per cent felt it causes Problems of teeth, gums & tongue; 37 per cent said it has an adverse impact on the stomach & liver, 28 per cent said it leads to sore throat; while 5 per cent stated that kharra consumption causes cancer of the mouth & throat.

8. Social aspects of chewing kharra

The habit of chewing kharra is associated with social gathering, meeting discussions among friends, morning & evening walks, welcoming guests who chew kharra,etc. It was observed that most youth prefor to chew & share kharra with friends, colleages, fellow- co workers, class or school mates, etc. They enjoy having kharra with other. Only those who are psychologically dependent on the substance love to have it alone with few exceptions.

9. Cultural implications

It us a traditional custom in Vidharba to offer betel leaf, clove, betel nut, & Phoenicum vulgare to a guest. Tribhuwan Robin (1998) , (2003) stated that it is a custom among the Thakars & Warli tribes to offer tobacco & bidis (cigars) to the guests during weddings , engagements & other community riyuals. Tribhuwan Robin & Kharche Jayshree (2013) have highlighted the ritual significance of toddy – an intoxicating drink, among the Warlis, in various rites of passage. Offering pan (betel leaf) to guests & friends is very common among the muslims. This custom is very popular in north India.

Kharra is offered to friends, relatives & guests, who consume kharra. These gestures of offering tobacco, pan, badi sauf, supari, cigar, and clove to the guests & friends is a mark of gratitude & respect for them.

10. Impact of kharra chewing on economic life

Data gathered from the field has revealed that the habit of chewing kharra certainly has an adverse impact on the economic life of an individual and his family. Given below are three case studies that will make the above point clear.

Case Study No. 1

Mr. DM, aged 30, a married agricultural labourer, with two kids & a house wife, earns Rs. 35000/- per year. He spends Rs. 15000/- to 18000/- on purchasely kharra for consumption per annual. He is hardly left with Rs. 17000/- to meet the expenditure of his family. For the sake of kharra, Mr. DM deprives his wife & children of their rights to basic human needs.

Case Study No. 2

Mr. Xy, aged 23 unmarried male , an under graduate, who has completed a certificate course in data entry, works for a Government Office on monthly basis as a temporary worker. He earns Rs. 5000/- per month, but spends Rs. 900/- on kharra. Thus, from an annual income of Rs. 60000/-, Mr. Xy Spends Rs. 10800/- on purchasing kharra.

Care Study. No. 3

Mr. SN, aged 16 a male student, studying in XIth grade, started chewing kharra when he was 11 years old. Today , he consumes at least 10 to 20 grams of kharra everday, He manages to get Rs. 10/- from his father and then requests his friends to give him the other 10 grams for the day. Thus, on an average Mr SN spends Rs: 300/- per month on kharra and Rs. 3600/- annually. Instead of using his pocket money on purchasing fruits, or biscuits, he prefers to chew kharra.

Out of the 400 respondents interviewed, it was observed that; 15 per cent spend Rs. 1000 to 3600/- per year 35 per cent, Rs. 3601 to 8000/- per year 40 per cent spend Rs. 8001 to 11600/- per year 10 per cent spend above Rs 11601/- per year.

The practice of consuming kharra not only influences personal expenditure , but shatters the economics if the family,

Concluding Remarks

The habit of chewing kharra is particularly prevalent on a higher side among the males and more so among youth and adults. Women too consume kharra, but their percentage is less as compared to males. The youth get addicted to this habit between the age range of 9 to 14 and more particularly from 15 to 18.

The addicts tend to spend 10 to 20 per cent of their annual income on kharra, depriving their family members the right to basic needs. The pan stall owners too consume kharra. In the cities it was observed that within a distance of 1 km there are 8 to 20 pan stalls on either sides of the road, especially near residential areas, market places, railway stations, and bus stops.

There are hardly any government offices, public places and even schools and colleges, where we do not come across red stains of kharra sputum. Well, spitting in a public is a social problem, that calls for educating people.

The stair case walls of the office of the Additional Commissioner, Tribal Development in Nagpur have posters of Hindu deities and important freedom fighters. These walls are clean. The Government officers and workers do not spit on these posters. Religious, patriotic faith and respect for the deities and freedom fighters prevents them from spitting on the walls.

In the rural areas there pan stalls number 5 to 15 for a population of 800 to 1000 . In Gadchiroli city alone, where there is 35,800 population, there are over 287 pan stalls. Out of there 287 pan stall, about 50 pan stalls are situated in the administrative complex area. The pan stall owners earn Rs 500/- to 2000/- per day from kharra & other items.

Kharra consumptions is deeply rooted in social & cultural habits of youth & adults from Vidharbha region. The problem of kharra consumption also gives rise to yet another problem and that is spitting. people spit around in toilets, bathrooms ,corners of walls and mess up public places.

Recommendations

In order to check the habit of chewing kharra and spitting, we recommend following suggestions.

1. Create awareness

There in an urgent need to create awareness in schools and colleges regarding the harmful effect of kharra chewing among student as well as their parents.

2. Ban on kharra

Ban on ghutaka was a good move by the Government. Similarly there should be ban on kharra consumption, especially in schools, colleges, offices, hospitals and public places. Consumers having kharra in public places and spitting should be heavily fired if taint habit be heavily fired if taint habit has to be controlled.

3. Posters of detain and freedom, fighters

Putting posters of deities and freedom fighters has been successful to some extent. This can be strictly implemented by combing it with reality of time. There used to smoke in the buses and trains but with strict laws and rulers then is a rapid change in the attitudes of smokers. Consumption of kharra in public places can be controlled to a great extent.

4. Teachers must take lead

Next to parents, teachers are guardians and parent. They must set an example by not consuming kharra and than preach, what they practice. They can play a major role in convincing the students of the ill effect of this habit.

5. Role of parents

Parents too, should set an example by giving up the habit of kharra consumption & then tell then children to prevent getting addicted to this habit.

6. Role media

Media should take initiative to create advertisements, short films, messages and testimonies by celebraties on ill effect of kharra consumption.

7. Role of saints and religious leaders

The respected saints and leaders can play an important role by speaking about the addiction of kharra and the impact on social economic and life and health of people.

8. Role of friends

Friends should create awareness amongst their friends to prevent getting addicted to kharra.

9. Counseling to kharra addicts

Rural hospitals, Primary Health centers, civil hospitals ,colleges and schools should organize counseling sessions for kharra addicts . There awareness - cum-counseling camps should be sponsored by the Public Health Department.

REFERENCES

Kurian J.C., 2013, The Problem of Drug Abuse in the World in South Asia and a Microcosm, in Patil K.S. and Tribhuwan Robin (eds), Social Problems and Development Issues of Youth, Discovery publishing House Pvt. Ltd., New Delhi.

Tribhuwan Robin ,1998, Medical World of Tribal , Discovery Publishing House, New Delhi.

Tribhun Robin and Finkenauer Maike , 2003.Thereads Together, Discovery Publishing House, New Delhi.

Tribhuwan Robin and Kharche Jayshree, 2013, Warli Youth & Toddy Rituals, in Patil and Tribhuwan (eds), Social Problems and Development Issues of Youth Discovery Publishing House Pvt. Ltd., New Delhi.

Dr. Fulzele Pandit, 2001, Consumption of Ghutka in Colleges, A Rapidly Increasing Trend, Maharashtra State Secondary and Higher Secondary Board, Pune 2009.

Warli Youth and Toddy Consumption Rituals

– Dr. **Robin D. Tribhuwan**
– Dr. **Jayshree V. Kharche**

Introduction

This chapter is based on several field trips to the Warli villages for the last 8 years or so. Dr. Tribhuwan the first author, in fact has conducted several fieldwork expeditions to the Warli villages for over 20 years. He has written five books to his credit on the Warli and several papers. He was also associated with documentary producers who made three films on Warli tribe. In order to understand the patterns and toddy consumption among the Warli Youth and more precisely the ritual significance associated with the same, the authors conducted over 30 focused group discussions in ten Warli villages with the youth. The objectives of the present research paper are as below:

1. To study the various types of traditional drinks among the Warlis.
2. To explore the traditional methods of preparing these drinks.
3. To understand the causes of toddy consumption among the Warli Youth.
4. To unveil the rates of these traditional drinks.
5. To highlight the rituals, ceremonies and occasions, the Warli Youth associate with toddy consumption.

Literature Review

Tribal's world over love music, dance and liquor. They drink the locally prepared liquor and intoxicants on several occasions, ceremonies and rituals.

(Vidyarthi L.P. &Rai B. K. 1984; Tribhuwan Robin, Krull Peter & Peter 2004; Tribhuwan Robin &Tribhuwanpreeti, 1999; Tribhuwan Robin &Mandke M. B.; Tribhuwan Robin &FinkenauerMaike 2003; Tribhuwan Robin, 2004) Tomar Y.P.S. &Tribhuwan Robin 2005).

Well, the Warlis are no exception to the rule. This paper throws light on several aspects of toddy drinking among the Warli Youth.

Traditional Alcoholic Drinks Among the Warli

The authors observed that there are three major traditional alcoholic drinks among the Warlis. These are as follows:

1. **Toddy:** Popularly known as "tadi" is an alcoholic drink, which is enjoyed by the children, teenagers, youth and the adults. The season for drinking toddy is from October to June. It is a drink, which is collected in a pot, which is hung over night to a Khajri (Phoenix sylvestrous) palm.

   The owner of the palm makes a deep cut at the bottom of the spathe, from which oozes toddy and gets collected in the earthen pot. Fresh toddy collected in the morning hours, that i.e. from 8.00am to 10.00am, is not fermented. If fresh toddy is kept for long time, it gets fermented and is intoxicating.
2. **Madi:** Madi is yet another alcoholic drink extracted from the spathe of a palm using the same technique as that of toddy.
3. **Mauha:** Mauha liquor is prepared from fresh as well as dry flower of a tree called *Mahua* (Madhucaindica). These flowers are mixed with water and soaked in a pot for 3 to 4 days. The fermented water is then boiled in a container. This container is attached to a bamboo or tube through which the vapors fall into a brass container, which is put in a pot having water. The condensed vapors fall into the vessel drop by drop and the pure form of Mauha liquor is collected in the brass vessel. The process of preparing Mauha liquor involves two processes namely fermentation and distillation.

Current Rates of Liquor

The current rates of toddy, Madi and Mauha liquor are as follows:

1. Toddy – 25 rupees per liter.
2. Madi – 25 rupees per liter.
3. Mahua – 50 rupees per liter.

These rates are for non-tribal, however for Warlis the rate of toddy and madi isRs. 20/- per liter and mauha for Rs. 45/- per liter. The rates are reduced to Rs. 15/- per liter during wedding season for the Warlis in case of toddy and Madi and Rs. 40/- per liter in the case of mauha. The Warlis prefer toddy for Mauha as it is cheap and available abundantly.

These days a number of Warli Youth have started consuming Beer, Rum, Whisky and even country liquor. It was surprising to note that, Beer shops in Warli hamlets have become more popular than toddy joints. In fact a guest who gives Rs. 100/- to the groom or bride is given a bottle of beer, if he gives 200/- rupees, he is given a bottle of whisky. The Warlis drink a way to glory during weddings. Given below are some rituals, ceremonies and occasions on which they consume toddy.

Occasion, Rituals and Ceremonies and Toddy Consumption

It was observed, that there are hardly any occasions, festivals, social celebrations and rituals during which the Warlis do not drink toddy. The young and the old, males and females drink toddy together on following occasions.

1. **Guests are welcomed by serving toddy.**

   It is a compulsory and strict norm among the Warlis to serve toddy to male and female guests above the age of 6 to 80.

2. **Birth Rituals:** Toddy, Madi or Mauha liquor is consumed on birth rituals by the Warlis.

3. **Wedding Rituals:** The Warli youth especially go crazy and drink away to glory during the wedding season, wedding occasions while fixing marriage dates, paying bride price, engagement ceremony, the "ghan rite" on the first day of the wedding, the "Mandav" rite on the second day, the "Bashing" (Wearing head gear) rite on the third day and the "Varat" rite on the fourth day.

   It was observed that minimum 500 liters to 2000 liters toddy is consumed by the Warlis during the four day wedding season. These days they also drink 50 to 100 bottles of beer and about 20 to 50 bottles of whisky. Wedding celebration becomes more colourful and lively with "Dhumsa dance" Music and liquor gives them great joy during the wedding rituals and occasion.

4. **Death Rituals:** The Warlis drink toddy after a dead is buried. The mourners donate Rs. 5/- to 200/- on a loin cloth or towel. This money is used by the family members in whom death has taken place to purchase and serve toddy to the mourners who attend funeral. The remaining money is kept for the family.

   Even on the 10th day (*dahava*) the day on which soul migration rates are performed, the people who participate are served toddy, madi or mauha liquor.

5. **Dance and drink:** Tribhuwan Robin & FinkenauerMaike (2004) have classified four major dance forms and the Warlisnamely :

   1. ***Gauri dance*** – performed during the Holi festival in March-April, before sowing.
   2. ***Kambad dance*** – performed during (avni) sowing and transplantation of rice saplings during June-July. This dance is performed by males only. It is symbolic presentation of the fertility

dance performed by "Narandev" (god of rains) for Kansari (the goddess of food grains), associated with a Warli myth (Tribhuwan Robin and FinikenauerMaike, 2004).

3. *Tarpa dance* – This dance is performed by males and females during October – November after the harvest and worship of "Kansari" to celebrate their joy over harvest.
4. *Dhumsa dance*– This dance is performed by Warli males and females during the weddings.

It is pertinent to note that majority of the participants in the above mentioned dance forms are youth. They drink toddy, madi or mauha on these occasions.

1. **Waghdev worship:** Drinking of toddy, madi&mauhaliquor is a common feature among the Warlis after the "Waghdev puja" (the worship of tiger god) during the months October – November, that is after the harvest.
2. **Kansari worship:** An important ritual observed by the Warlis is the worship of Kansari, performed by a family every year or once in five years. On this occassion too drinking is a common feature among the tribes men.
3. **Festivals:** Drinking is common during all the festivals celebrated by the Warlis.
4. **Social Occasions:** Drinking toddy on social occasions and gatherings is common among the Warlis. These occasions could be visits by the relatives, fixing marriages etc.
5. **Hard labour and work:** The Warlis, especially the youth, who work hard every day in the field, forest or elsewhere get tired. In order to overcome tiredness, they drink toddy, mauha or madi. The Warlis believe that their nerves and muscles are released by drinking toddy. That they get sound sleep.
6. **Drinking Vs. Punishment:** In case a person is found guilty of breaking traditional laws of the Warlis. The members of the traditional panchayat council summon him/her cross examine and then fine the culprit. One of the forms of punishment is to feed the members of the village council and offer all of them toddy, madi or mauha liquor. There and several occasions are associated by the Warlis with drinking.

Why Warli Youth drink toddy ?

Focused group discussions with the Warli Youth revealed that they consume toddy for the reasons given below:

1. Toddy is available in abundance.
2. Toddy drinking is intertwined with several cultural events, rituals, ceremonies practices and occasions.

3. Warli Youth drink a lot of toddy, because they get habituated to it, since the age of 6 to 7 years.
4. All the family members including father, mother, brothers and sisters drink toddy.
5. Drinking toddy, madi and mauha liquor is socially and religiously sanctioned.
6. Rates for toddy are less.
7. Majority of the Warli families have their own toddy palms.

Quarrels and Fights

Quarrels and fights after drinking is a common feature among the Warlis. Quarrels with in the family, among relatives, friends and the tribesmen were observed among the Warlis.

Concluding Remarks

Consumption of toddy, madi and mauha liquor according to the Warli Youth is not a social problem but a cultural tradition. Drinking, they say is socially accepted and sanctioned. Both males and females drink. Drink and dance goes together. Toddy consumption is a dietary ritual, among the Warlis.

Quarrels and fights that take place after drinking are solved in the traditional Warli counsels. What is considered as a social problem from an etic (outsiders) respective, may be a cultural tradition from an emic (insider's) perspective. The authors, however, recommend creation of awareness among the Warli Youth regarding harmful effects of excess alcohol consumption.

REFERENCES

Tribhuwan Robin & Finkenauer Maike (2003) Threads Together, Discovery Publishing House, New Delhi.

Tribhuwan Robin & Tribhuwan Preeti, 1999 Tribal Dances of India, Discovery Publishing House, New Delhi.

Tribhuwan Robin & Krull Peter, 2004.

Tribhuwan Robin & Mandke M.B.

Vidarthi L. P. & Rai B.K., Tribal Cultures in India, Concept Publishing House, New Delhi.

Part – V

Health Issues of Youth

High Risk Pregnancy and Access to Health Services Amongst Women in Rural Wardha

– Dr. **Kasturi S. Pesala**

Introduction

Women represent almost half of the total population of our country. The status of women in India has been seen ups and downs. The fact however, remains that the women's conditions are still not up to the mark. High-risk pregnancy is broadly defined as a pregnancy in which there is or will be increased risk of morbidity and mortality of mother, fetus or neonate before or after delivery (Dutta, D.C., 1992: 641). As per the world health report for more than 30 million women, each year suffering from pregnancy and childbirth related ill health or death. More than half a million women die annually of pregnancy related complications, 99 per cent of them in developing countries yet most maternal deaths and disabilities could be avoided through better quality health services and good maternal nutrition.

Every year some eight million women suffer pregnancy related complications and over a half a million die. In developing countries, one in 16 women may die of pregnancy related complications compared to one in 2800 in developed countries. (Beyond the number; WHO Geneva 2004).

One in 48 women in India are at risk of dying during childbirth. According to the National Health Policy (NHP) 2002 the maternal mortality ratio (MMR) in India is high 407 per 100,000 live births. To reduce maternal mortality by 2015 is a Millennium Development Goal (MDG) for all countries including India. Achieving this means reducing the maternal mortality ratio to 100 by 2015.

Objectives of the Study

The proposed study is based on the following objectives.

General Objective

To study and evaluate the high-risk pregnancy, access to health services, role of primary health center and social work Intervention in rural area of Wardha District.

Specific Objectives

1. To study the most causing factors for high-risk pregnancy in rural area.
2. To study various health aspects of rural women.
3. To find out the right to choice and decision making of women in health care.
4. To explore their access to health services in rural area.
5. To study about the primary health center equipped with facilities during emergency.
6. To find out the well equipped staff in the primary health center.
7. To assess the impact of National Health Policy on the health status of the women in rural areas.

Methodology

The Wardha district has a network of government run health facilities consisting of the district hospital offering tertiary level care with rural hospitals at the secondary level care and primary health centers, sub-centers and dispensaries providing basic health care to the rural population. Besides the medical services provided by the Government, Zilla Parishad, Muncipal Councils and trusts also maintain the general health of the citizens. There are in district, 24 Hospitals, 48 Clinics, 18 Maternity homes and 54 Primary health centers having the capacity of 911 beds.

The health scenario in Wardha district from April 2002 to November 2002, there was 16894 ANC cases out of which 13486 were delivered where as 41 i.e. 0.30 per cent by untrained " Dai" and 2935 i.e. 21.76 per cent by trained "Dai" and 1091 i.e. 8.08 per cent by health workers and 9419 i.e. 69.84 per cent in primary health centers/sub center. The total abortions cases were 428, followed by 399 MTP and 286 stillbirths. (DHO office, Wardha Dist., Maharashtra, India).

The research felt the necessity to select this topic taking in to view the totality and vulnerability associated with the health problems of the rural women, the study is proposed to carry out in 27 primary health centers (PHC) at Wardha District, Maharashtra State.

There are 27 primary health centers and 180 sub centers in Wardha dist. Primary health centers are only selected for the study as many pregnant women are referred from sub centers to the primary center. It is also observed that there are many vacant posts in 27 primary health centre and in many centers there are minimal facilities such as equipments, manpower, electricity etc.

The researcher has taken representative sample size of 405 for the present study from 27 primary health centers within the jurisdiction of 8 Panchayat Samiti of Wardha district For this purpose from each rural block through probable random sampling technique about 15 pregnant women is covered during the study.

Major Findings

India's maternal mortality rates in rural areas are among the highest in the world. A factor that contributes to India's high maternal mortality rate is the reluctance to seek medical care for pregnancy. The estimates nationwide are that only 40 per cent -50 per cent of women receive antenatal care. Evidence from the states of Bihar, Rajasthan, Orissa, Uttar Pradesh, Maharashatra and Gujarat find registration of Maternal and Child Health services to be as low as 5 per cent -22 per cent in rural areas and 21 per cent -51 per cent in urban areas. (Carnood S.Carol, June 1998.)

As per the reports published by the Govt. of India,, Ministry of Human Resources Development Department of Education in the year 1999 (WHO Geneva, 2003) the drop out rate of girls in high school is as high as 72 per cent.

There are 1694 primary and 159 secondary schools, 82 junior and senior colleges and 13 adivasi ashram schools and only one University (Hindi) in Wardha district. The literary rate in Wardha district is 80.50 per cent i.e. out of total population of 12,30,640 only 86,9673 are literate. Besides this the male literacy rate is 87.70 per cent i.e 4, 89,417 and female literacy rate of 72.80 per cent i.e 3, 80,256. (http://wardha.nic.in, 9th Feb 2007)

Considering the socio economic status & other aspects related to health and the respondent's non-approachability to access to health services at the time of urgency put them on risk. The researcher tried to focus on health, access and other issues towards the vulnerability of the rural women in the Wardha district.

Education Status: The education status reveals that 37.0 per cent of the respondents are high school drop outs and 7.4 per cent of the respondents are illiterate. 27.4 per cent have done their education till higher secondary, 15.3 per cent have studied up to primary, 9.1 per cent have studied upto graduate, whereas 3.7 per cent have completed there studies till post graduate.

Educational Level

Educational Level	Count
Primary	62 (15.3%)
Higher Secondary	111(27.4%)
Graduate	37 (9.1%)
Post Graduate	15 (3.7%)
Drop outs	150 (37.0%)
Illiterate	30 (7.4%)
Total	**405**

Age at Marriage and Manifestation of Gender Discrimination

To reduce the incidence of child marriage the Child Marriage Restrain Act, 1929 was passed and amended in 1979. Under this act, unless there is anything repugnant in subject or context (a)"child" means a person who is male under 21 years of age and if a female under 18 years of age; (b)"child marriage" means a marriage to which either of the contracting parties is a child; (c) "contracting party" to a marriage means either of the parties whose marriage is or is about to be thereby solemnized; and (d) "minor" means a person of either sex who is under 18 years of age.

However, women are affected disproportionately more than and in different ways from men. Some manifestation of gender discrimination are lower investment in a girl child's education, the pressure on girls to marry early, restrictions on women's mobility which constrain their educational and income earning opportunities and laws which deny women the same rights as men. The combination of poverty and gender discrimination increases women's risk of illness and limits their ability to take care of themselves when ill.

The table representing age at marriage reveals that 20.8 per cent of the respondents got married at the early age between 15 yrs –18 yrs. 23.5 per cent got married at 19yrs-22yrs,48 per cent of the respondents got married in the age between 23-26 years and only 8 per cent got married from 27yrs-30 yrs.

Age at Marriage

Age at Marriage	Count
15 yrs. -18 yrs.	84 (20.8%)
19 yrs. - 22 yrs.	95 (23.5%)
23 yrs. - 26 yrs.	194 (48%)
27 yrs. - 30 yrs.	32 (8%)
Total	**405**

Different criteria have been kept to know respondents view about manifestation of gender discrimination. 48.8 per cent of the respondents say that there is pressure on girls to marry early; 17.2 per cent feels there is less education and income earning opportunities; 14.0 per cent say lower investment in girl child education; 16.0 per cent are of the opinion that there is restriction on women mobility; whereas 4.7 per cent of the respondents says that there are laws which deny women the same right as men

Manifestation of Gender Discrimination

Manifestation of Gender Discrimination	Count
Lower investment in girl child education	40 (9.8%)
Pressure on girls to marry early	148 (36.54)
Restriction on women mobility, which constrains	36 (8.8)
Educational and income earning opportunities	45 (11.11)
Laws, which deny women, the same rights as men	19 (4.69)
Can't Say	117 (28.8)
Total	**405**

Thus, the finding suggests that women should be made aware about their rights and also about their decision making capacity which will not only help them in their social development but will also encourage them to educate themselves and also help regarding income earning opportunities.

Domination of patriarchal values and traditions in family and Causes of ignorance of family planning methods in Indian society:

As per the study conducted by Syeda Nahid M. Chowdhury, (WHO Geneva 2003), Parents arranged the marriages and girls did not get opportunities to meet their prospective husband before marriage. Further women have little idea about what to expect during pregnancy and delivery and only vague ideas about possible complications. Objections of in-laws and financial concerns were major barriers to seeking health care. All young women knew the name of some family planning methods but none had actually used them. Their perception was that once they were married they would have a baby. Nevertheless in-laws had a general expectation that couples should have a baby soon after marriage.

Cultural factors however play a major role in shaping the socio-economic profile of the region's women, some traditional beliefs and social pressures disadvantage women. In spite of constitutional guarantees of women's rights and equal status, discrimination is visible in many areas. In certain countries a preference for sons is openly expressed.

The data shows that 54.0 per cent of the respondents feel there is domination of patriarchal values and traditions out of which 27.7 per cent feels there is son preference, 16.3 per cent feels there is seclusion and 10.1 per cent feels there is restriction on mobility and 45.9 per cent feels there is no domination.

Respondents are of the opinion that the causes of ignorance of family planning methods in Indian society mainly due to desire for son as old age security i.e. 65.7 per cent, 7.4 per cent are of the opinion say that large family issues are still considered ideal whereas 3.5 per cent of the respondents feels mainly the desire of motherhood and desire to compensate for child loss and 20.0 per cent are of the opinion that they don't know about the family planning methods. Though 45.9 per cent are of the opinion that there is no domination of patriarchal values and traditions in family but still there is ignorance of the family planning methods such as 29.6 per cent due to some extent their is desire for son as old age security.

Respondents 1st Preference as a Child and have gone through Sex Detection Test

One of the studies documenting the widespread practice of sex selective abortions was in 1980. Examining the records of one hospital in Pune, Maharashtra the authors found that 700 women had sought sex detection tests during June 1976-June 1977. Of these 450 women were informed that the sex of the fetus was female- 430 (95.5%) of them terminated their pregnancies. All of the 250 women who were informed that the fetus was male continued with their pregnancies. (Women Health in South East Asia, www.unaid.com, 2003)

The reveals that 56.8 per cent of the respondents have given 1st preference to male child, It is shocking to know that 49.4 per cent of the respondents have gone through sex detection test eager to know boy child, The statistical analysis reveals that still in rural areas the first preference is given to male child and majority of them have gone through sex determination test to know about sex of the fetus.

Anemic during Pregnancy

Anemia is common in pregnant females especially of low socio-economic strata. Mostly the anemia is due to iron deficiency, although other factors are also involved. The anemia's of pregnancy can be attributed to poverty, malnutrition, multiparty, abortions etc. (Ratan Vidya, preventive and social medicines, 1994:292)

It has been observed that inadequate nutrition is a significant factor contributing to maternal deaths in India, the average weight gain of pregnant women is just 7 kg compared to almost 9kg in Thailand and Philippines and 12 kg in the developed countries. One rural study in Gujarat and Maharashtra found that 90 per cent of pregnant women were anemic by WHO standards. The WHO criteria for hemoglobin levels indicative of anemia gives a count of less than 12gm for non pregnant women and a count of less than 11gm for pregnant women. (www.google.com: India; Issues in Womens health Jan 25th 1996).

Domination of Patriarchal Values and Traditions in Family and Causes of Ignorance of Family Planning Methods in Indian Society

			Causes of Ignorance of Family Planning Methods in Indian Society					Total
			Early Mother-hood	Large Family Issue are still Considered Ideal	Desire for Son, as Old Age Security	Desire to Compensate for Child Loss	Don't Know	
Domination of Patriachal Values and traditions in family	Son Preference	Count	5	12	76	1	18	112
		% of Total	1.2%	3.0%	18.8%	.2%	4.4%	27.7%
	Seclusion	Count	2	4	42	9	9	66
		% of Total	.5%	1.0%	10.4%	2.2%	2.2%	16.3%
	Restriction on mobility	Count	2	4	28	4	3	41
		% of Total	.5%	1.0%	6.9%	1.0%	.7%	10.1%
	No domination	Count	5	10	120	0	51	186
		% of Total	1.2%	2.5%	29.6%	.0%	12.6%	45.9%
	Total	Count	14	30	266	14	81	405
		% of Total	3.5%	7.4%	65.7%	3.5%	20.0%	100.0%

Respondents 1st Preference as a Child and have gone through Sex Detection Test

			Respondent done Sex Detection Tests Q50			Total
			Eager to know Boy Child	Eager to know Girl Child	Not Aware about Sex Determination Test	
1st preference as a child	Girl	Count	26	12	16	54
		% of Total	6.4%	3.0%	4.0%	13.3%
	Boy	Count	137	28	65	230
		% of Total	33.8%	6.9%	16.0%	56.8%
	Both of them	Count	32	17	32	81
		% of Total	7.9%	4.2%	7.9%	20.0%
	Don't know	Count	5	3	32	40
		% of Total	.7%	7.9%	9.9%	1.2%
Total		Count	200	60	145	405
		% of Total	49.4%	14.8%	35.8%	100.0%

In Maharashtra severe anemia rose from 32 per cent the first trimester to 47 per cent in the third trimester, with 68 per cent and 94 per cent of women, suffering any kind of anemia in the first and third trimesters respectively. (July 2002 Reproductive and child health module for Medical Officer)

The table depicts that 58.8 per cent of the respondents are anemic,21.2 per cent say they are not anemic, and 20.0 per cent say they don't know whether they are anemic or not.

Anemic during Pregnancy

Anemic during Pregnancy	Count
Yes	238 (58.8%)
No	86(21.2%)
Don't Know	81 (20.2%)
Total	**405**

Access to Health Services

Women's access to health services is constrained by several factors. First, the time spent on child care, housework and in the occupational sphere leaves them with little time to think about their health, often resulting in neglecting their illnesses in the early stages. Second, the clinics offer women no privacy. Third, most clinics are staffed by men and women show a great reluctance to be treated by them. Fourth, the expense and time incurred in traveling long distances and in meeting clinic and drugs fees are also constraining influence. (State of India's Health, 1992:269)

One of the Indian study was hospital based and examined factors associated with 100 maternal deaths that occurred during 1994-1996. Distances and difficulties in transportation were important factors delaying treatments. The average distance covered by the women who died was 72 kilometers, and except for eight women who were transported by ambulance, the others traveled by buses, taxis or three wheelers. Most had been carried to the nearest road on cots or on the backs of relatives before being transferred to an automobile. (Women of South East Asia,WHO, 2000:191)

The study reveals that 24.7 per cent of the respondents home is 11-15 km from primary health center, 21.2 per cent of the respondents home is 1-4km away from primary health center, 17.3 per cent stay at a distance of 5-10km, 16.3 per cent of the respondents stay away more than 20 km, where as 8.6 per cent stay in about 16-20 km. 11.9 per cent don't know how much is the distance between their home and primary health center.

Distance of Primary Health Center from Residence

Distance of PHC from Home	Count
1-4 km	86 (21.2%)
5-10 km	70 (17.3%)
11-15 km	100 (24.7%)
16-20 km	35 (8.6%)
More than 20 km	66 (15.3%)
Don't know	48 (11.9%)
Total	**405**

19.8 per cent say due to shortage of trained health personal they unable to access health care in times, of urgency, 16.5 per cent say due to transportation times and costs, 11.4 per cent are of the opinion that due to working hours of government employees, 10.6 per cent say health centers are few and far. Whereas 3.0 per cent and 2.0 per cent say delivery at home by dais and cultural basis i.e. less priority to women health respectively and 36.8 per cent say none of the causes affects their access to health services.

68.9 per cent of the respondents are satisfied upto some extents with the functions of primary health center, 8.9 per cent say they are satisfied upto large extent and 22.2 per cent of the respondents are not at all satisfied. 60.0 per cent say there are not adequate infrastructure facilities available in the primary health center 14.3 per cent say there is adequate infrastructure facilities .36.8 per cent of the respondents say there is no sufficient staff in primary health center, 95.3 per cent are not aware about Rashtriya Janani Suraksha Yojana.

Concluding Remarks

Social work can play a major role in this context where more focus should be on Integrated Child Development Services (ICDS), which covers children 3 to 6 yrs old as well as pregnant, and lactating women. The Good nutritional status in a reproductive woman is of vital importance for the successful outcome of pregnancy. Therefore more emphasis should be given on pregnant and lactating women as well as on children below 5yrs of age.

Maternal death is an avoidable tragedy. It can be prevented if women have access to basic and emergency medical care during pregnancy, childbirth and the post partum period. If safe practices with trained birth attendants are followed for delivery then home delivery can be motivated in our country. This will prove to be an effective and safe delivery with proper training and precautions. And a boon to our rural people who most of the time cannot afford institutional deliveries.

The new government policy should focus on Information education and communication (IEC) in order to promote maternal care in the community especially among women. The knowledge, attitude and practice (KAP) of the rural women need to be studied in order to develop Information education and communication (IEC) materials.

People are in immediate need of adequate infrastructure in primary health centres. If adequate infrastructure is provided and training is given to staff there would be an improvement in services and people can take advantage of it during emergency. After training and equipping when a team is fully functional then random and sudden transfers of the members should not be allowed as it disturbs the functioning of the team. Multi-functionality must be emphasized so that work will not hinder due to absence of one particular member of the team.

Workshops for health workers should be conducted quarterly once at panchayat samiti/ PHC to upgrade their knowledge so that reproductive and child health programmes can be positively implemented. Appointment of professional medical social workers/ efficient counselors in all primary health centers will help to concentize the community. They also need counseling on symptoms of problems to help them prepare for birth, and where to seek care if complications arise. It is very essential that health services should begin at the time of conception. Prenatal supervision helps to avoid, prevent, recognize and treat anemia in women during pregnancy.

REFERENCES

Books

Sachdeva D.R. (1995), Social Welfare Administration in India, New Delhi: Kitab Mahal, pp. 285

Dutta, D.C (1992), Text Book of Obstetrics, Calcutta: New Central Book Agency Fact Sheet on Women in India (2005), National Institute of Public Cooperation and Child Development, pp. 641

Ratan Vidya (1992), Handbook of Preventive and Social Medicine, New Delhi: Jaypee Brother, pp. 292.

Journals

Beyond the Numbers, Reviewing Maternal Deaths and Complications to Make Pregnancy Safer (2004), WHO Geneva.

Fact Sheet on Women in India, National Institute of Public Cooperation and Child Development (2005), New Delhi.

National Family Health Survey-2 (1999-2000), International Institute of Population Sciences, India.

Syeda Nahid et.al M. Chowdhury (2003), Postpartum Experience Among First Time Young Parents in Bangladesh - Preliminary Observations, WHO Geneva.

Knitkar Tara and Mistry Malika, July 2000. The Indian Journal of Social Work, Volume 61, Issue 3, Tata Institute of Social Work, Mumbai.

Module for Medical Officer July 2002 Reproductive and Child Health State of India's Health, 1992:269

Women of South East Asia, WHO, 2000:191.
DHO Office, Wardha Dist., Maharashtra, India.

Websites

www.unaid.com Women Health in South East Asia (2003).
http://wardha.nic.in, 9th Feb 2007.
www.unaid.com India; Issues in Women's Health (1996).

Health Effects of Migration Among Youth in Pune, Maharashtra

– Dr. **Robin D. Tribhuwan**
– Ms. **Beena Rajan**

Introduction

Migration is a process of social change during which a person moves from one cultural setting to another in order to settle for a longer period of time or permanently [1]. Reasons for migration can be divided into push factors (driving the individual out of the country of origin) and pull factors (attract- ing the individual towards the recipient country). Push factors include war, poverty, hunger etc., while pull factors include employment opportunities and political and religious freedom [1, 2].

Migration is one of the important factors contributing to the growth of urban population. The total urban population of the country, excluding Jammu and Kashmir increased from 217.6 million in 1991 to 283.6 million in 2001 registering a growth rate of 30.3 per cent. Maharashtra witnessed largest in-migration of population during the last ten years from different states. The total number of in-migrants in to the state was 3.2 million. Reasons of migrations shows ,in Maharashtra 42.2 per cent migration of persons (0-9 yrs) 62.6 per cent were male and 7.7 per cent female is for work/employment.

The Economic Survey of Maharashtra, 2008-09, recently presented in the state legislature pointed to a decline in the ratio of Marathi-speaking population, and this trend, particularly in Pune, has been corroborated by a study conducted by the University of Pune. "The total number of migrants coming from other states to the city will be 7,40,287 in 2021 and 22,98,264 in 2051, if the present trend continues. Intra-state migration to Pune city in 2021 will, however, be 67,453 people, which will come down to only 441 in 2051," says Vijaya P Khairkar, reader in the geography department, in her paper 'Migration, Quality of Life and Sustainable Development of Pune City'.

The decline in migration to Pune from other parts of Maharashtra, says the researcher who based her findings on past trends, is due to the fact that places like Nashik, Baramati and Aurangabad have been developing and providing employment to its people over the past few years. With the Maharashtra Industrial Development Corporation (MIDC) being set up in the rural parts of the state, migration from villages to Pune has also come down.

On the other hand, such schemes have not taken off in states like Bihar, Uttar Pradesh, Madhya Pradesh and Karnataka that face an acute job deficit, forcing people to migrate to other states, especially Maharashtra. The trend is likely to continue for many more years, says the study.

Khairkar, who specialises in migrant patterns and also had her earlier research 'Migration and Social Economics of Pune City', published by Diamond Publications in 2007, adds that the total migrants in Pune in 2021 will be 14,11,887 people, which in 2051 will go up to 27,21,447.

The relationship between migration and health is a complex one: it operates in both directions and is mediated by socio-political factors, environment and disease exposure .The relationship can produce either positive or negative effects, on both the migrant him/herself as well as on other family and household members. In order to explore migration as a risk factor, information is needed on the type of migration and reasons for it, factors in both the sending and receiving communities, including political, socio-economic, cultural and environmental factors, disease prevalence, dietary and lifestyle factors, and the integrity or fragmentation of social networks.

On the positive side, a move for work is likely to result in increased income and hence better nutrition and ability to access health care. Education may be more readily available and of higher quality in more developed areas where employment opportunities exist. Certain jobs, however, expose workers to particular occupational hazards, for example tuberculosis, pneumoconiosis and accidental workplace injury experienced by migrant mine workers. Temporary circular migration leads to family breakdown, fragmentation of social networks and psychosocial stress. Extended sexual networks result in sexually transmitted infections (STIs), including HIV/AIDS, which affect temporary migrants themselves as well as their permanent partners residing in the sending communities. Commercial sex workers based near those workplaces employing temporary migrants bear a heavy burden of STIs and HIV infection.

Changes in Labour Migration Trends

Large scale migration of labourers from Hindi speaking , especially from Bihar, has led to violent opposition to them in various parts of India, such as Maharashtra, Assam, Karnataka and Punjab. The labour migration of younger adult males aged 15-34 years show increase and Pune is showing shift in labour driven market towards formal and informal sector. With 73 per cent of the population of Pune below 40 years of age, the city is among leading ones in the country with a large youth. The finding is part of a survey by Karve Institute of Social Service, to act as a reference for preparation of the new Development Plan.It indicates that 32.68 per cent of the population is below 20 while 40.23 per cent is between 20 and 40(4).

Vulnerability Among Migrants

While the link between circular migration and increased risk of HIV infection is supported by a variety of literatures, Lurie identifies an important gap in our understanding, i.e. the implication for the rural communities to which the migrants regularly return (Lurie, 2000). The social disruption institutionalized by a century of extensive labour migration affects not only the migrant in the work-place, but also the extent of sexual networking in the sending area (Dladla, et al, 2001). HIV discordance among migrant couples was investigated in a cohort study involving migrant workers and their partners in Kwazulu Natal. Preliminary data showed that nearly 40 per cent of discordant migrant couples contained an HIV infected woman and an uninfected male migrant partner (Lurie, et al, 2000).

The Spread of HIV/AIDS and Sexually Transmitted Diseases

The migrants show 8 times higher prevalence rates 2.35 per cent.than Gen Population (0.3%). Two to four times more number of Migrants has non-regular partners or visit sex workers. Condom use is reported as infrequent and unprotected sex leads to rising prevalence of STDs. Maharashtra was one of the earliest states in India where the disease manifested itself, registering its first AIDS case in Mumbai, in 1986. First cluster of HIV infections was detected among female sex workers sent back from Mumbai to Chennai in 1986. Historically, Mumbai and Pune are well-known as epicentres of HIV infection in India. Among states reporting generalized HIV epidemic, except in North-eastern India, the epidemic is driven by sex work whereas it is driven by migrants in low prevalence states.

Research evidence from India and abroad demonstrates that urban migration is a strong co-factor accelerating HIV prevalence. A study conducted among 6747 migrant youths in PCMC area (Bhatlavande, 2010) Single male migrants mostly coming from low HIV prevalence states. Contrary to the perceptions, their HIV prevalence rates are not high but they continue to have high behavioural & biologic vulnerability.

Health Risks during Migration

Migrants may be exposed to health risks before, during and after leaving the states (source state.). The migrants may experience stay in unhygienic condition, agglomerated labour camps, socio-economic hardships ,loss of relatives, language barrier, hostile political scenario, lack of knowledge of health providers etc. Some of the risks experienced after arriving in the recipient country include imprisonment, long-lasting asylum seeking processes, language bar-riers, lack of knowledge about health services in the new social con-text, discrimination and marginalization [8]. These hardships and impacts may happen directly through higher stress response leading to unhealthy behaviours e.g drug abuse, lack of sources to prioritize disease preventing behaviour and to seek health care when needed, or poorer adherence to medical advice [9-12].

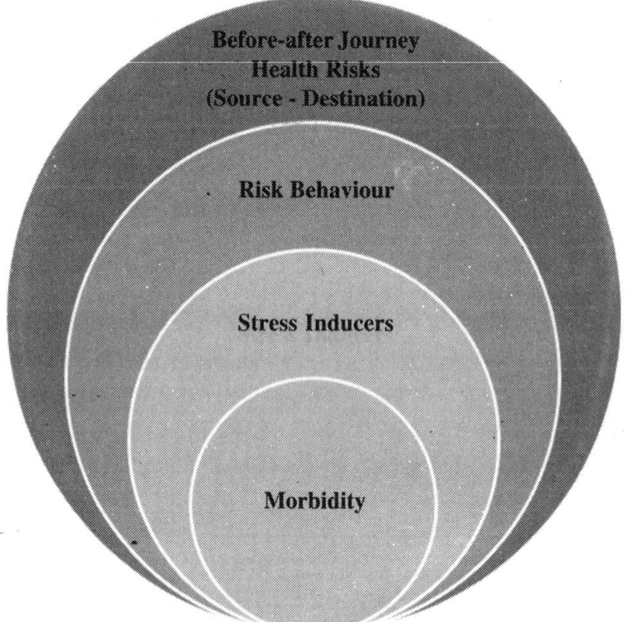

The Influence of Migration Process on Migrant's Health

Lack of Knowledge of Health Providers

Marginalisation, discrimination lack of knowledge of health providers in the new social context and inexistent social security leads to mortality and spread of infectious diseases like Tuberculosis, HIV/AIDS , STI, etc all leading to stress reactions with negative health impacts The stress inducers may be labour camps, sexual networking, risk behaviour, vicious circle of dept, social alienation etc. Lack of authentic data also makes the migrants in the informal sector more can be categorised as 'biologically vulnerable group'.

Conclusions and Recommendation

Several studies demonstrate how overtime migrants in host societies, after an initial period of general improvement to their health condition known as "migrant health effect", become more vulnerable to a vast array of health risks including *inter alia* reproductive health related issues, psycho-social affects particular to their age, sexually transmitted diseases, substance abuse and eating disorders. These risks are often exacerbated by poverty, social exclusion and limited access to social security benefits. Migrant's health can probably be improved through number of initiatives like targeted interventions based on linking source and - destination, special emphasis of needs of vulnerable groups with social and economic security. Health providers should be roped into the migrant's nexus to convert negative effects on health to positive.

REFERENCES

1. Syed HR, Vangen S. Health and Migration: A Review. Oslo: NAKMI, 2003.
2. Carta MG, Bernal M, Hardoy MC, Haro-Abad JM. Migration Carta MG, Bernal M, Hardoy MC, Haro-Abad JM. Migration and Mental Health in Europe. The State of the Mental Health in Europe Working Group: appendix 1. Clin Pract Epidemol Ment Health 2005;1(13).
3 Sunanda Mehta; 'Quantum Leap in Migrants from Other States in Next Few Decades', Pune ,Tue June 16 2009, Indian Express.
4. '73 per cent of City's Population Below 40 Years of Age' December 21,2010: Indian Express.
5. Dladla AN, Hiner CA, Qwana E, Lurie M. 2001. Speaking to Rural Women: The Sexual Partnerships of Rural South African Women whose Partners are Migrants. Society in Transition. 32(1).
6. Lurie M. 2000. Migration and AIDS in Southern Africa: A Review. Southern African Journal of Science. Vol. 96, June 2000.
7. Bhatlawande Prakash, Pattar Shrinivas, Rajan Beena Belsangvikar Ambadas Bhat Priti. Cross Sectional Study on Single Male Migrant Workers in Pimpri Chinchwad Municipal Corporation, District Pune: IPH Conference Karad 2012.
8. Packness A. Indikatorer af Betydning for Voksne Asylsøgeres Mentale helbred [Indicators with Importance for Adult Asylum Seekers' Mental Health]. Copenhagen: University of Copenhagen, 1998.
9. Mygind A, Kristiansen M, Krasnik A, Nørredam M. Etniske Minoriteters Opfattelse af sygdomsrisici - betydningen af etnicitet og migration [Riskperception Among Ethnic Minorities - the Influence of Ethnicity and mi-gration]. Copenhagen: The National Board of Health, 2006.
10. Bhugra D. Migration and Mental Health. Acta Psychiatr Scand 2004; 109: 243-58.
11. Thomas SL, Thomas SD. Displacement and Health. Br Med Bull 2004; 69: 115-27.
12. Carta MG, Bernal M, Hardoy MC, Haro-Abad JM. Migration and Mental Health in Europe. The state of the Mental Health in Europe Working.

Health, Nutritional and Compensation Issues of Stone Quarry Workers

– Dr. **Robin D. Tribhuwan**
– Dr. **Jayshree V. Kharche**

Introduction

In the recent years there has been a growing awareness of the existence, importance of the needs of the unorganized sector. The concept of unorganized sector as defined by subrahmanya R.K. and Jhabwala R. (2000) as "no clear cut employer-employee relationships and lacks most form of social protection."

The occupational categories of un-organized sector include agricultural labourers, sugar cane cutters, Rag pickers, brick kiln labourers, stone quarry workers, construction workers and so on.

This chapter focuses on the health, nutritional and health compensation issues of the stone quarry workers keeping in view following objectives.

Objectives of the Study

1. To understand the various health and nutritional problems faced by the stone quarry workers.
2. To unveil the issues of health compensation.

Research Methodology

The present study was carried out in two villages of the two blocks of Pune district, namely Haveli and Pune. An interview scheduled was prepared, pre-tested and finalized to gather data from 150 stone quarry workers. These respondents belonged to four major caste groups namely the Lamans, Wadars, Beldars and Tirumals. Quantitative data was analyzed using excel software. The data on nutritional status of children and women was collected and analyzed using weight for age criteria adapted by the Indian Academy of pediatrics. The Chart developed by the IAP was used to grade the degree of malnutrition. Qualitative data was analyzed manually.

Major Findings

Some of the major findings are as below:

1. Accidents and Injuries

Stone quarrying work involves several procedures and operations including, blasting, drilling, stone breaking, stone cutting, stone crushing, loading, unloading and transporting. The workers are employed at different places as per the nature of the work.

The mining and quarrying sector posses large risks to occupational health and safety. The research revealed that the most important occupational risks to the stone quarry workers are:

(i) Fatal accidents

(ii) Physical injuries requiring medical treatment.

(iii) Work related illness : respiratory diseases such as silicosis and tuberculosis due to inhalation of dust.

(iv) Death due to stone slides.

2. Respiratory and hearing problem

A study by Ghotkar V.B. and Maldhure B.R. and Zodpey S.P. has revealed that the prevalence of respiratory morbidity was among 32.5 per cent of the stone quarry workers they studied. Our study revealed, that it was among 44 per cent of the respondents. Another common problem of occupational hazard in quarrying involves hearing impairment due to long term exposure to noise.

3. Injuries and cuts

Injuries of fingers, hands, legs and even eyes were observed to be very common.

4. Place of delivery

The study revealed the 81 per cent of the women delivered at home, 4 per cent in private hospitals, 5 per cent in Municipal Corporation Hospitals, 3 per cent in Government Hospitals, and 7 per cent did not respond. Women, who delivered at home, went to their native place. The stone quarry workers send their women for delivery to their native villages, due to threats of respiratory problems for the new born and the mother.

5. Personnel Conducting Deliveries

It was observed that 74 per cent of the deliveries were conducted by Traditional Birth Attendants, mothers, mother-in-laws or elderly women.

6. Abortion

Only 5 per cent of the women studied had to undergo abortion, one or more times.

7. Contraceptives

It was observed the 95 per cent of the respondents did not use contraceptives.

8. Deaths

Out of the 150 respondents studied, it was observed, that in 29 families (19%) death occurred due to landslides and blasts. Out of the 29 death victims 15 belonged to the Wadar community, 8 to Laman, 5 were Beldars and only 1 was from the Tirumal community.

9. Malnutrition among stone quarry children

Out of the 121 children measured, 64 per cent were malnourished of these 14 per cent were severely malnourished. The prevalence of mal nutrition was maximum among the Wadar Children, followed by the Beldars, Tirumals and Lamans.

10. Impact of pollution

Quarrying not only pollutes human bodies, but also pollutes the environment at large scale. It lays extensive dust on land and water resources leading to fundamental changes in local environment and biodiversity. It causes respiratory problems to the workers.

11. Health compensation

The owners of the stone quarries did pay for the medical expenses of the workers for injuries and accidents on duty. However, no financial compensation was given to the families of the workers who died on duty. The concept of leave including medical, casual, earned etc. is absent. Maternity leave to pregnant women was not granted.

Concluding Remarks

The stone quarry workers certainly face several health and nutritional problems. They are not given any financial compensation for death on duty. There is a need for the health and family welfare department to evolve programmes for workers in unorganized sector.

REFERENCES

Tribhuwan Robin & Patil Jayshree, 2009, Stone Quarry Workers, Social Insecurity and Development Issues, Discovery Publishing House, New Delhi.

Part – VI

Development Issues of Youth

Role of Maharashtra Cosmopolitan Education Society (MCES), Pune in Promoting Education for the Youth of Weaker Sections

– Mr. **Azimuddin F. Sherkar**

Introduction

This research paper is based on primary and secondary data furnished by the Maharashtra Cosmopolitan Education Society (MCESociety). The paper aims to high light the hard work, transparency, honesty and the consistency to face challenges by the founder members of the society in providing education to the economically, educationally and socially weaker sections of the society. One of the oldest education institutes in Pune city has been a boon to students and youth of the weaker sections and more precisely to the Muslim youth and children.

Maharashtra Cosmopolitan Education Society (MCES), Pune, Azam Campus: An Excellent Educational Campus

MCE Society, Azam Campus, Pune is centrally located on 24 acres of land. It has been 30 institutions from K.G. to P.G. and Research Centres including 12 professional colleges (Dental, Physiotherapy, Unani, Law, NBA, MCA/MCM, Diploma/Degree Pharmacy, Hotel management, Under-graduate/Post Graduate Architecture, D.Ed., B.Ed, M.Ed/Fine Arts etc.) Boys and Girls Hostels. Clean and green, the well disciplined campus with its beautiful landscape has 32 well maintained buildings and 5 state-of-the-art conference halls. The campus has 3000 computers, 24/7 internet with 100 per cent computer literate staff. 25000 students of all castes, creeds, religion and regions, with Board and University Toppers, make it a symbol of true national integration. A super sports complex with pavilion has given India – 2 international sports persons and 57 national sports persons in addition to 153 district players. It is the best living example of an excellent educational institution for the poor and deserving students to mould them into human resource and assets to society. *'Seeing is beliving!'* Whoever enters this vibrant complex is pleasantly shocked.

History

The MCA Society, Pune was established in 1948 by Late Mr. Abdul Kadir Khan and others with an objective of providing education to the economically, educationally and socially weaker section of the society. It is registered under the Society Registration Act, 1860 and also under Bombay Public Trust act, 1950.

In the year 1982 when the election of MCE Society was held, the entire panel of the Awami Mahaz – under the able leadership of Mr. P.A. Inamdar – came on the Governing Board.

The society had a land of 24 acres on a prime location, donated by Late Mr. Haji Gulam Mohammed Azam in the year 1924. Till 1982 they had 2 primary schools, 2 secondary schools and just 2000 students. There was no compound wall, encroachments abounded and it was a hideout for criminals. There was no water, no greenery, no money and the academic performance was very poor. All that has changed drastically, *now* !

The MCA Society is one of the oldest educational institutes of Pune and has done pioneering work in the field of education within a span of last 28 years. The MCA Society from a humble beginning of 4 schools has been transformed into an excellent educational complex of higher, technical and professional academic institutions in the field of Arts, Science, Commerce, Computer Science, Law, Education, Pharmacy, Management Science, Architecture, Dental Science, Hospitality Studies and Information Technology.

The MCE Society firmly believed that talent is available in all the students irrespective of whether poor or rich. The only thing the students need is the right opportunity, encouragement and proper guidance at proper time.

The Campus with its scenic beauty is equipped with modern libraries and reading rooms, laboratories and classrooms. The society has made tremendous progress in the field of academics, sports and extracurricular activities. The infrastructure comprises of 32 beautiful buildings, well laid internal roads, picturesque landscape, well equipped laboratories and libraries with computers as well as well-furnished hostels for both – boys and girls, CCTV for security. The V.M. Gany Sports Complex and Pavilion constructed in accordance with the national standards has brought international, national, state and district players to the upfront. The moral and value education enhances the personality of the students and develops their self-confidence, self-respect and positive attitude towards life.

Micro Planning

In the year 1984 the Governing Board prepared a master plan to execute their vision into action. A few of them are mentioned as follows:

- To construct a commercial complex on the outer ring facing roads to be leased out on rent and to have perennial source of income.
- To build educational institutions in inner side in a phased manner.
- To have play ground in the centre. The Governing Board constructed the 'Parwaz' building for which they had to face 150cases including criminal one.

However, they worked with courage, organised planning, dedicated efforts with the aim to have both – quantitative as well as qualitative growth.

In the year 1989, Mrs. Abeda Inamdar donated a huge amount to establish the Abeda Inamdar Junior College for Girls (Arts, Science and Commerce) with an intention to enhance the status of females in the male dominated society. She gave her time, money and energy for imparting quality education to girls as she dedicatedly says – *'to express the sense of gratitude towards Almighty Allah and to repay the debt of the society.'* She believes that the education is the only field through which one can bring social, economic and political change in any society. In the year 1991, she again donated substantially to establish the Abeda Inamdar Senior College for Girls (Arts, Science and Commerce).

From 1991 onwards, the MCE Society started studying the Constituent Assembly Debates, Constitution of India, Article 30(1) related to Fundamental Rights, various judgements delivered by Hon'ble Supreme Court of India as well as by various High Courts relating to minority rights to establish and administer educational institutions of their choice.

Since 1991, every year one institute was started getting adding up to the existing ones, after a deep study of all norms, Acts, rules and regulations, infrastructure, finance, inspections, appointment of HR, etc. Whenever required the MCESociety approached the Hon'ble High Court of Judicature Bombay, filed Writ Petitions and followed them up to the logical end. After getting favourable orders, the MCESociety approached the concerned authorities and then compelled them to do the needful as per the law of the land. This was done with personal involvement, commitment, determination and dedication.

The following table shows various institutes and their year of establishment:

Sr. No.	Name of the Institute	Year of Establishment
1.	Abeda Inamdar Junior College Arts, Science and Commerce	1989
2.	Abeda Inamdar Senior College Arts, Science and Commerce (UG/PG)	1991
3.	H.G.M.Azam College of Education – B.Ed., M.Ed.	1993
4.	A.K.K.New Law Academy 3 Yrs./5 Yrs./LL.M.	1994
5.	Allana College of Pharmacy – B.Pharm./M.Pharm.	1996
6.	M.A. Rangoonwala Talent Search and Promotion SC	1998
7.	Allana Institute of Management Science (MBA/MCM/MCA)	1998
8.	Allana College of architecture – B.Arch./M.Arch.	1999
9.	M.A.R.College of Dental Science & Research Centre – BDS/MDS	2001
10.	MCES Junior College of Education – D.Ed. Eng/Marathi/Urdu	2003
11.	MCES Institute of Pharmacy – D.Pharm.	2003
12.	Allana Institute of Information Technology	2004
13.	M.A.R. College of Physiotherapy (U.G./P.G.	2004-05
14.	M.A.R College of Hospitality Studies and Research	2006
15.	Azam Sports Academy	2007
16.	MCE Society's School of Art	2008
17.	MCE society's Arts and Commerce Night College	2009
18.	PAI International Learning Solutions	2010
19.	Inter Disciplinary Science and Technology Research Academy	2010
20.	B.A., B.Ed.and Ph.D. in Education	2011
21.	Ph.D. in Law	2012

All the above institutes are recognised by respective councils (DCI/ AICTE/NCTE/Bar council etc.) and affiliated to University of Pune and Maharashtra Health University, Nashik.

The following philanthropists came forward and voluntarily gave huge donations to establish educational institutes and the sports complex after seeing our zeal and zest:

Sr.No.	Name of the Donor		Educational Institute
I.	Rangoonwala Foundation (U.K.)	1.	M.A. Rangoonwala College of Dental Sciences and Research Centre
		2.	M.A.Raongoonwala College of Physiotherapy
		3.	M.A.Rangoonwala College of Hotel Management
		4.	V.M.Gany Sports Complex
II.	Allana Foundation (Mumbai)	1.	Allana College of Pharmacy
		2.	Allana Institute of Management Sciences
		3.	Allana College of Architecture

The Governing Board also studied Article 15 and Article 16 of the Constitution of India and established a cell for OBCs to collect all the information and also passed on this information to the society to create awareness.

In 1998, they started the M.A.Rangoonwala Talent Search and Promotion Scheme sponsored by late M.A.Rangoonwala, Banobai Rangoonwala and Asif Rangoonwala with the prime intention of nurturing talent amongst the students from society in general and muslim community in particulat at 10+2 level for Science Faculty. Now, thousands of Doctors, Engineers, Lawyers and others have successfully completed their studies and passed out with flying colours.

In the year 2000, the Governing Board executed computer literacy programme and made it compulsory for all teaching and non-teaching staff. They stated the MKCL, MSCIT courses for the students of 7th standard as value added courses and today thousand of students have cleared the MSCIT course. The teaching staff cleared this course (100%) and the non-teaching staff to a great extent (87%). The management has appointed special computer instructions to teach computer literacy.

Students are taught to use computer key boards to type English, Marathi and Urdu words. The ICT is compulsory. 20,000 books have been scanned and put on our intra-net i.e. e-Library. Students are learning to prepare various projects of their interest during vacation making use of the internet. All classrooms are equipped with LCDs and computers.

Keeping pace with the international development, they emphasized on learning English language in Urdu medium schools and for that purpose, the management appointed special English teachers to teach English to all students.

- **Brilliant Academy:** An academy that provides industry relevant I.T. courses to the students through unique I.T. certification methods from Class VIIIth to Class Xth.

- **Value Added Courses and Certificates:** Our students are learning the softwares – such as Ink Scape and Gimpshop through value added courses conducted by PAI International Learning Solutions functioning in the Campus.
- **Sports Academy:** To promote sports persons scientifically and systematically at national and international levels and to centralise all schools and colleges of Azam Campus under one banner of the MCE Society forming MCE Society's Azam Sports Academy. The Academy provides Coaches, Sports Kits, Diet Supplements, Equipment, Medical Assessment and Financial assistance to the eligible students.

How

I Administration

1. Optimum utility of Infrastructure.
2. Time Management.
3. In time applications and built infrastructures, as per Acts, Rules, Regulations and all norms/H.R./Finance.
4. Quick Decisions.
5. Transparency in money matters.
6. Result oriented development programmes.
7. Personal donation/contribution for all educational work.
8. Modern Technology were adopted immediately i.e. e-larning e-Teaching, e-Administration and e-Accounts.
9. Admission of students on merit.
10. Financial assistance to poor and needy but meritorious students.
11. Scientific approach and practical solutions.
12. No loan policy proper financial management.

II Academics

(a) Excellent staff, encouragement of their new ideas, support to their extra work, accountability of staff, motivating them for research and further education.

(b) Special coaching for bright students/remedial studies for below average students, reading facilities, experts in various subjects were invited as visiting faculty. The examination patterns were explained and various internal tests were conducted.

III. Environment

1. Clean and Green, Strict Discipline (for e.g. Parking, Security etc.)
2. Lots of trees planted and their maintenance.
3. 6 bore wells for ample wate.

The Visionaries

Rome was not built in a day

. . . this is the result of self confidence, honesty, hard work,
. . . perseverance, positive attitude, ready to face the challenges,
. . . sincerity of purpose and courage of conviction.

Behind every successful man is a woman. Mrs. Abeda Inamdar truly and sincerely supported her husband to achieve the noble goal of education. Both Mr. & Mrs. Inamdar were a guiding force to make this dream come true. There is not a single educational institute in Pune, that has provided a platform for the children and youth of weaker sections of the society, and more particularly the Muslims. The Inamdars were supported by their team. As aptly pointed out by the Inamdars, *"If you put your heart and soul into anything you will succeed."*

The credit goes to the entire team: the President, Mr. P.A.Inamdar; the Vice President, Mrs. Abeda Inamdar; the Hon.Secretary, Mr.Latif Magdum; the Treasurer, Mr. Muzzaffar Shaikh; the Joint Secretary, Mr Irfan Shaikh; Chairman of Haji Gulam Mohammed Azam Education Trust, Mr. Munawer Peerbhoy; Hon.Secretary, Mr. Zubair R. Shaikh; and, other Trustees. They had unity in purpose. Courage conquers and boldness pays. All of them worked with visionary goal and missionary zeal. Each member of the team is sharing responsibility for this noble cause of education.

Today there is a change in the attitude of parents, social workers and various authorities associated with all the institutes of MCESociety and this transformation in the society is in itself the first step of revolution. The hard and sincere efforts of the MCESociety's founder members, administrators, academicians and the staff has brought the work of the MCESociety to an excellent stage. Several people have been employed because of the MCESociety. Needless to say, besides the work of this Society in the field of education, it has penetrated into other fields such medicine, social work, sports etc.

After a long span of almost three decades – 28 years to be precise – Mr. P.A.Inamdar, Mrs. Abeda Inamdar, Chairman of Haji Gulam Mohammed Azam Education Trust even today give their time, money and energy for the social cause of upliftment of the poor and deserving students and bringing them on par with the best institutes in India. *All with the unitary intention of pleasing the Almighty Allah.*

Sanjay Nahar – The Man Working in India's most Troubled Zones

– Mr. **Shailesh Wadekar**

Introduction

This article presents the work done by Sanjay Nahar , through an NGO called SARHAD. Sanjay hails from Maharashtra. His work has been presented as below:

Inspiration

Driven by a desire to do something constructive for the country, Sanjay Nahar took to social work very early in life. His uncle, Shri Dhanraj Nahar being a social worker in his time who worked closely with eminent leaders like Yashwantrao Chavan, Bhausaheb Hire and Keshvrao Jedhe, could well be the seed that got sowed in Sanjay's young mind. Even when he was still in college and all of 15 years old, he always felt compelled to think seriously about the issues of social and national importance.

During the communal riots in Pune, Maharashtra around the beginning of the '80s decade, Sanjay got to see the stark reality of human pain. The polarization of the society on communal lines threatening to weaken the very social fabric that holds the country together disturbed young Sanjay Nahar. Unity in diversity that is so unique to India must be preserved through integration of communities and religious tolerance, he was convinced. He was also convinced that rather than mere rhetoric, concrete work needs to be done at the grass root level. Sanjay Nahar, had found the mission of his life: To work towards bonding people and communities together.

Beginning

In the year 1984, on 23rd March, Sanjay Nahar founded Vande Mataram, a social organisation dedicated to the cause of national integration, along with a few like minded fellow young men. Like his own birthday, coinciding with India's Independence Day, the formal beginning of working for national cause coincided with the anniversary of the day the great freedom fighters of India, Bhagat Singh, Sukhdev and Rajguru were hanged by the British, observed as Martyr's Day. Pune, in Maharashtra, which is a hallowed place where many major national movements have started in its history, once again proved the ideal incubator for Vande Mataram. The date was especially significant on the backdrop of severe violence that had gripped Punjab.

Punjab

The year 1984 was when the Punjab issue was at its peak and in October it culminated into the assassination of the then Prime Minister of India, Mrs. Indira Gandhi. Sanjay Nahar was quite disturbed by the turn of events like every other Indian. He had started his activities with a visit to Punjab in the form of a Peace March in the most violence-affected districts in Punjab.

Sanjay Nahar and his colleagues kept visiting Punjab, establishing people to people contact and spreading the message of peace in the strife torn state. In all 21 peace marches were organized during the subsequent period. Even at that early stage, Sanjay succeeded in organizing peace talks between different streams of thought. A major example of this was the meeting between Prof Darshan Singh Raagi and Jain muni Sushil Muni that took place after the Rajeev – Longowal accord.

Their efforts at that young age endeared them to the people as well as the authorities. During a flood situation in Punjab around that time, one of the activists Dattatraya Gaikwad drowned while valiantly trying to save a Sikh family. He was conferred posthumously, the President's Medal.

In the process of such humanitarian work Sanjay Nahar got introduced to and appreciation from eminent leaders of the time in Punjab, like Jathedar Jeevansingh Umranangal, Satypal Dang, Amrita Pritam, editor of Punjab Kesari Vijay Kumar Chopda, J.F. Ribeiro, Sardar Beant Singh, Prakash Singh Badal, Jagjit Singh Anand as well as (now ex- DGP Maharashtra and Punjab) S.S. Virk. Even three former prime ministers of India, Rajeev Gandhi, Chandrashekhar and I. K. Gujral had appreciated his work.

Sanjay Nahar's role proved pivotal in many youths abandoning the path of militancy and starting a normal life, though he himself had received many threats to his life during this period apart from two actual attempts of it.

Kashmir

Around 1990 when Punjab was cooling down, another border state of India, Jammu & Kashmir had begun experiencing militancy and related tensions. By now married, Sanjay Nahar went to Kashmir along with his wife Sushama. That eventful visit from which he had almost decided to return, discouraged by the advice given by many about the life threatening situation in the valley, in fact opened a new chapter in Sanjay's life.

Zain-ul-Abideen Peace March kicked off the activities in Kashmir and later on the Know India Tours for the Kashmiri children became a regular annual event in which they are shown the peaceful, accommodative and tolerant side of India and indeed life.

Sanjay Nahar was instrumental in naming a chowk near Sarhad Bhavan as Pune-Kashmir Friendship chowk to celebrate the close ties the city has with the valley.

Sanjay's other initiatives in Kashmir in brief are as follows:

1. MOU between the municipal corporations of Pune and Srinagar.
2. Visit of the PMC corporators, journalists and newspaper editors from Pune to Kashmir.
3. Helping Kashmiri youths get admissions in the educational institutions in Pune.
4. Creating the Mughal Garden in Pune.
5. Arranging visits of the Kashmiri children to eminent personalities like Amitabh Bachchan, Shah Rukh Khan, Late Bal Thackeray, Raj Thackeray, Sonia Gandhi, Hrithik Roshan etc as well as places like the Science Center, Film City, various important destinations in and around Pune, Mumbai and Delhi etc.
6. AAASH project in Kashmir employing the local widows, half-widows in handicraft work.
7. Annual Kashmir Festival of dance and music in Pune, where thousands of Kashmiri Pandits and Muslims come together and relish the moments steeped in their rich, shared cultural heritage.
8. Inviting eminent people from Kashmir like artists, poets and writers to Pune 4 Kashmir, a project dedicated for exploring the opportunities of creating a better future through cooperation for the people of Kashmir.

There are many more initiatives in the offing.

North East: Around 1987, prior to visiting Kashmir, Sanjay's attention was drawn to North East, where the AGP agitation was in full cry. He in fact established contact with the AGP leader (later elected CM of Assam) Prafulla Kumar Mahant and started exploring ways to start working to build bridges between people in that part of the country and Pune. Eventually however, work in Kashmir engulfed him for more than two decades before he could refocus his attention on the North East.

Visit to Pakistan: In March 2012, Sanjay Nahar visited Pakistan as a member of a peace delegation led by veteran journalist Kuldip Nayyar. His public speeches were well received by the journalists and people of Pakistan. He met with the then Pakistani Prime Minister Yusuf Raza Geelani, Sherry Rehman, Shazia Marri etc

Current Status

- Having worked closely with people and authorities in two Border States of India, Punjab and J&K, Sanjay Nahar founded Sarhad, a social organisation dedicated to work in the border areas, in 1995. Today, that small sapling has become a large tree in the form of a reputed organisation which has created a great name and place for itself in history with a number of initiatives. Notably, this has been achieved without any foreign funding whatsoever in any form.
- Having faced enormous difficulties in having the Kashmiri students admitted in the reputed educational institutions in Pune, especially those from the lower income groups and orphans, Sanjay Nahar decided to create a world class educational facility for the students in Kashmir and other troubled border states, himself. Starting with 105 Kashmiri children, of whom 22 are from Kargil, today Sarhad has Sarhad School, Sarhad College of Arts, Commerce and Science, Sarhad Research Center for Conflict Resolution and Peace, Sarhad Vocational Training Center, Dr. Raghunath Mashelkar Science Lab and Research Center and Sarhad Cricket Academy.
- Kashmir Festival in Pune in which the culture and art forms of the Kashmiri artistes is on display in Pune.
- Sant Namdeo National Award for the outstanding contribution to the nation in any field of endeavor. The recipient of the award each year is strictly a person belonging to Punjab and the award is a token of appreciation by the people of Maharashtra.
- Bhagvan Mahavir International Peace Award.
- Bhupen Hazarika Award for the outstanding contribution to the nation in any field of endeavor by a person belonging to Northeast.
- Helpline for tourists to Kashmir whenever there trouble erupted in the valley. This helpline is operated by Kashmiri orphan students to help especially Maharashtrian tourists visiting the valley.
- From the academic year 2013-14, 75 students from the North East would be admitted in Sarhad, Pune. Sarhad will bear the lodging, boarding and educational expenses of these students.
- The initiative in the education field has to do more with the intention of helping the youths from the border areas find their footing in the outside world. In that, Sanjay Nahar didn't just bring children to Sarhad, he also helped many young men and women from Kashmir secure

admissions in the reputed educational institutions in Pune. He convinced the managements of these institutions to accord a special consideration to these youths so that they are not deprived of a chance to build a good life for themselves because of the strife-filled atmosphere back home. Through this, Sanjay Nahar also succeeded in increasing the awareness in the minds of ordinary citizens of Pune and Maharashtra about the ground reality in Kashmir.

- Sanjay Nahar is a regular panelist on various TV channels when there are discussions related to Punjab, Kashmir, Northeast, Pakistan, Bangla Desh and Afghanistan. He is also invited to write articles in leading Marathi dailies like Sakal, Loksatta, Maharashtra Times, Lokmat and Pudhari on these subjects.
- Plans are afoot to set up a World Music University to promote peace through music. The proposed university would be headed by Dr. M. Rahman, Ex - VC, Aligarh Muslim University and the proposal is currently under consideration of the concerned authorities
- Chinar Publishers, a publishing house which brings out books by well know authors on subjects in which Sanjay Nahar and Sarhad work.
- Sanjay Nahar's work has been duly recognized at national and international level however his aim is not personal glory but the cause he has chosen.

An Impact Analysis Study of the Swindia Project

– Dr. **Usha Varghese**

Introduction

The Swindia Project was initiated in 1996 at Bharati Vidyapeeth Deemed University – Social Sciences Center and since then it has been an on-going Programme. The Primary objective of the project is to promote interaction between Swedish Social Work students and their Indian counterparts and provide glimpses into the Indian Society and Social Welfare Development through a cross cultural perspective.

Every year, since 1996, a group of on an average thirty six Swedish students in two batches of 18 each have been visiting Bharati Vidyapeeth, Deemed University – Social Sciences Center. These Swedish students are undergraduate Social Work students doing their $4^{th}/5^{th}$ or 6th Semesters in Social Work at various Swedish Universities. Till date, approximately 600 Swedish students from the following prominent universities in Sweden have participated in the Swindia Project.

1. Orebro university;
2. Ostersund – Mid – Sweden university;
3. Umea university;
4. Lund university; and
5. Gotenberg university.

Each batch goes through a one week programme at the Bharati Vidyapeeth Deemed University – Social Sciences Center. During this week efforts are taken to expose them to the maximum variety of experiences possible. The students are given several inputs of social work and the Indian Society, and this is achieved through lectures, field visits, rural project visits, presentations, family visits and Cultural Programmes.

Sweden Indian Project has completed 16 years. It has trained around 600 students in cross cultural sensitivity and global social work – a key skill for social work students.

The Swindia Project has been one of the most sought after International field practice programme among Swedish Universities. It was though worthwhile to research and access how much of an impact it has made on the Swedish students in making them into the fine and culturally competent social workers. Hence this study has been designed to research and document the experiences of the Swedish respondent over a period of five years i.e. from 2005-2010.

Objectives of the Study

- To assess key learning outcomes of the Swedish Social work students in terms of getting an insight to Indian professional social work.
- To assess the impact of the project in creating cross cultural sensitivity and understanding of global social work.
- To assess relevance of the project to Sweden and Swedish socio-cultural realities.

Major Findings of the Study (Key Learning Outcomes)

- All the respondents without exception opined that the Swindia Project had been one of many impressions; experiences, feelings and thoughts and those they had learned a lot. It had been an enriching and fruitful experience for all participants.
- Majority of the respondents remarked that they had a very positive interaction with the social work organisations. It had been inspiring for them to see how the organisation worked with the deprived and marginalized sections in society in order to empower them.
- The respondents had got very valuable insight to the Indian society, especially the student community. A major learning had been that the stereotype views and theories, they had about the Indian society weren't really applicable. They had been able to break the myths.
- There was a realization among the respondents that material things are not always the key factor in social work. It is not all about money wealth does not solve all the problem and that problem can be worked with without an affluence of material resources.
- An interesting observation was how important religion and traditions are in the Indian society which is a very dynamic and complex society

full of paradoxes. The paradoxes in India are more obvious and function in a different way than in Sweden. There are more obvious and function in a different way than in Sweden. There are great paradoxes in Sweden as well but they are hidden. Extremes are not as obvious – ex. in India, one can see a beggar right next to a BMW, or a luxurious apartment not far away from the slums which would not be the case in Sweden.

- From the global perspective it is worthy to note that social work does not look the same the world over and it needs to be put in context. What strategies work in one country need not work in another and strategies/models that may be applicable to a certain community or a group of people might not work for another. A professional social worker has to stop categorizing and think out of the box and realize that everything is not just black and white but there are all kinds of shades in between.
- A major learning outcome related to the Ralegaon Siddhi Rural Development Project was the concept of people – mobilization and the amazing transformation that can be achieved when people work together motivated by charismatic leadership. One can achieve great outcomes within small means and a few people can make a big difference. It was a key example of rural transformation through people's participation.

Feedback of the Sweden India Programme

Every batch offers a detailed feed back of the one week programme at the College. This feedback enables the coordinators to modify the programme accordingly so as to make it more effective, fruitful and exposure oriented. This feedback includes aspects like:

(a) Focus of the Project

(b) Learning outcome for the students

(c) Relevance to Sweden

To date, Swedish students have unanimously expressed their appreciation for the very professional manner in which the programme has been conducted. Most of the participants have opined that the Swindia experience has made an ever lasting impression on them. The week with Bharati Vidyapeeth has given them new perspectives and dimensions in the diversity of Social Work in India.

Some first hand experiences recorded by the Swedish students have been enclosed as follows:

Martina Mattisson

Mid Sweden University, Ostersund, Sweden

Baharatiya Vidyapeeth Deemed University,

Social Work Teaching Institute.

Report, Week 5.

Project Focus

I believe the focus of this week lay in getting an insight into Indian social work education and to meet and interact with the Indian students of social work. This included to see different fields of social work such as India's largest prison, Yerwada Central Prison with an open prison ward, one private hospital Ruby Hall Clinic which had three social workers guiding and giving counseling to the patients, Relagaon Siddhi, community work in one rural village and Intervida which worked in one urban slum area.

Learning Outcome and Relevance to Sweden

The first week was very intense and exhausting although extremely interesting. I think all these new impressions and experiences had to sink in before I could even start to think about what I really learnt from them.

First of all I have learnt a bit about social work education in India and that it seems to be more men studying to become social workers here than in Sweden. This I find to be a good thing that I wish will become more common in Sweden as well, because I fell it is much needed. From the interaction with the Indian students I also realized what it might be like to come as a complete stranger to a new country where you don't understand the language they are speaking, body language or social norms, that is what to do and what not to do to be seen as "normal" in the society you are in. Here I can see a big relevance to Sweden and social work in Sweden. I think it is good to have experienced "the other side", that is the experience of not doing "the right" thing all the time, not understand what people are talking about or laughing about, which gives you an uncomfortable feeling of being an outsider that don't belong anywhere. In working with refugees in Sweden this must be a good thing to have felt to get closer to understanding how the refugees feel and think. This will make me aware so that I don't talk over one persons head in Swedish or so that I try to remember to explain everything that may seem obvious to me, but which is not at all obvious for those who come from another part of the world.

Something that also caught my mind was the "classroom experience" when we had our cultural shows. When we presented our small show everyone in the audience kept talking giggling and looking at other things and at first I thought it was lack of respect but then I asked my self if there may be different ways of showing respect and that there might not be a universal way of doing this. I noticed that the Indian students did almost the same thing as they had their own show and that made me think that this might be a normal thing to do here. But I have really no idea ! These are just my thoughts and from this a learnt that we, as social workers and as humans, have to accept different ways behaving when there is not one right way of living.

The first thing I learnt during our visit to Yerwada Central Prison was that there is death penalty in India. This is something I do not believe in and it was the first thing I found to be uncomfortable and unfair, although I do know that one has to be open-minded and try to understand why and how and all that. In Sweden we don't have death penalty anymore but I am sure we have something that is equal to death penalty, but may be at another level ? I also found the power structures in the prison to be very strong and clear. This is something I think we have in Swedish prisons as well and I think it's something I think we have in Swedish prisons as well and I think it's something that you can find in almost all societies with prison as punishment. I have thought a lot about prison as punishment, and I don't know if I think that anybody has the right to take someone else's freedom. But at the same time I have no new constructive idea about what would be a good way to deal with people that have gone against the law. Is there a better way then prison in trying to scare people from committing crime ?

During our day at Intervida in the urban slum area in the outskirt of Pune I realized the importance of starting a project on the level where people are standing. There is no use in starting to educate and set up schools if the people feel that they need to start develop some other part in life. This is something that I really find as relevant to all sorts of social work in every country and it is something I will always try to remember in my social work in Sweden. I also find this to be relevant on all levels in society, from micro to meso and macro levels, where politicians and higher departments need to look at the whole population and see the bigger problems and try to start working with them at a level where the society are at that moment. I don't believe in rushing in to projects or development, which a society is not yet ready for.

An Intervida I also learnt that it is important to work with separate groups like women and men separately and young boys and girls in different groups as well as a whole group. They might have various problems and also have different understanding in life. Here I also saw the value of working with other organisations and NGO's. To build a network of helping each other is a good way to go forward in creating something better. This is something I find Sweden to be lacking a little bit. In different cities and communities in Sweden know there is a big struggle to make networking effective and I think this is something Sweden have to get better at. This is a responsibility for both higher departments who need to make sure that the single social worker will have time to both working with clients and start connecting and work with other organisations and institutions such as hospitals and unemployment offices and for the social workers to really set up and maintain these networks so they work properly. I wish to Swedish government or who every is "in charge" will make sure that social workers get more time to clients and to networking. I also wonder what it would be like if social work in Sweden wasn't so much individual oriented but more group oriented ? Would social problems and social structures look different then ?

I feel that I could go on forever with all the other experiences and learning outcomes that I have got this week. There has been so much information about Indians which I know will help me a lot in understanding various actions and problems during the following weeks and this week has given me a small understanding of the role social work plays in India. I also believe that all these experiences will make me look at Swedish social work in a different perspective and that it will help me to be more critical in my way of viewing social work on different levels in the society.

Name : Marvi Manty

University : University of Orebro

Organisation : BVP Social Work Teaching Institution

Project Focus : Meeting Indian Social Workers and Students.

Observation Home for Boys, Yerwada Central Prison,

Intervida, Relagon Siddhi, Family visits, Lectures.

This week has been very interesting. I have seen things I have never seen before, met new people, seen differences and similarities between Sweden and India, lived with 8 other people in the same apartment, tried new food ... the list is long.

What have I learned ?

1. **Empowerment:** Empowerment is a successful method social work e.g. in the slum where INTERVIDA was placed, Ralegan Siddhi and self supporting groups for women. The method is good because it strengthens people's self-esteem and helps them to take responsibility for their situation and be in charge of their lives. I don't know whether this method is common in Sweden or not, but this certainly is something to applicable in the Swedish society. e.g. Many teenagers in Sweden feel as they don't have anything to say and that their voices are unheard and meaningless. They have a very pessimistic view of their future and feel like victims. Empowering them, who feel like this, would promote both the individual and the social climate.
2. **Group thinking:** From may point of view, the whole range of social work, that I've seen this week, is based on group. In Yerwada Prison the prisoners lived together and maintained the prison together. In the slum, where INTERVIDA was, there were many self-help groups and hobby groups. The Indian family is solid, and divorces are rare. At the observation home for boys there were groups of approximately 40 children in a class. In Sweden that big groups are seen as a handicap, not a strength.
3. **Education:** At the observation home for boys education was considered as rehabilitation. This is very different from the Swedish way of taking education for granted. In Sweden education is a right, in India education is valued and many times a "tool" to get a better life. My thought is

that Swedish children should be informed about the world's situations and what a privilege it is to have schools "free of charge."

4. **Being a Foreigner:** All of a Sudden, I'm here in India, I realize: I'm a foreigner ! People look at me, most of them smile and seem friendly. Rickshaw drivers try to fool me.

Conclusion

Academic learning, interaction with faculty members and Indian students, field supervisors, institutional visits, field visits, cultural exchange – all these inputs in varied ways had a deep learning impact on the Swedish participants, which would continue to influence them all their lives both professionally as well as personally. The Swindia Programme has most certainly been successful in creating cultural sensitivity among Swedish Social Work students.

31

Motivating Madia Youth Towards Progress

– Adv. Lasu Narote

Introduction

The Madias of Maharashtra are one of the particularly Vulnerable Tribal Group (PVTG'S). The other two being, the Katkaris of western Maharashtra and Kolams of Nanded & Yavatmal. The Madias are predominantly found in Bhamragad tahsil, of Gadchiroli district. In India, they are found in Madhya Pradesh, Chattisgarh, Maharashtra and in few pockets of Andhra Pradesh, Orissa & Jharkhand. The tribe is socially, economically, educationally very backward & is geographically isolated.

I belong to the Madia tribe and my native village is juvvi, in Bhamragad tahsil of Gadchiroli district, in the state of Maharashtra. I completed my primary & high school education in the Ashram school of Lok Biradari Prakalpa, Hemalkasa village of Bhamragad, block in Gadchiroli district. Dr. Prakash Amte – the famous social worker helped me to join the Anand Niketan Mhahavidyalaya- a college in Anandwan of Warora block in Chandrapur, where I complete 11th and 12th grade. I am grateful to Dr. Vikas Amte for his co-operation during these two years. During these two years I was fortunate to take the guidance of Dr. Baba Amte.

Later on, I completed bachelors degree in Marathi, in Pune's famous college called Ferguson. After this, I completed graduation in journalism and communication. Further, I got an opportunity in law. I completed two masters, one in sociology and the second one in journalism and communication. By 2005, I could compete my education with the help of Tribal Development Department, Dr. Dharyasheel Shirole and other well wishers. I returned back to Nagpur to practice law as on apprentice with Adv. Surendra Gadling Later on I got an opportunity to work with an Yavatmal bosed N.G.O under the able guidance of Ajay Dolke. While learning and earning in pune, Nagpur & Yavatmal , I always felt that, I shall motivate my community youth to wards progress.

The Motivational Strategy

In order to motivate the Madia youth,I visited several youth dormitories, locally called "ghotuls". Several meetings with the Madia youth and their parents were organized. As a result of this motivation, monitoring and follow-up, the result was satisfying.

Impact of Motivation

Over a period of 12 long years of motivation, monitoring and follow-up, I was able to send 150 Madia youth to Pune for higher education, make their arrangements in Government tribal hostels, help them to get scholarships and admissions, meet them frequently to boost their morale and so on.

As on today, 100 Madia youth have completed their masters in Journalism and communication, English, Sociology, graduation in law, one girl became a Homoeopathic doctor, while the rest 47 completed graduation. Out of this 150 Madia youth, 4 are employed in Government sector, 15 in private educational institutes, one is practicing medicine, two are practicing law,while others are studying for MPSC, UPSC NET & SET. Of course some are unemployed, but are in their respective villages helping their parents in agriculture.

The Result of my motivation was as follows:

1. The Madia youth were exposed to city life, modernization, urbanization, Mass communication & to the concept of globalization.
2. They realized the significance of formal education.
3. They become aware of few Government programmes & their constitutional rights.
4. A few of them got jobs in private & Government sector.
5. Our interaction with a few well-wishers in Pune, helped us to form an association called the friends of Madia.
6. The Madia youth have realized the importance of competitive examinations like the:
   (a) National Education Test (NET)
   (b) State Education Test (SET)
   (c) Maharashtra Public Service Commission (MPSC)
   (d) Union Public Service Commission (UPSC)

7. Out of the 150 Madia youth, nearly 100 received training at the Tribal Research & Training Institute, Government of Maharashtra, Pune.
8. Many more Madia youth are coming forwards to be educated in Pune, Nagpur, Chandrapur, Delhi, Mumbai etc.
9. I was fortunate to visit Manila, at the University of South Whales for a 15 days course.
10. I was able to start an NGO of the Madia youth, by the Madia youth, for the Madia youth. The objective of the NGO is to help the Madia youth to progress & develop in par with the main stream.

Counseling and Guidance Centers for Slum Women
An Imperative Need

– Ms. **Laurie M. Anderson**

Slums "are the outgrowth of a particular development process by which the means of production, employment opportunities, wealth and urban amenities concentrates around an area or place." (Jayaswal, 1955, p. 183). They usually develop, as they have in Pune, where employment is available, near mid to upper scale housing, central business districts or construction sites. They can be identified by a number of characteristics and there is considerable variance with respect to things such as housing, density, sanitary conditions, availability of basic amenities, drainage and sewage facilities, and garbage disposal. A variety of people make slums their homes.

Slums are primarily made up of low caste workers who have migrated from rural areas to urban centres in search of employment. Migration may be a result of famine, pressures of joint family, caste group exploitation, or may be a search for better economic livelihood. In any event, slum development can be firmly linked to industrialization and urbanization. Slum communities remain intact for a number of reasons.

People remain in slums primarily because the land is cheap to rent and transportation costs are low. Slum dwellers are hesitant to leave as result of 'fatalism, illiteracy, distrust towards development programmes, psychological fears, apprehensions, and restricted social mobility.' (Jayaswal, 1993, p. 187) Women, of course have little to say about leaving.

Women who reside in slums are often being forced, due to circumstances beyond their control, to migrate to urban centres with their husband and children. As the primary caretakers of their households, women have to deal with a number of miseries in their new homes. With limited access to amenities, facilities and far removed from their traditional support systems, they are vulnerable and very much at the mercy of this new environment.

Women, who are firmly connected with the roots of their traditions, who are faced with and deal with the realities of their current circumstances, must ultimately be included in any development undertakings that it is hoped will succeed in the future. Because of the key role that they play in the maintenance of their house holds and their communities, any type of long term development plan must focus on the empowerment of women in the slums. Long overlooked as simple servants in patriarchal homes, the inclusion of women is now clearly imperative.

The failure of the various level of government in India, in conjunction with non-government organisations (NGOs), to recognize women as the key to empowering entire communities, is deplorable. It is absolutely critical that women be provided with the tools necessary to build a better community. The establishment of 'Counseling and Guidance Centre for Slum Women' is the first step towards a new reality.

The aim and goal of Centres of Counseling and Guidance would be to assist women in identifying their own needs, and the needs of their communities, to provide them with a direct support group, and to provide a motivating force. The ultimate goal would be for a network of efficient, effective Centres to be established which are self-sufficient and fully operated by women of the slum communities.

In order to consider the feasibility and potential viability of the centre concept, and to ensure that the voices of slum women were reflected, a number of research methods were used. Data was collected through observations, informal interviews with social workers and with non randomly selected women in three local slums. These slums were Indira Gandhi Vasahat and Ambedkar Vasahat in Ganeshkhind post region, and Maldhakka Vasahat in Shivajinagar region. In addition to this primary research, secondary sources were also utilized.

After completing this initial research, a number of key areas in which Counseling and Guidance Centres for Slum Women would be most useful – health, education, economic, social, political, financial and legal – were identified. These have been set cut below along with a discussion of the specific role a centre would play in the identified area.

Health

(a) Emotional well-being

Slum conditions contribute to the low self-esteem and unhappiness of the women who live there and "lack of essential facilities like sewage etc.

further deteriorate the self dignity of the community. Scenes of violence and drunkenness, family quarrel, crying, mark the living atmosphere of slums. In sum, the poor living conditions of the slum create an all round deterioration in the urban environment." (Jayaswal, 1993, p. 184).

Severe stress related to uncertain health and economic conditions leads to tension related emotional ailments.

(b) Hygiene and sanitation

Slums have deplorable hygiene conditions. There are insufficient toilets for the number of inhabitants, children are often seen defecating and urinating wherever convenient, and play in the fetid water. Women are forced to wash household utensils and clothing in the immediate vicinity of raw sewage. General information about hygiene is not available.

(c) Disease and infections

The data which have been collected in surveys and studies from India's major cities indicate that the tuberculosis, gastro-intestinal, skin and venereal diseases are most common among the slum dwellers." (Jayaswal, 1993, p. 183).

Various conditions lead to a high rate of infection and disease in slum areas. Compact living conditions mean that illness spreads rapidly unless curbed quickly. Women are particularly vulnerable because they are the main caretakers of the health of the family. Skin irritations are rampant.

(d) Garbage removal

The number of women who make their living by rag picking, and the fact that slums are almost devoid of any garbage disposal systems, leaves them particularly prone to the ravages of rodents and insects. Further, the lack of effective garbage removal increases the danger of infection and disease.

(e) Family planning

Families in the slum areas are often large for a number of reasons and limited resources mean that little has to be shared by many and ill health and unhappiness are often the result. Family planning is perceived to mean sterilization and general information about contraception is not understood.

(f) Childbirth

Slum women are very vulnerable to complications of death due to childbirth. Often they need to rely on the services of local mid wives who may not have the support they need for particularly difficult births. The early death of a mother often leaves children vulnerable and neglected.

(g) Pre-natal care

Women in the slums generally have no pre-natal care. This is not the case in the communities from which they come originally but is the result of a disjointed migratory community where not all traditional resources may be available. "Women in India continue to die at childbirth owing to anemia and toxemia' although appropriate medical treatment during the course of pregnancy, or during the pre-natal period, could prevent much of this. (Varma, 1991, p.60)

(h) Nutrition

Adequate nutrition is a serious problem for slum women. As they are the main food preparers in their families, and as they tend to feed the husband and children first, they rarely receive an adequate caloric intake given the amount of energy they require for survival or reasonable health. Nutrition plays an important role in the prevention of illness and disease. Women in the slums commonly describe a meager food intake of tea, rice and assorted vegetables. "... an average Indian takes only 94 per cent of the total calorie requirement daily with women taking much less. As many as 5 per cent of India's children under 5 years old are extremely malnourished..." (Varma, 1991, p. 58).

Long term caloric deprivation, particularly prevalent in the case of female children and adults, can lead to impaired mental faculties as well as physical deformities and ailments.

(i) Early marriage

Early marriages are still prevalent in the slum communities. This is largely due to the concern with female pre-marital sexual activity and the need to remove the burden of young women from the family.

Early marriage is a critical health issue because it generally means the early production of children. Children born to young mothers are often less hardy and resilient to the environment. The young women who bear the children are also put at risk for short and long term health complications.

(j) Dental care

Preventive dental hygiene programmes are not available in the slums. Long term neglected often leads to related health problems.

(k) Immunization

Immunization programmes for children, though classified as "primary health care" and therefore provided by the Government, are inadequate in the slum areas. More established tracking, recording and follow-up is needed as well as emergency immunization programmes in case of epidemics.

Role of Counselling and Guidance Centres in Health

The effective functioning of a community centre which would contributed to improved living conditions in a variety of ways, which sought to empower women to take control of their lives where possible, with effectively provided programmes of assistance and support identified in conjunction with the input of the community, would serve to increase the emotional well being of slum inhabitants. Besides the provision of specific mental health assistance, this holistic approach would have a holistic result.

An established Centre could provide the tools for hygiene and sanitation to the community women given that this is almost exclusively their domain within the household and community. Women could monitor the result of their efforts by tracking the reduction of illness and infection in their communities. The Centre would play only a coordinator role in this project as it would seek to empower slum women to disseminate health information. On occasion, representatives from different centres could be drawn together to compare notes on progress and success in respective communities. Given that slum dwellers make up such a sizable proportion of the community, an investment in the health of slums would be an investment in the health of entire urban populations.

The Centre could provide information by way of audio-visual tools operated by trained women in the community, about the causes and symptoms of diseases. As women are the primary care givers in the family, their inclusion is crucial to the success women are the primary care givers in the family, their inclusion is crucial to the success of the Centre in this area. A community health worker could be trained within the community for more critical diagnosis and solutions once Centre women had determined a serious situation existed. Respected women within the community could be responsible for the implementation and management as well as success monitoring by way of reduced spread of illness and disease in the slum.

The Centre could provide a voice to slum women who need to be heard by landlords and civic administrations with respect to garbage removal. A Centre project could be to follow-up on community complaints about inadequate or irregular garbage removal. The slum community as a whole could see that their voices were being heard and acted upon.

The Centre could provide information about contraception and the value and benefits of controlling family size. Information geared particularly to women would be most effective. The stigma attached to "family planning" due to the nature of Government programmes in the mid-1970s could be reduced or eliminated. Women, provided with the tools to prevent unmanageable families might well be motivated to implement family planning concepts once they could see an increased survival of infants and became aware of their own abilities to provide viable futures for their children A Centre were women could gather to discuss issues of family planning, where women could find their own voices, would result in positive changes.

The provision of information through Centres to local slum midwives and their inclusion in discussions of new techniques could dramatically reduce the death of women during childbirth.

The provision of regular medical check-ups for women coordinated through a community centre would be very beneficial. Early detection of pregnancy could assist in the necessary pre-natal care for improved heath and survival of infants and the reduction in the birthrate in slums.

The Centre could provide on going information relative to the nutritional needs of the body, particularly the needs of children, based particularly on an affordable range of food. Recipes and combinations of affordable products could be shared and discussed by the women of the slum community and perhaps recorded for the audio-visual benefit of other communities through their own centres. These audio-visual tools could be provided, with appropriate training, to women of the slums. This would increase empowerment through the shared knowledge of women. New skills and capabilities provide a sense of certainty that the information women hold is valuable and worthwhile to others.

The Centre could act as a clearing house of information relative to the high economic value of a young woman to her household, and the fact that her contribution in waged and unwaged work far outweighs the good and foods she consumes within her household. Further, the Centre could help to provide information about the benefits, both short and long term, of later marriages for both young men and women.

Information on dental hygiene for long term dental health could be disseminated through local centres. Again the key to the success of such a programme would be the inclusion of the primary care givers, women in both the implementation and the follow up of such a programme.

While immunization is provided by the government, the current system is insufficient for the needs of slum communities. A Counseling and Guidance Centre could provide women with the tools to record new births and determine the immunization needs of its members. Not only could it co-ordinate the provision of immunization shots, it could also communicate the importance of such shots through local women, to the community at large. Thus those women of the slum unable to travel to medical facilities could utilize on site services periodically provided for their benefit. Again, women would play a primary role in the effective implementation of such a programme.

Education

(a) Illiteracy and drop out

According to the 1981 census of India, women made up 57 per cent of the illiterate population of India and females made up 70 per cent of the children of school age who did not participate in the format education system. Further, the dropout rate for girls is over 60 per cent at the primary level. (Varma, 1991, P.57). Illiteracy is particularly high amongst women in the slums.

Some groups such as the Wadaris, or stone cutting castes migrating from Andhra Pradesh and Karnataka, have particularly high rates of uneducated women and often pull young girl from school as soon as they are old enough to wash vessels.

Men, and the community as a whole, see little reason for young women to be educated since they are expected to commit themselves to household and family responsibilities at a very young age. They are unsupportive of extended (formal) education of young women and encourage the withdrawal of female children from school prematurely.

Illiteracy means that women are unable to support their young children is a monitoring capacity and thus, generation after generation may be unable to reach full potential due to a lack of educational support in the home (and in the community).

Illiteracy often compounds a woman's feelings of inadequacy and certainly limits her economic options.

(b) Vocational/technical training

Women in the slums are often unaware of advanced vocational or technical training opportunities available or such opportunities are far from the slums or are economically inaccessible. Again, communities tend to be unsupportive of such pursuits in any event as they see the role of "women" as clearly defined and static.

Role of Counseling and Guidance Centres in Education

A Centre could serve as a funneling mechanism for information with respect to the long-term benefit of staying in schools. It could provide onsite periodic visits by members of the community who had completed education to pursue women and youth with a vision for the future. Written and audiovisual material could assist in conveying this 'stay in school' message to parents who might be anxious to pull young children from school once they are old enough to do manual labour.

The provision of onsite monitoring and discussion classes for women and youth, as well as periodic networking with other communities, could assist in the building of self-esteem relative to the education. A place to go to seek guidance, and to discuss difficulties in a non-violent setting, would also be helpful. A centre could assist in the process of upgrading the education levels in a community must see that the goals of increased prosperity and well-being are both desirable and attainable.

As women, often illiterate, spend much time with their children, it is crucial to seek their support in retaining children, primarily little girls, in the education system for as long as possible. One way to do this would be to provide ongoing literacy programmes through Counseling and Guidance Centres for adult women. These could be scheduled around women's waged and unwaged work hours so that they could make themselves available to participate on a regular basis. This would serve not only to empower the women but would also to create an awareness of the importance of education.

The Centre could function as a clearinghouse of information with regard to the values of education, could be a source of monitoring assistance to young people as well as a support in terms of tutoring facilities. It is often said that part of the difficulty with the advancement of the disadvantaged is the lack of tools they have access to. The Centre could provide an area for young students to read and study, could provide access to the guidance of others, more senior students or local volunteers who make their time available periodically. Once again the critical success of this programme would be dependent upon the participation of the community. Until slum dwellers see part of the education programmes being implemented, feel that their voices are being heard, and that their words are given credence, little will change. This means that women, who play a vital part in the informal education of young children in slums, must be included in any effort to change participation in school needs to be internalized and then shared with others by the women of the slums. With the support of community women, and the increasing success of self-monitored programmes of Student improvement Centres could help to facilitate change in this critical area. Further, the conveyance of messages via the Centre with respect to the increased economic value of a girl child to a community with her advanced education, might also help to reduce the drop-out rate.

Economic

(a) Maidservants

The most common type of employment for women in the slums is as maidservants. Maidservants may work for as little as 100 rupees per month and the responsibility of several houses may provide as 400 to 500 rupees per month Maidservants in some local slums have organized associations but many remain unrepresented. Exploitation in a variety of forms is common.

(b) Rag-picking

Another common job for women in the slums is rag-picking. This is grueling and arduous work and involves spending a lot of time with garbage. It is back breaking and pays in the order of four to five rupees per day. Exploitation due to illiteracy is common. Women are very much reliant on the honesty of those who procure their gathered items to receive fair payment. The rainy season makes rag-picking work more difficult and the length of time it takes to dry collected items means a severe reduction in income during these periods.

(c) Construction

Construction, yet another common employment of slum women, is generally seasonal. The work is often as assistants or head loaders. The work is hard, and despite legislation to the contrary, women are sometimes paid half of a man's wage for the same work. A typical working week consists of an eight hour day, for six days a week, for approximately 25 rupees per day.

(d) Industry

Slum women often do piece work for local industries. While the companies may have unions and benefits for full time employees, these do not apply to piece workers. Work may involve leather goods, rubber parts, and a variety of other manual labour chores.

One woman interviewed cut 200 pieces of rubber parts per day from molds which was compensated with four rupees. The work is monotonous, stress inducing and exhausting. Work may be rejected if not precise. If a woman was employed on site for this type of work she would be paid 25 rupees per day. This is an effective and exploitive way to save the company 21 rupees per day. It was astonishing to learn that this woman's salary had doubled to two-rupees per 100 pieces over the course of six years. She had to walk one-and-a-half kilometers per day to pick up the supplies for her work.

(e) Vegetable/fruit handcarts

Vegetable and fruit selling is another source of income for slum women. They may pool resources with other sellers to hire an auto-rickshaw to obtain a load of vegetables or fruits from the market to sell in other areas. Because of the limited supply of goods they can procure to sell, profits are meager.

(f) Caste, religious beliefs and entrepreneurial endeavours

Unfortunately, the joint family system, the caste system and religious beliefs have impended the development of industry because young people are not encouraged to be entrepreneurial and the caste system has, to some degree, restricted people's entrance into new occupations. The belief in Karma, i.e. predetermined fate, may have further confined others. Caste regulations over the activities of women have certainly limited their opportunities for economic divergence.

(g) Child labour

Young girls are often put to work as soon as they are old enough to contribute economically to the family. Although this provides short-term gains to her family, it may also guarantee long-term limited economic opportunities for her.

Role of Counselling and Guidance Centers Relative to Economic Problems

Clearly, Centres could provide assistance with disseminating information to maidservants with respect to organizing and creating associations that would help to curb exploitation and increase wages. The Centre would function as an intermediary and could approach a variety of private and industrial employers to try to ease the burden of both maid servants and piece work employees. Representatives from various slum areas could use the Centre as a meeting point to discuss and lobby on a variety of issues.

Centres could facilitate the locating of temporary storage sites for drying materials of rag-pickers during the rainy months and could assist with finding alternative seasonal work to ease the burden of this season as well. A Centre could also provide basic skills in weights and measurements and this new knowledge would help to ensure that women were getting fair prices for their collected goods.

Centres could provide basic constitutional rights' information to women construction workers to assist them in organizing against discrimination on the basis of sex relative to wages. The Centre could also assist with lobbying and approaching industrial sites for better wages for contract or piece work. Perhaps it could also act as a Centre for picking up piece work dropped off by companies each day so as to avoid the need to walk to the site each day.

A co-operative system could be established through the Centre so that larger or more diverse others could be filled at the market and thus improve the profits of the vegetable and fruit sellers in the suburbs. A collective system of pooling resources in order to maximize the profits of everyone would be beneficial.

Sharing information amongst women in the slums could lead to the predicting of short falls in the community economics so that alternative possibilities for income could be suggested. Input by slum women themselves would not only help to, in the long term, break down the barriers built by religion and caste, but would also aid in determining useful programmes for economic development which are worth pursuing. Creating a sense of empowerment at an economic level may alleviate an entire set of social problems in slum areas.

Part-time jobs could be developed by the community, with the help of the Centres, which offer "earn while you learn" opportunities. This would serve to provide women with new skills and would increase self confidence. Boosted self-confidence would benefit the immediate family and the community as a whole.

The Centre could promote small-scale business ventures but rather than being only an instigator of such centres, it would serve as a clearinghouse of information and a meeting place for those who wish to pursue alternative or accidental opportunities.

The Centre would also be an appropriate place to convey information about the hazards of child labour as well as to provide ways for women to avoid this as an option for acquiring funds for the family.

With the changing economic needs of urban environment the Centre could facilitate a number of workshops and discussion groups, held on a regular basis, to try to enable slum women to stay one step ahead of changes in the economy relative to types of work.

Social

(a) Prostitution

As a result of social problems such as separation, desertion and divorce, women may have to turn to prostitution in order to support their children.

The practices of the Devdasi cult continue even today. This religiously sanctioned prostitution leaves few options available to the women who are drafted into it.

(b) Juvenile delinquency

Children moving from rural areas to urban slums are ill prepared for their new realities and often women, who are the primary care givers encounter new difficulties with juvenile delinquency.

(c) Violence

Women in slums are regularly abused by their husbands and are relatively powerless to stop the abuse. The violence is socially sanctioned by the society and women are often brutally raped, doused with kerosene etc. with little recourse. They are far removed from their extended families and from the support of their original communities.

Rape in slum areas is a common occurrence. Due to the social stigma attached to this violent crime, young women often do not pursue the matter. In Indian society, rape is commonly thought to be a crime of passion rather than a violent act and this ensures that offenders are rarely prosecuted or punished in any way. No rape counseling is available to women in the slums.

Sexual abuse by employers is a common form of violence endured by slum women. Women, young and old, are often subjected to coercive threats which result in sexual exploitation.

(d) Alcohol/drug abuse

Abuse of alcohol and drugs is often associated with depression, marital problems and economic hardships. Men who do heavy labour or manual work believe that alcohol adds strength and vigor to their bodies. (Madan, 1992, p. 155) This not only results in a drain of family finances, battery of women and children, and ill health of all concerned, it contributes to a long-term pattern of escapism which never benefits the community. Women are often the primary victims of substance abuse as they have to bear the brunt of the violence and have to find a way to stretch finances.

The infants are often doped with opium in poor houses to keep quiet and allow their mothers to carry on their work." (Madan, 1992, P. 176).

Opium and other drugs such as charas, ganja, bhang and cocaine are consumed mostly by the poor and the labouring classes. (Madan, 1992, P. 176).

(e) Separation/divorce/desertion

Separation, divorce and desertion often leave woman destitute. They rely heavily on the economic support of their husband for survival.

(f) Widows

After the death of a husband a woman may be left completely destitute. Often women in slums are abandoned by their sons who have either become burdened with their own family responsibilities or who have not migrated and are therefore unable to provide any support. Social stigma attached to widowhood remains strong.

Role of Counselling and Guidance Centres Relating to Social Problems

A Centre could provide a meeting place for women in prostitution to discuss difficulties of the trade as well as alternative options available. Information about issues such as sexually transmitted diseases could also be funneled through the Centre.

The Centre could help to monitor the levels of Juvenile Delinquency in the slum community and provide women with a place to obtain information about combating delinquency as well as a location for discussion and sharing ideas. The Centre could also provide counseling to disenchanted youth feeling the pressures of urban life.

The provision of rape counseling and information about leaving violent households could be provided through and by the Centre. It could also assist with supporting women in their attempts to get police action in cases of violence, as well as legal advice relative to their constitutional rights.

Emotional support for women living in substance abused households could be provided through the Centre as well as a place for group discussion with other women. Information about the danger of drugging children could also be disseminated. Again, the key to the success of such programmes would be the empowerment of the women of the slum communities themselves to take charge of the organisation.

Family breakdown is particularly difficult for women and assistance with acquiring economics skills for survival is crucial to their recovery and survival. The Centre could play an active role in assisting women in equipping themselves with new skills. Widows would also benefit from such systems.

Political

(a) Voting banks

Typically, slum women migrate to the cities with their husbands and children to settle on a piece of land owned by a particular landowner. The new tenant is given a piece of paper setting out conditions of the agreement and these acts as a receipt. The paper is not legal or binding. This paper is then taken to a corporator who belongs to a political organisation. Through the legal process of the Municipal Corporation the corporator provides an identity card (residence card) and adds this new individual to his voters list. Thus, slum dwellers are added to voting bank. Corporators have organizers within the slums who, for a price, guarantee, through violence and intimidation, the votes of the masses in the slums. Women often vote as they are told to by their husbands.

(b) Cheap labour pools

Slums provide a cheap source of labour for industrialists without their having to provide any facilities or housing. It is obvious that ".... the problem of slum is associated with the exploitive system of the capitalist society. The city is for the rich and the middle class who can pay for the infra structure and other urban facilities and luxuries. The city administration safeguards the rights of the propertied classes and the corporation or the Municipality renders services to those who reside in authorized areas and who pay taxes for these services." (Rao, 1984, P. 101).

(c) Government apathy and failure

It is clear that there has been some failure at an administrative level to consider the needs of slum dwellers which may be as high as 45 per cent in some urban centres. Government 'has become flabby, slack, demoralized, callous and answerable to none' (Nimbkar, 1992, P.7). Unfortunately, as a result of this breakdown. 'the public utilities and civic and social welfare services have never been worse.' (P. 7) Citizens have come to rely on Government instead of being given the tools to help themselves. This reliance of funding has provided too much support without any real concern about what funds are being used for, or accountability of any kind. 'To keep the system of government propped up in power and to keep political parties functioning without accountability, citizens have been reduced to function as mere voting entitles in the name of democracy. Programme planning for social good have become exercises in futility' (P.9). Financial allocations, resources, and programmes have failed to be properly administered, implemented and monitored.

Role of Counselling and the Guidance Centres Relating to Politics

Slum dwellers do not realize that they function as huge voting reservoirs and that they do have the political power, if they have the political will, to force change to their advantage. Women too need to realize the power of their votes within the slum communities. What they need is a cohesive voice, a forum in which to air their grievances and to relay their concern to those who have power to implement change on their behalf. Public opportunities and a safe space in which to voice concern is needed. A Counseling and Guidance Centre could provide information at a community level about political parties (acting in a non-partisan capacity), could provide a forum through which speakers could be both seen and heard, and could also provide workshops on how and why voting takes place. It could serve as a meeting place for women who wished to discuss particular political concerns for them, and could provide assistance to anyone who appeals for help because of political intimidation.

Corporators get funding from municipal corporation for a greeting slums but improvements seldom get done. Slum dwellers, for the most part women and children, are valuable tenants. They are also valuable to those who employ their services, to politicians and local industries. Slum girls and women are a cheap source of labour that growing cities cannot do without. They need to be made aware of their value in Society. They need a voice. Organized women could provide a powerful lobby group.

Centres would operate as clearing houses of information slums in different communities, they could facilitate meetings and focus on sharing political strategies and success stories. Centres could help to make women aware of the power of forming associations and co-operatives.

Financial

Slum women have few finances to manage and no information about services, programmes, or options available to them.

Role of Counselling and Guidance Centres Relating to Finances

Information about saving money and multiplying financial resources could be provided by the centres. Funds, loans and development schemes could be conveyed to those who could benefit from them through the Centre.

Legal

(a) Legal rights

Slum women are unaware of their legal rights. They have no representation, and no access to information about contracts, agreements and labour laws, or their constitutional rights as citizens of India.

(b) Abuse

Battering is a serious problem for women in the slums. Situations are often exacerbated by economic woes and family breakdown, both of which are not uncommon in the slum. While woman report incidents of abuse to the police, they advise that assistance and follow up is rare.

Women are commonly victims of exploitation by landlords and employers partly because they are unaware of their rights to legal recourse.

Role of Counselling and Guidance Centres Relative to Legalities

Legal representatives, through the Centre could assist in providing new arrivals to slums with information about what they might expect to find, what they need not tolerate, and how to exercise the options available to them. Women, in particular, could be warned of common infractions and resources available to them.

Women also need an advocate relative to sexual abuse and exploitation. A Centre could not only assist with individual abuse cases, it could also operate as a clearing house for various slums about particular problem employers. Publicity shared information about infractions might also assist in preventing such abuses.

All of the legal avenue representations could be offered in conjunction and coordination with the informal, traditional legal system of the slum itself. This would be a participatory effort, an empowerment effort, a convergence of knowledge and information to provide tools.

Other – Failure of NGOs

(a) NGOs alone cannot solve the slums. They "work in diverse fields like family welfare, slum improvement, women's development, care of street children etc. They try to find solutions in their own limited ways, to the problem of the target-affected population. There is however, little mutual cooperation among the NGOs.".(Haldule, 1993, P.19).

Role of Counselling and Guidance Centres in NGO Efficiency

There is a distinct need to coordinate the efforts of NGOs operating in slum areas. An effort to coordinate would increase the efficiency of the NGOs and maximize the benefits to women of their work. The centres could help to alleviate the wastefulness of duplicated efforts.

In summary, it is clear that the establishment of Counselling and Guidance Centres is an immediate imperative. Volunteer boards reflecting ethnic and gender diversity, as well as caste diversity, should be drawn from various walks of life. Representatives should be included from : law, education, medicine and social work. They should work with a rotating group of community women from the slums to help guide the centres in projects and programmes. Centres, with a non partisan, social mandate, would serve to uplift skills and spirits, and motivate people to empower themselves all within a traditional societal framework combined with the realities of modernity. This would help to reduce macro level plans to micro level plans.

Slums in India have become looming reminders of the failure of a nation and people to find adequate solutions to the growing problems of poverty and unemployment. The effects of these issues have been particularly devastating to women. Slums in many cities make up close to half of the urban population, yet, despite attempts on the part of all levels of administration as well as development organisations, little has changed. The problem continues to grow and the plight of women continues to worsen. The answer to the problem is not continued contributions of mis-managed, unmonitored Rupees and Dollars to the system, but a change in administrative attitudes and approach to strategies of assisting slum women of India.

Counseling and Guidance Centres could effectively be a participatory project supported by government, NGOs and solicited funds from private industry. Information about the accumulation and distribution of funds would be readily available public knowledge and limits of financial participation could be established to keep in check the power of any individual or organisation. Meetings would be a matter of public record and the Centres would be held publicity accountable. The sole goal of the centres would be to improve short and long term conditions for women in the slum. Having a strong representation of slum women on the board of the centres would ensure that their voices could be heard and a rapport established with the surrounding community.

It is critical that strategic planning, implementation and follow up are in place with the establishment of centres in slum communities. It is imperative that success and failures be monitored and recorded for improvement and adjustment. Slum women will, in this way, be able to use the commitment of the larger community, to the success of this project.

The resources of slum are the women themselves. They increase the value of the land they inhabit by turning marshy waste land into useful property. They use every resource at their disposal to improve their lives. Slum women have the ability to find alternatives to their current reality but they need support and empowerment to do this. Centres that are independent entities built by the commitment of slum women and their communities will be investments in the future of India. Centres that can curb violence and the propagation of the social ills that will inevitably interfere with the middle and upper classes, can only be considered an investment.

Slum are a reality of urbanization and industrialization and Counseling and Guidance Centres are an effective way to empower women, to provide hope where there is none, and guidance to those who need it. Most importantly centres will serve to develop a sense of community and consciousness within the slums. A holistic approach is long overdue; Counseling and Guidance Centres for women are clearly an immediate imperative.

REFERENCES

Anita, The HCM Rajasthan State Institute of Public Administration (ed.). Women's Quest For Equality, Jaipur, 1991.

Gulati, Leela. Profiles in Female Poverty. New Delhi; Hindusthani Publishing Corporation, 1981.

Haldule, S.B. "Networking The NGOs – Some Suggestions", Joint Council of Citizens – Pune, Third Information Bulletin, Pune: Dr. Krishnabai Nimbkar, May, 1993, p.19-21.

Harriss, Barbara, S. Gahan, R.H. Cassan (eds.). Poverty in India: Research & Policy. Bombay: Oxford University Press, 1992.

Jayaswal, R. "Psyche of Slum Dwellers : Some Emerging Patterns". Man in India, Vol. 73, 2, June 1993.

Madan, G.R. Indian Social Problems : Social Disorganisation and Reconstruction. New Delhi : Allied Publishers, 1982.

Nimbkar, Krishnabai. "What It Aims At", Joint Council of Citizens – Pune, First Information Bulletin. Pune : Dr.Krishnabai Nimbkar, February, 1992, P. 7-24.

Rao, K. Ranga and M.S.A. Rao. Cities and Slums : A Study of Squatters' Settlements in the City of Vijayawada, New Delhi : Concept Publishing Company, 1984.

Seabrook, Jeremy, Life and Labour in a Bombay Slum. London: Quartet Books Ltd., 1987.

Tribhuwan Robin D., Consulting Anthropologist, C-2 West View Society, Salisbury Park, Pune, India. Numerous Discussions and Field Trips, Sept. to Nov. 1993. (Discussions)

Tribhuwan, Robin D. and P. Tribhuwan, 1994, "Community Development : An Integrated Effort to Enable People to Help Themselves. In Journal of Rural Development, Vol. 13 (1). pp.133-137, NIRD, Hyderabad.

Varma, Sudhir "Status of Women in India, Policy Planning and The Implementation Machinery : Some Crucial Issues", Women's Quest for Equality. Published by : Anita, The HCM Rajasthan State Institute of Public Administration, Jaipur, 1991, pp. 57-67.

33

Involvement of Slum Women in Plan Process

– Dr. **M.L. Santhanam**

Introduction

The cause and consumer of the fruits of development are people and it is imperative that any programme planned for their welfare should necessarily involve them. The national and international agencies have recognized this fact and stressed the need for organizing the people for development activities. Based upon the various studies and experiences, it is often emphasized that the individual approach to any development or welfare programme need to be substituted by group ventures and collective action to project the beneficiaries from the adverse operational forces. (Santhanam, 1985).

In the context of rural development, the World Conference on Agrarian Reforms and Rural Development (WCARRD) while stressing for growth with equity also emphasized that development would succeed only by involving the rural poor as much as possible in the development process viz., policy making, planning and implementation. The Conference also highlighted the importance of organizing the rural poor as the best mechanism for involving them for development, since they make it possible for people to participate in the systems governing them, which is a fundamental human right. (FAO, 1984 quoted).

Social Change

When we talk about development, the underlining concept is to bring about social change in the community. Analysis of the steps or the patterns of process involved in community change has been attempted by several writers most of whom have concentrated on change in smaller rural communities rather than large urban areas. As a result several action models have developed. (Clinard, 1966). The model suggested by Sehnert (1961) considers the process of social change involving the following activities: *(i)* initiation of idea; *(ii)* preliminary study; *(iii)* planning and establishment of goals; *(iv)* establishment of a structure to co-ordinate the development process; *(v)* training and election of leaders; *(vi)* operational period in which action is undertaken; and *(vii)* continuation with evaluation and follow up.

An action model developed by Taylor and others (1965) suggested the following steps: *(i)* systematic discussion of commonly recognized needs by the members of the community; *(ii)* systematic planning by the residents for first self-help undertaking selected by the community; *(iii)* almost complete mobilization and harnessing of the physical, economic and social potentialities of the community and the development of group aspirations. Lippitt and others (1958) have outlined six phases of planned change, viz.: *(i)* the client system discovers the need for help sometimes with stimulation by the change agent; *(ii)* the helping relationship is established and defined; *(iii)* the change problem is identified and clarified; *(iv)* alternative possibilities for change are examined; *(v)* change is generalized and stabilized; and *(vi)* the helping relationship ends, or different type of continuing relationship is defined.

Concept of Planning and Development

Planning may be defined as an organized, conscious and continued attempt to select the best available alternatives to achieve goals. Planning involves economizing of scarce resources, human, natural, capital and other resources. (Shah, 1972)

A plan's success depends on public acceptance of its objectives. If planners fail to include those who will execute the plan in the plan process it is not likely that the plan may be successfully implemented. Of course the quantitative data viz., the targets may be achieved but the desired social impact in terms of social change will not occur.

The first phase of any project is planning, appraisal and design, Within this phase, there are three basic tasks: *(i)* the identification and formulation of the project; *(ii)* the design of the project. The basic aim of all plans is to achieve welfare of the people. This can be achieved by integrating the social planning which caters to the needs of the particular community and viewing planning as a bottom up approach rather than top down approach. This is particularly true of not only rural communities but also urban areas. In the context of urban community development Sanders (quoted by Shaha, 1990) is of the opinion that the term Community Development is a comprehensive one which may be viewed as process focusing on changing social relations, where community may be accustomed to decision making by few leaders. In the process of community development, the community makes decisions by themselves about matters of common concern. This concept has been emphasized as early as 1980, in the Third Five year plan which emphasized the need for each city to mobilize its own resources to help create better conditions for its citizens.

A Rural-Urban Relationship Committee was set up to examine the role of Municipal Government, which reported lack of awareness among people that municipality was there to serve their needs. The report suggested a need for constant discussion of local problems with the people so as to help them to verbalize their felt needs, motivate change and encourage them their own initiative in planning and carrying out improvements in various projects. (Shah 1990). Even though it is popularly said that India lives in its villages, the alarming growth of urban population indicates the fast changing urban scene in India. The following table indicates the growth of urban population from 1951 to 1991:

Year	Urban Population as Percentage of Total Population
1951	17.29
1961	17.97
1971	19.91
1981	23.34
1991	25.72

Individual Vs. Group Action

In many situations, individual action cannot produce result. This is true of the weaker section/population and hence, a group approach is a more effective proposition. This is particularly a case with a woman both in rural areas as well as in urban slums. Women could not take advantage of various development programmes planned and implemented for their welfare. But everyone recognizes the potential of the women power and the need to get women organized for collective action. The question is how to bring about women to participate in the programmes.

Ever since, the planning exercise began in India, the slogan is need based area specific plan, but what was really happening is the top down approach where the bureaucrats, administrators and planners, draw plans and programmes to the areas of which they have little or no knowledge. The old saying that the plans prepared in the air conditioned rooms of the state head quarters to be implemented in the remote areas of the state is still hold good. The reason given by them is that the people are not capable of designing the plan for them, and considered the would be beneficiaries as only receivers of the programmes. In the words of Chambers, (1989) "I manage, you participate" has been the dominate underlining principal of involvement behind the government projects. The primary step in securing involvement of people particularly women is to bring about a change in the attitude of officials both government and the non-government. People should not be looked upon merely as those dependent on relief to be given by that government or other agencies but on the contrary they should be viewed as executors of their development programmes with necessary facilities provided by the implementing agencies to carry out their plan of action.

It was only during the Sixth Five Year Plan, the Government of India for the first time devoted a whole chapter to Women's Development. It spoke of the need to inspire women with self-confidence and to increase their managerial and supervisory skills. The Seventh Plan also had a similar chapter. An exclusive department of Women and Children was set up at the end of the International Decade of Women to emphasize the importance given to women and their involvement in programmes.

Involvement of Women – Suggested Strategies

There are a number of studies to show that women can effectively participate and reap the fruits of the efforts. In the field of education Mahila Samakhya Programme implemented by Government of India (1991) is an example of where women organized themselves to remove illiteracy. In a study, Mukherjee (1993) points out that if rural women are able to participate in planning, decision making and implementing different programmes the results are expected to be much better and practical.

Based on the studies on rural communities (Santhanam, 1982; 1984; 1984a) and the experience gained by the author in working with non-governmental organisations, an attempt is made to suggest an approach to involve slum women in plan process.

The premises presented by the author in a paper presented in this volume give clues for possible strategies which one might adopt. The following are the few strategies suggested:

1. One of the most important strategies would be, that the planning process should be of "bottom-up" approach, i.e., start from where the people are. The user of the programme should also be the decision maker of the programme. Hence the present "top-down" approach where the programmes/schemes are formulated at higher levels for the people in the rural areas should be changed to an approach called "bottom-up" with "support-down" where the slum women plan the programme based on their need and the officials concerned given them support in the form of guidance so that the people can plan the programmes meaningfully.

2. Approach to the person should be based on the concept of "total person". This requires an integrated approach of economic and welfare oriented programmes. In this, the role of external agency is to develop the "self" of the individual.
3. Before organizing the slum women, the officials (both government and non-government) need to be convinced with regard to the potential for and capacity of people to deal with their problems. Once this is done. The officials would build community consultations into the planning process and become participatory in their approach to the problem.
4. Developing a sense of ownership and responsibility for a programme is yet another strategy. To develop such feelings, the outside agency should be prepared to make the community responsible for certain activities and gradually withdraw from the scene.
5. There is a feeling of dependency on the government that it would do everything for the people and they are only to receive the benefits which have been nurtured over the decades. Hence, a process of unlearning of this idea should be initiated, which would start a thinking process that people are important and they can bring about a change in the community, both social and economic.

The following steps are suggested, in operational zing the above strategies which the Urban Development Worker can adopt by organizing Vikas Mandals (Citizen Development Councils), Vikas Parishads (Neighbourhood Councils), Mahila Samitis (Women's Councils), and Mohalla Committees (Clinard, 1966):

1. Build up a rapport with the local people of the area where the implementing agency would like to have a programme is the foremost step for brining people together for action.
2. To make an assessment of the local needs by conducting a survey with the help of the local people themselves. This survey would also find out the resources available in the community, social structure and the existence of various groups in the area.
3. Once the assessment of local needs are made, the people of the area need to be educated about various schemes available for their development and also their slum area. Hence a sound information dissemination system needs to be developed. It has been found from studies that because of the existing illiteracy, there is less mass media contact and a low awareness and contact with officials. People's involvement in activity is influenced by literacy and therefore education, formal or informal, should be made available to all to enhance their capacity to plan, initiate, implement and follow-up the schemes.
4. Organising the women is to be done through a process of conscientization so that they become aware of their rights and privileges

as per the law and also their duties and responsibilities. This step is essential because the local power structure would play a role in not allowing the women to get the information necessary for action. Added to this, the fatalistic attitude of the women, their dependency on the men, cultural barriers and lack of faith in the government programme deter them from participation. They always look upon their men folk for advice and guidance. In these circumstances. It is proposed to organize small homogeneous groups, whose needs, requirements and social positions are almost equal, and it is an effective starting point to give the least advantaged groups their own organisation. These small groups may be classified based on land holdings, income, social status/caste or a combination of these. These groups need to be harnessed. It is necessary to work with several small groups till they become strong enough to come into the larger organisations.

5. To work with these small groups, make them identify the needs, priorities, plan and initiate action for their own development and also their area. The implementing agency should act as a catalyst in the group for their activities. Emotional and psychological support need to be given constantly because the people have organized themselves breaking the hierarchical nature of the existing social structure.
6. To identify the leaders of the group because whenever and wherever a group emerges, a leader also emerges along with the group. The potential leaders should be identified by the group in terms of their capability and initiative to take action.
7. To provide adequate training facilities to the leaders as well as group members so as to enable them to understand and do things effectively and efficiently.
8. To form a small committee (a functional group) of the larger community group which would be responsible for planning and implementation of the programmes. This committee will be accountable to the people in the entire plan process.
9. To make the committee aware of the allocated budget for programmes so that the planning process would be meaningful.
10. To inform the progress of the programme to the people at periodic intervals. This would be a continuous process. It is always found that the knowledge of results of the efforts is a motivating factor.

REFERENCES

Chamber Robert et. al., To The Hands of the Poor – Water and Trees, Oxford and IBH Publishing Co., New Delhi, 1989.

Clinard, M.B., Slums and Community Development : Experiments in Self-help, The Free Press, New York, 1966.

F.A.O. Organising for Change : The People's Participation Programme, 1984. (Quoted)

Government of India, Mahila Samakhya : A complication from Reports, Dept. of Education, Ministry of HRD, 1991.

India, Planning Commission, Third Five Year Plan, New Delhi, 1961.

India, Planning Commission, Sixth Five Year Plan, New Delhi, 1985.

India Planning Commission, Seventh Five Year Plan, New Delhi, 1985.

Lippitt, R., et.al., The Dynamics of Planned Change: A Comparative Study of Principles and Techniques, Harcourt, Brass and World, Inc., New York, 1958.

Mukherjee, Neela, "Women's Participation and Jawahar Rozgar Yojana", Yojana September, 15, 1993

Purao, Prema, "Women's Participation in Policy and Decision Making Process", Reading Material of the Court on Involvement of Women in Plan Process, Feb, 28th March 05 1994, YASHADA, Pune.

Santhanam, M.L., et. al., "Human and Social Factors in People's Participation", Journal of Rural Development, Vol. 1., No. 5 Sept. 1982.

Santhanam, M.L., et.al., "Community Participation – A Case Study", Social Change, Vol. 14, No. 2, June 1984.

Santhanam, M.L., et.al., "People's Participation : Some Psychological Dimensions", Journal of Rural Development, Vol. 3, No. 4, July 1984.

Santhanam, M.L., "Strategies of Organising the Rural Poor for Development", Partnership in Progress – Issues 11, Luthern World Service, Calcutta, June 1985.

Sehnert, F.H., A Functional Framework for the Action Process in Community Development Carbondale, Dept. of Commerce Development, Southern Illinois University, 1996.

Shah, Kırtee, Community Participation in the Hyderabad Urban Community Development Project, Economic Development Institute, The World Bank, New York, 1990.

Shah, S.H., "Sectoral Planning in India" in Lalit K. Sen (Ed) Readings on Micro-level Planning and Rural Growth Centres, N.I.R.D., Hyderabad 1972.

Taylor, C.C., et. al., India's Roots of Democracy, A Sociological Analysis of Rural India's Experience in Planned Development since Independence, Orient Longmans, Bombay 1965.

Educating Youth on HIV and AIDS
An Imperative Need

– Dr. **Pranali K. Patil**

Introduction

The youth of India have great creative energy with the positive potential to take them to spiritual heights. If human creativity is a special quality, then the "Never say die!" spirit is its apex. Demographically, today's India is at its youngest best and has the power to meet any challenge with the collective consciousness and effort of all people, especially young people. Swami Vivekananda believed that working for any social change required massive energy and spirit. Hence, he requested the youth to amplify both their mental energies and physical fitness. What Vivekananda wanted from the youth were 'muscles of iron' and 'nerves of steel'. Today, the youth are exceptionally responsive and they just need to be encouraged in their quest for justice for common benefit. Swami Vivekananda was the and is not only the medium; he is himself the message as well for the youth of India. This is the perfect time when youth is alert and aware and provoked by the environment and lack of values. India is a nation facing incredible challenges. Here we want to discuss on HIV Aids among youth in India (Mithun Dey).

According to Survey results, reported in the Financial Express, on March 26th, 2010: India's youth population grew at over 2 per cent to 459 million in 2009 from 390 million in the 2001 census, while the literate youth population grew at a more rapid 2.5 per cent to 333 million from 273 million. Growth was faster in urban India (3.15% a year) than in rural India (2.11%).

Of the country's total youth population of 459 million, literate youth constitute around three-fourths, numbering 333 million. Literate youth in rural India number 207 million (62.1% of the total) and 126 million (or, 37.9%) in urban areas. A large proportion, over 41 per cent, is in the older 25-35 age group, followed by teenagers (36.7%), with the rest in the20-24 age bracket (22.1%).

HIV/AIDS in India

Acquired Immune deficiency Syndrome (AIDS) is a deadly, new sexually transmitted disease now spreading rapidly in much of the world. The First AIDS patients were detected in New York City in the year 1981 and now there are more than two core patients around the world. Every day, on an average 10,000 people is affected with AIDS (HIV-Virus). Aids result from a viral infection that damages the immune system. The damage immune system cannot protect the body against even simple infections let alone cancers and this will leads to death. At present Heterosexual or Homosexual, intercourse is the major way through which AIDS is transmitted. In some countries, Condoms provide the best protection against sexually transmitted Aids. AIDS can be transmitted from mother to fetus during pregnancy or childbirth. Mostly AIDS cases are occurring among sexually active person. India is one of the largest and most populated countries in the world, with over one billion inhabitants. Of this number, it's estimated that around 2.4 million Indians are currently living with HIV.

AIDS is the name of a most dreaded disease, and the most understand as well. And the acronym represents "Acquired Immune-deficiency syndrome" caused by the HIV virus which stands for the "Human Immunodeficiency Virus." AIDS is currently considered incurable; where treatments are unavailable (mostly in poorer countries) most sufferers die within in a few years of diagnosis. Recent estimates suggest that of all people living with HIV in the world, 6 out of every 10 men, 8 out of every 10 women, and 9 out of every 10 children are in Sub-Saharan Africa. These figures provide sufficient evidence to make HIV/AIDS both a regional and a national priority.

Acquired Immune deficiency Syndrome (AIDS) is a deadly, new sexually transmitted disease now spreading rapidly in much of the world Jain, Jacob, and Gerald, (1994). The First AIDS patients were detected in New York City in the year 1981 and now there are more than two core patients around the world. Every day, on an average 10,000 people is affected with AIDS (HIV-Virus). Aids result from a viral infection that damages the immune system. The damage immune system cannot protect the body against even simple infections and this will leads to death. India is one of the largest and most populated countries in the world, with over one billion inhabitants. Of this number, it's estimated that around 2.4 million Indians are currently living with HIV Biswas, (2010).

The History of HIV/AIDS in India

At the beginning of 1986, despite over 20,000 reported AIDS cases worldwide, India had no reported cases of HIV or AIDS. There was recognition, though, that this would not be the case for long, and concerns were raised about how India would cope once HIV and AIDS cases started to emerge. One report, published in a medical journal in January 1986, stated: "Unlike developed countries, India lacks the scientific laboratories, research facilities, equipment, and medical personnel to deal with an AIDS epidemic. In addition, factors such as cultural taboos against discussion of sexual practices, poor coordination between local health authorities and their communities, widespread poverty and malnutrition, and a lack of capacity to test and store blood would severely hinder the ability of the Government to control AIDS if the disease did become widespread.

India's first case of HIV was diagnosed among sex workers in Chennai, Tamil Nadu. It was noted that contact with foreign visitors had played a role in initial infections among sex workers, and as HIV screening centers were set up across the country. There were calls for visitors to be screened for HIV. Gradually, these calls subsided as more attention was paid to ensuring that HIV screening was carried out in blood banks. In 1987 a National AIDS Control Programme was launched to co-ordinate national responses. Its activities covered surveillance, blood screening, and health education. By the end of 1987, out of 52,907 who had been tested, around 135 people were found to be HIV positive and 14 had AIDS. Most of these initial cases had occurred through heterosexual sex, but at the end of the 1980s a rapid spread of HIV was observed among injecting drug users in Manipur, Mizoram and Nagaland - three north-eastern states of India bordering Myanmar (Burma). At the beginning of the 1990s, as infection rates continued to rise, responses were strengthened. In 1992 the government set up NACO (the National AIDS Control Organisation), to oversee the formulation of policies, prevention work and control programmes relating to HIV and AIDS. In the same year, the government launched a Strategic Plan for HIV prevention. This plan established the administrative and technical basis for programme management and also set up State AIDS bodies in 25 states and 7 union territories. It was able to make a number of important improvements in HIV prevention such as improving blood safety.

At the beginning of 1986, despite over 20,000 reported AIDS cases worldwide (NFHS-3 2005-06), India had no reported cases of HIV or AIDS. The factors such as cultural taboos against discussion of sexual practices, poor coordination between local health authorities and their communities, widespread poverty and malnutrition, and a lack of capacity to test and store blood would severely hinder the ability of the Government to control AIDS if the disease did become widespread Ministry of Health and Family Welfare (May, 2007). At the beginning of the 1990s, as infection rates continued to rise, responses were strengthened. In 1992 the government set up NACO (the National AIDS Control Organisation), to oversee the formulation of policies, prevention work and control programmes relating to HIV and AIDS. In the same year, the government launched a Strategic Plan for HIV prevention.

There was recognition, though, that this would not be the case for long, and concerns were raised about how India would cope once HIV and AIDS cases started to emerge. One report, published in a medical journal in January 1986, stated: "Unlike developed countries, India lacks the scientific laboratories, research facilities, equipment, and medical personnel to deal with an AIDS epidemic. In addition, factors such as cultural taboos against discussion of sexual practices, poor coordination between local health authorities and their communities, widespread poverty and malnutrition, and a lack of capacity to test and store blood would severely hinder the ability of the Government to control AIDS if the disease did become widespread."

Later in the year, India's first cases of HIV were diagnosed among sex workers in Chennai, Tamil Nadu. Time magazine (1986, 1st September), It was noted that contact with foreign visitors had played a role in initial infections among sex workers, and as HIV screening centre's were set up across the country there were calls for visitors to be screened for HIV. Gradually, these calls subsided as more attention was paid to ensuring that HIV screening was carried out in blood banks. NACO (2005), Kakar and Kakar, (2001).

In 1987 a National AIDS Control Programme was launched to co-ordinate national responses. Its activities covered surveillance, blood screening, and health education. Panda S. (2002), by the end of 1987, out of 52,907 who had been tested, around 135 people were found to be HIV positive and 14 had AIDS NACO (2007). Most of these initial cases had occurred through heterosexual sex, but at the end of the 1980s a rapid spread of HIV was observed among injecting drug users (IDUs) in Manipur, Mizoram and Nagaland - three north-eastern states of India bordering Myanmar (Burma) Nath, (1998).

At the beginning of the 1990s, as infection rates continued to rise, responses were strengthened. In 1992 the government set up NACO (the National AIDS Control Organisation), to oversee the formulation of policies, prevention work and control programmes relating to HIV and AIDS. In the same year, on May 22, 2001 the government launched a Strategic Plan, the National AIDS Control Programme (NACP) for HIV prevention. This plan established the administrative and technical basis for programme management and also set up State AIDS Control Societies (SACS) in 25 states and 7 union territories. It was able to make a number of important improvements in HIV prevention such as improving blood safety.

What is HIV/AIDS?

Acquired immune deficiency syndrome or acquired immunodeficiency syndrome (AIDS) is a disease of the human immune system caused by the human immunodeficiency virus (HIV).This condition progressively reduces the effectiveness of the immune system and leaves individuals susceptible to opportunistic infections and tumors. The virus breaks down the body's immune system. It destroys the body's ability to fight infection and illness. By pre-venting HIV infection, you can prevent AIDS. HIV is transmitted through direct contact of a mucous membrane or the bloodstream with a bodily fluid containing HIV, such as blood, semen, vaginal fluid, preseminal fluid, and milk. This transmission can involve anal, vaginal or oral sex, blood transfusion, contaminated hypodermic needles, exchange between mother and baby during pregnancy, childbirth, breastfeeding or other exposure to one of the above bodily fluids. AIDS is now a pandemic. AIDS was first recognized by the U.S. Centers for Disease Control and Prevention in 1981 and its cause, HIV, identified in the early 1980s. Although treatments for AIDS and HIV can slow the course of the disease, there is currently no vaccine or cure. Antiretroviral treatment reduces both the mortality and the morbidity of HIV infection, but these drugs are expensive and routine access to antiretroviral medication is not available in all countries. Due to the difficulty in treating HIV infection, preventing infection is a key aim in controlling the AIDS pandemic, with health organisations promoting safe sex and needle-exchange programmes in attempts to slow the spread of the virus.

HIV Affects the Body

A healthy body has CD4 helper lymphocyte cells (CD4 cells). These cells help the immune system function normally and fight off certain kinds of infections. They do this by acting as messengers to other types of immune system cells, telling them to become active and fight against an invading germ. HIV attaches to these CD4 cells. The virus then infects the cells and uses them as a place to multiply. In doing so, the virus destroys the ability of the infected cells to do their job in the immune system. The body then loses the ability to fight many infections. Because their immune systems are weakened, people who have AIDS are unable to fight off many infections, particularly tuberculosis and other kinds of otherwise rare infections of the lung (such as Pneumocystis carinii pneumonia), the surface covering of the brain (meningitis), or the brain itself (encephalitis). People who have AIDS tend to keep getting sicker, especially if they are not taking antiviral medications properly. AIDS can affect every body system. The immune defect caused by having too few CD4 cells also permits some cancers that are stimulated by viral illness to occur - some people with AIDS get forms of lymphoma and a rare tumor of blood vessels in the skin called Kaposi's sarcoma.

Process of Infection

The AIDS virus causes a weakness of the Immune system. When it infects the body it prefers to attach certain cells of your defense system these cells are called helper T cells which are a fundamental part of our immune system. The AIDS virus is fully specialized on these white blood cells since these helper T cells have CD4 molecules on the surface to which the AIDS virus binds. The Aids virus, to put it simply consists of genetic information on the inside and protective outer shell of protein and glycoprotein. Since virus use the host cell's resources for reproduction, they don't need to contribute much it. That's why they are smaller than host cells, E.g. helper, Cells in the host cell's nuclease. Displayed in blue here, there are more than T cells. In the host cell's nucleus, displayed in blue here, there are more than 100000 times as much genetic information stored then under the protein shells for the AIDS virus once the cell has been infected. Infection proceeds in the manner. The virus Anchors itself to a special protein (CD4) on the surface of the helper T cells Thus causes of virus membrane to fuse with the host cells membrane. This way to genetic information gets inside the cell.

The AIDS virus belongs to a special group of viruses. Its genetic information is not encoded as DNA, but instead of RNA ribonucleic Acid and therefore has to be reversing Tran scripted into DNA. The tools for this are delivered by the host cell itself, except for a little helper protein (reverse transcriptase) which the virus has been brought itself. The DNA is now legible for the cell as a transfer to the nucleus. This process already finishes I half of a day after infection. The foreign piece of DNA is than inserted randomly into the host DNA and it is now ready to be transcribed. At the binging of AIDS, The Viral DNA is being transcribed to form many RNA molecules the single which causes this is unknown. The accruing RNA is carried to the cytoplasm of the cell, where it can start making proteins. The Ran with the help of the resources begins to make many copies of the different part of the AIDS virus. After everything has been copied, thousands of bubbles like these are produced and migrate to the cell membrane surface and fuse with it .Finally copy of RNA genetic information is added to the bubbles. Than this section of cell membrane turn inside out and new virus leave the cell. Naturally, the release of the new AIDS of the viruses weakened the host cell which soon dies. That's how the Immune system weak and AIDS starts.

Signs and Symptoms

Severe symptoms of HIV infection and AIDS may not appear for as long as 10 years (or more for some people). The people with HIV may not notice any signs that they have the virus for years leading up to that how long it takes for symptoms of HIV/AIDS to appear varies from person to person. Some people may feel and look healthy for years while they are infected with HIV. It is still possible to infect others with HIV, even if the person with the virus has absolutely no symptoms. You cannot tell simply by looking at someone whether he or she is infected. Doctors diagnose someone with AIDS when that person's blood lacks the number of CD4 cells required to fight infections. Doctors also diagnose AIDS if the person has signs of specific illnesses or diseases that occur in people with HIV infection.

- Extreme weakness or fatigue;
- Rapid weight loss;
- Frequent fevers that last for several weeks with no explanation;
- Heavy sweating at night;
- Swollen lymph glands;
- Minor infections that cause skin rashes and mouth, genital, and anal Sores;
- White spots in the mouth or throat;
- Chronic diarrhoea;
- A cough that won't go away;
- Trouble remembering things;
- In girls, severe vaginal yeast infections that don't respond to usual treatment.

Primary Routes of Transmission

1. *Sexual:* 0.1 per cent-1 per cent risk, 70 per cent-80 per cent of all global HIV infection.
2. *Vertical:* 10 per cent-30 per cent risk, In utero, during labour and delivery, and through breastfeeding.
3. *Parenteral:* Blood transfusions (estimated risk from a single unit of HIV-infected whole blood is over 90%).
4. Needle sharing among drug users (risk of 0.1%, responsible for 5%-10% of global HIV infection) and needle pricks among health workers.

Stages of HIV Disease

- Acute infection (2-8 weeks)
- Asymptomatic (2-10 years)
- Symptomatic
- Late

Disease Recognition through HIV Testing

- Negative during first 3 months after infection (window period)
- Two tests required plus a third to confirm if results conflict
- Repeated test recommended 3 months after initial test
- False positives very possible in children under 18 months old

Types of HIV Test

Blood tests for antibodies against HIV

- Enzyme immune assay/enzyme-linked immuno sorbent assay (ELISA) is most common
- Western blot is more specific than ELISA and used as a confirmatory test
- Radio immuno precipitation assay (RIPA) is expensive and used as a confirmatory test when antibodies low
- Dot-blot immunobinding assay is a rapid screening blood test that is cost effective
- Polymerase chain reaction (PCR)looks for HIV genetic information

Urine tests

Tests for Antibodies in Urine

- Not as sensitive as blood tests
- Enzyme immune assay
- Western blot
- Oral fluid tests

Tests for Antibodies in Oral Fluids

- Enzyme Immune Assay
- Western blot

A retrovirus, the Human Immunodeficiency Virus (HIV) was identified in 1983 as the pathogen responsible for the Acquired Immunodeficiency Syndrome (AIDS). AIDS is characterized by changes in the population of T-cell lymphocytes that play a key role in the immune defense system. In the infected individual, the virus causes a depletion of T-cells, called "T-helper cells",

Indian Scenario at National Level

The 'Time of AIDS' in India had its beginning in 1986, when serological testing found 10 of 102 female sex workers in Chennai (Madras) HIV positive (John et al., 1987). The earliest confirmed cases of HIV infections were concentrated in Chennai, Tamilnadu and also in Mumbai, Maharashtra. Throughout the 1980s and early 1990s some governmental and private health authorities downplayed the significance of the spreading epidemic. In those early days it was thought to be a 'Western Problem', which would not affect India very much because (it was believed) of lower rates of multi-partner sexual activities and other risky behaviours among Indians. On the other hand, in 1986 the Indian Council of Medical research (ICMR) had already set up 30 IV testing centre has to monitor the spread of infection (Nag, 1996).

The evidence of HIV was first documented in Chennai in southern India in 1986. From then until March 2004, 68,809 AIDS cases have been reported to the National AIDS Control Organisation. Heterosexual route is the predominant mode of transmission, followed by injecting drug use. Nationwide, annual HIV sentinel surveillance (HSS) was started in 1998 and so far six rounds have been completed. The numbers of ANC sentinel sites have increased considerably over the years; however, the vulnerable population groups such as MSMs, IDUs and CSWs remain largely underrepresented (http://www.naco.nic.in). Soon after the first case were identifies, a National AIDS Control Committee was established. A Central AIDS Cell was established in New Delhi, and all the states were encouraged to develop plans for AIDS surveillance (Sethi, 1999). The next step was a National AIDS Control Programme, developed in 1987 and reviewed in consultation with the World Health Organisation (WHO in 1990).

New, more accurate estimates of HIV indicate that approximately 2.5 million (2 million: 3.1 million) people in India were living with HIV in 2006, with national adult HIV prevalence of 0.36 per cent. Although the proportion of people living with HIV is lower than previously estimated, India's epidemic continues to affect large numbers of people. The revised estimates are based on an expanded and improved surveillance system, and the use of more robust and enhanced methodology. The inclusion of the results of the recent national household survey (the National Family Health Survey 3, conducted in 2005–2006) in the estimation process contributed significantly to the revised estimates. Over 100 000 people were tested for HIV in the survey which was the first national population based survey to include a component on HIV (NFHS-3, 2007). In addition, India has expanded its HIV sentinel surveillance system in recent years and the number of surveillance sites increased from 155 in 1998 to 1120 in 2006. Data from pregnant women attending antenatal clinics, people attending sexually transmitted infections clinics and population groups that are at a higher risk of exposure to HIV are included in the surveillance.(AIDS Epidemics Update, 2007)

In 2006 UNAIDS estimated that there were 5.6 million people living with HIV in India, which indicated that there were move people with HIV in India than in any other country in the world. However, NACO disputed this estimate, and claimed that the actual figure was lower. In 2007, using a more effective surveillance system, UNAIDS and NACO agreed on a new estimate between 2-3.6 million people living with HIV. This puts India behind South Africa and Nigeria in numbers living with HIV (http://www.naco.nic.in). Recent estimates of HIV infection show that, of the 2.5 million PLHIV in 2006, 88.7 per cent are adults (15-49 yrs), 7.5 per cent are aged 50 and above, while 3.8 per cent are children (15 yrs). The proportion of infections among children and adults above 50 years age has been increasing during the past five years. Females constitute 39.3 per cent of the PLHA in the country. At the end of August 2006 total cumulative AIDS cases were 124995 out of which 36,750 were female (http:www.avert.org). Sexual transmission was 85 per cent, Mother to child transmission 4 per cent, Blood to blood products 2.0 per cent, Injecting drug users 2 per cent and from other sources 6 per cent.

Mode of transmission: HIV is transmitted from one person to another through the following modes.

1. **Blood transfusions**

HIV infection can occur in medical settings; for instance, through needles that have not been sterilized or through blood transfusions where infected blood is used. In wealthier countries this problem has virtually been eliminated, but in resource-poor communities it is still an issue. The largest scale case of infections among children resulting from contaminated injections and unscreened blood transfusion occurred in Romania between 1987 to 1991 when more than 10,000 babies and children were infected with HIV as a result of unsafe medical practices.

Unsafe blood transfusions have also led to hundreds of HIV infections in countries in the Central Asia region, namely Kazakhstan, Kyrgyzstan and Uzbekistan from 2006-2008. The widespread reuse of injection equipment as well as encouragement by doctors motivated by financial reasons to carry out 'unnecessary blood transfusions', led to the infection of at least 119 children in Kazakhstan and at least 150 in Uzbekistan from 2007-2008. Although official statistics claim that unsafe injections account for a small percentage (2.5%) of HIV infections in sub-Saharan Africa, this is contested by a number of researchers. HIV prevalence in children can be 1 to 3 times higher than that of pregnant women in antenatal clinics and in one study as many as a fifth of children who were not sexually active had HIV negative mothers

Suggesting that the children were infected through contaminated medical procedures.

1. **Injecting drug use**

In central and Eastern Europe, where injecting drug use fuels the spread of HIV, young people living on the street are found to be especially vulnerable to HIV through injecting drug use. In St Petersburg, a study of more than three hundred year olds living on the street found that 40 per cent of them were HIV positive. In Ukraine, one study found a variety of HIV risk behaviours like sharing needles and unprotected and forced sex were prevalent among year old street children, while a multicity study found an HIV prevalence of per cent among street youth (aged 15-24). Police harassment and the general attitude of society that sees street children as 'outcasts' and 'criminals' means that that they are difficult to reach with health and social services.

2. **Sexual transmission**

Sexual transmission does not account for a high proportion of child infections but in some countries, children are sexually active at an early age.

This is potentially conducive to the sexual spread of HIV among children, especially in areas where condom use is low and HIV prevalence is high. In sub-Saharan Africa 16 per cent of young females (aged 15-19) and 12 per cent of young males reported having sex before they were 15 in 2007. In Lesotho, these figures are 16 per cent and 30 per cent, respectively; in Kenya, 15 per cent and 31 per cent. In developing countries overall it is estimated that 6 per cent of boys and 11 per cent of girls have had sex by age 15. The lower the age of first sex, the higher the lifetime risk of HIV infection. This is because early sexual debut is often associated with older lifetime partners, higher rates of coerced sex and lower rates of condom usage. Children are also at risk of becoming infected with HIV through sexual abuse and rape. In some parts of Africa, the myth that HIV can be cured through sex with a virgin has led to rapes, sometimes of very young children by infected men - although whether or not this is a significant factor in child sexual abuse in the region is disputed. In some cases, young children are trafficked into sex work, which can put them at a very high risk of becoming infected with HIV.

Mother-to-Child Transmission of HIV

In 2011, UNAIDS produced 'The Global Plan towards the Elimination of New Infections among Children and Keeping Their Mothers Alive'. The plan recognizes the need to consider different ways of preventing MTCT, and to integrate HIV interventions into other family planning, maternal health and child health services. The following are broader strategies for preventing HIV among children: International HIV & AIDS charity Donate Fundraising. Global HIV/AIDS response: epidemic update and health sector progress towards universal access: progress report 2011 Joint monitoring tool on the health sector response to HIV/AIDS Global HIV/AIDS response: epidemic update and health sector progress towards universal access: progress report 2011. Each year, many children are newly infected with HIV, mainly through mother-to-child transmission. An overwhelming majority – more than 90 per cent of HIV infections in infants and children are passed on by mothers during pregnancy, labour, delivery or breastfeeding. Without any intervention, between 15 per cent and 45 per cent of infants born to mothers living with HIV will become infected (5-10 per cent during pregnancy, 10-20 per cent during labour and delivery and 5-20 per cent through breastfeeding). Approximately 50 per cent of infants infected with HIV from their mothers die before their second birthday. The transmission of HIV infection from mother to child can be sharply reduced if antiretroviral drugs are administered to a woman during pregnancy and delivery and to her infant shortly after birth.

Reducing HIV transmission from a pregnant woman living with HIV to her infant requires a range of interventions beginning with voluntary and confidential counseling and testing for pregnant women; followed by antiretroviral prophylaxis for pregnant women with HIV and their newborn baby or antiretroviral therapy for the mother if eligible; and safe delivery practices and guidance in selecting a suitable infant-feeding option in order to prevent mother-to-child transmission (PMTCT) of HIV. With growing political support for prevention of mother-to-child transmission, an important push is now being made to virtually eliminate mother-to-child transmission by 2015. Specific, time-bound targets have been developed at global level and adapted by countries to support this goal.

Children, HIV and AIDS

More than 1,000 children are newly infected with HIV every day, and of these, more than half will die as a result of AIDS because of a lack of access to HIV treatment. In addition, millions more children every year are indirectly affected by the epidemic as a result of the death and suffering caused in their families and communities. Preventing HIV infection, providing life prolonging treatment and relieving the impact of HIV and AIDS for children and their families and communities is possible. However, a lack of necessary investment and resources for adequate testing, antiretroviral drugs, and prevention programmes, as well as stigma and discrimination, mean children continue to suffer the consequences of the epidemic.

The Number of Infected Children

The figures below show the number of children (defined by UNAIDS as under-15s) directly affected by HIV and AIDS: At the end of 2010, there were 3.4 million children living with HIV around the world. An estimated 390,000 children became newly infected with HIV in 2010. The 1.8 million people who died of AIDS during 2010, one in seven were children. Every hour, around 30 children die as a result of AIDS. There are more than 16 million children under the age of 18 who have lost one or both parents to AIDS. Most children living with HIV/AIDS– almost 9 in 10 live in sub-Saharan Africa, the region of the world where AIDS has taken its greatest toll. In countries with an HIV prevalence of above 5 per cent, child mortality rates have not fallen in line with global trends. This is most probably due to the high risk of mortality associated with untreated HIV infection in young children.

HIV/AIDS Scenario at Maharashtra State Level

Mumbai is the capital of Maharashtra state and is the most populous city in India, with around 20 million inhabitants. Maharashtra State is a very large state of three hundred thousand square kilometers, with a total population of around 97 million. The HIV prevalence at antenatal clinics in Maharashtra has exceeded 1 per cent in all recent years, and surveys of female sex workers have found rates of infection above 20 per cent. Very high rates also found among injecting drug users and men who have sex with men.(http://www.avert.org/aidsindia.htm)

In Maharashtra estimated cases were 750,000 and Tested HIV positive cases were 1,33,676 (Aug '86 to April 2004). High prevalence districts (2003) in Maharashtra State were Mumbai, Pune, Sangli, Satara, Kolhapur, Thane, Solapur, Nagpur, Chandrapur, Nasik, Aurangabad. Contributing Factors to the HIV/AIDS in Maharashtra State are High Mobility, Migration, Trafficking, Gender disparities, education, health care, Myths and misconceptions, Stigma and discrimination, Domestic violence etc (Bhardwaj, 2006).

Statistics in Maharashtra

Mumbai is the capital city of Maharashtra state and is the most populous city in India, with around 20 million inhabitants. Maharashtra is a very large state of three hundred thousand square kilometers, with a total population of around 97 million. According to Sheela, (2010) the HIV prevalence at antenatal clinics in Maharashtra was 0.75 per cent in 2006, and surveys of female sex workers have found around 20 per cent to be infected. Similarly high rates are found among injecting drug users and men who have sex with men. The 2005-2006 survey found an infection rate of 0.62 per cent in the general population of Maharashtra. This state is home to around one in five of all people living with HIV+ in India. HIV/AIDS State wise statistics India 2010As per the HIV Estimations 2010, India is estimated to have 23.9 lakh people infected with HIV in 2009 at an estimated adult HIV prevalence of 0.31 per cent. Adult HIV prevalence among men is 0.36 per cent, while among women, it is 0.25 per cent.

Indian Scenario on HIV & AIDS

The spread of HIV in India has been diverse, with much of India having a low rate of infection and the epidemic being most extreme in the southern half of the country and in the far north-east. According to NACO, (2007) the highest HIV prevalence rates are found in Maharashtra, Andhra Pradesh and Karnataka in the south; and Manipur, Mizoram and Nagaland in the north-east. Four southern states (Andhra Pradesh, Maharashtra, Tamil Nadu and Karnataka) account for around 63 per cent of all people living with HIV+ in India. In the southern states, HIV is primarily spread through heterosexual contact, whereas infections are mainly found amongst injecting drug users and sex workers in the north-east. 2.4 million People living with HIV/AIDS and 15 year and above HIV prevalence is 0.3 per cent. Previously it was thought that around 5 million people were living with HIV in India - more than in any other country. It is now thought that around 2.4 million people in India are living with HIV (NFHS-3 2005-06).

HIV Prevalence Among Different Population Groups

HIV infections are especially increasing among young women and youth 63 per cent of HIV infections reported among 13-19 year olds are among women African Americans account for 67 per cent of HIV cases reported among 13-19 year Weinstock, H., et.al. (1999). the average HIV+ prevalence among women attending antenatal clinics in India is 0.60 per cent (UNAIDS/ WHO, 2005). Much higher rates are found among people attending sexually transmitted disease clinics (3.74%), female sex workers (4.90%), injecting drug users (6.92%) and men who have sex with men (6.41%). Rates vary widely between regions, and in 2006 were found to exceed 15 per cent among female sex workers in Maharashtra and Nagaland; injecting drug users in Chandigarh, Maharashtra, Manipur and Tamil Nadu; and men who have sex with men in Maharashtra and Nagaland Afsar, (2010).

It is now thought that around 2.39 million people in India are living with HIV. Of these, an estimated 39 per cent are female and 3.5 per cent are children. Time magazine (1986, 1st September), WHO (2007), 6th July International Institute for Population Sciences (IIPS) and Macro International (2007) 'National Family Health Survey (NFHS-3) 2005-06' Back-calculation suggests that HIV prevalence in India may have declined slightly in recent years, though the epidemic is still growing in some regions and population groups.

Treatment for People living with HIV

Antiretroviral drugs (ARVs), which can significantly delay the progression from HIV to AIDS – have been available in developed countries since 1996. Unfortunately, as in many resource-poor areas, access to this treatment is limited in India; an estimated 285,000 people were receiving free ARVs in 2009 NACO (2008). The totaled with the number receiving ARVs through the private sector, amounted to 320,000 people receiving ARVs in 2009. According to NACO, this represents just over half of the adults estimated to be in need of antiretroviral treatment in India. However, according to WHO's latest treatment guidelines (2010), which recommend starting treatment earlier, revised estimates may indicate that only around 1 in 4 people in need of HIV treatment are currently receiving it NACO (2010, April). While the coverage of treatment remains unacceptably low, improvements are being made. The government has started to expand access to ARVs in a number of areas; by November 2009 there were 266 reported sites providing antiretroviral therapy, UNGASS (2010, March 31st).

Increasing access to ARVs also means that an increasing number of people living with HIV in India are developing drug resistance. When HIV becomes resistant to the ARVs the treatment regimen needs to be changed to 'second-line' ARVs. As with many other parts of the world, second-line treatment in India is far more expensive than first-line treatment. In 2008, NACO began to roll out government funded second-line antiretroviral treatment in two centers in Mumbai and Chennai. However coverage remains limited; of the 3,000 who needed to be on second line treatment, about 970 were receiving it as of January 2010, NACO (2008).

Kaiser Daily HIV/AIDS Report (2009, 6th January) One reason for this is expense; second line ARV drugs, unlike first line ARVs, are not produced on a large scale in India due to patent issues that control drug pricing. Therefore, they can be 10 times more expensive than first line ARVs. Ironically, India is a major provider of cheap generic copies of ARVs to countries all over the world. However, the large scale of India's epidemic, the diversity of its spread, and the country's lack of finances and resources continue to present barriers to India's antiretroviral treatment programme. The Indian government has also been criticized for not providing palliative care for HIV patients. UNGASS (2010, March 31st) to read about the challenges faced in increasing access to antiretroviral drugs around the world, see our Universal access to AIDS treatment page.

NACO (2008), UNGASS (2010), India has a population of one billion, around half of whom are adults in the sexually active age group. The first AIDS case in India was detected in 1986 and since then HIV infection has been reported in all states and union territories. The spread of HIV in India has been uneven. Although much of India has a low rate of infection, certain places have been more affected than others. HIV epidemics are more severe in the southern half of the country and the far north-east. The highest estimated adult HIV prevalence is found in Manipur (1.40%), followed by Andhra Pradesh (0.90%), Mizoram (0.81%), Nagaland (0.78%), Karnataka (0.63%) and Maharashtra (0.55%). In the southern states, HIV is primarily spread through heterosexual contact. Infections in the north-east are mainly found amongst injecting drug users (IDUs) and sex workers. Unless otherwise stated, the data on this page has been taken from a 2008 report by the Indian government's AIDS organisation-NACO (National AIDS Control Organisation) Posted on February 9, 2011 by Abigail.

Human Clinical Study

98 per cent inhibition against the causative agent HIV has been recorded in the Anti-retroviral Activity Testing Drug Sensitivity Testing made in a lab studies, revealing the highest inhibition rate among any anti-retroviral medicines against HIV in vitro studies.

Clinical Observation

Drug Sensitivity Study

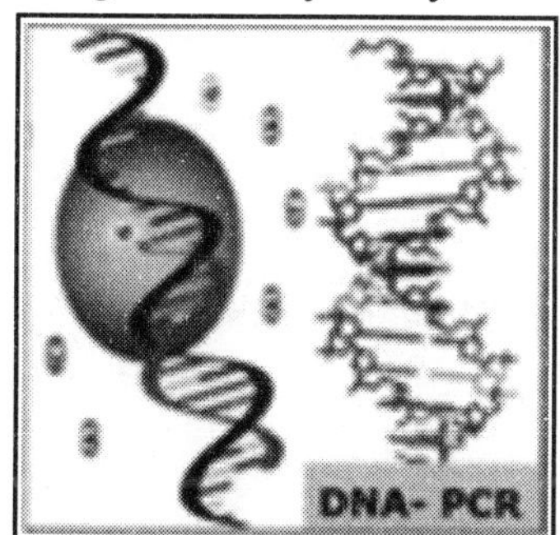

30 per cent increase in CD4 counts & 70 per cent decrease in RNA viral load Real time RT-PCR within first month of the treatment, and CD4 counts doubled & viral load down to less than detectable level within 3 months of the treatment in the patients possessing very high viral load counts.

Molecular Diagnostics

Viral Specific Antigen

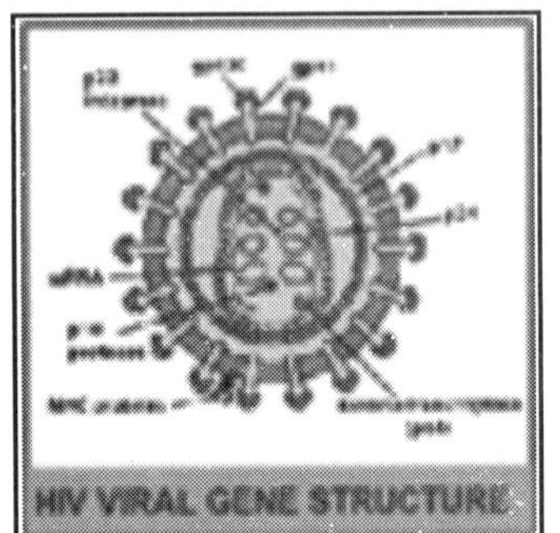
HIV VIRAL GENE STRUCTURE

The patients who were earlier confirmed positive through DNA PCR or Western blot antibodies test later after the treatment with this medicines has recorded 'Not Detected' in DNA-PCR Antigen test and the Sample of the patient is Negative for the presence of HIV.

Viral Structure Viral Specific Proteins

In the viral specific protein study the HIV-I intermediate Gag precursors P55, P39 and matrix protein P17 and Pol integrase P51 were found to be absent in patients after the treatment, thus indicating the absence in the process of new viral assembly of HIV in the body.

Prevention Education on Sexual Risk Factors: Today's youth need to be educated on prevention of sexual risk factors that result into a person-becoming victim of HIV/AIDS. Social science research has pointed out that several young migrants in the informal sector indulge into unsafe sex. Hence, it is necessary to educate both young males as well as females on the preventive aspects of AIDS and HIV. Studies also have reveals that the college and university students who migrate from their respective villages, districts, states and countries fall prey to the basic instinct of sex. It is observed that many of these students visit brothel and street based sex workers.

According to CDC's 2009 National Youth Risk Behaviour Survey (YRBS), many adolescents begin having sexual intercourse at early ages: 46.0 per cent of high school students have had sexual intercourse, and 5.9 per cent reported first sexual intercourse before the age of 13. Of the 34.2 per cent of students reporting sexual intercourse during the 3 months before the survey, 38.9 per cent did not use a condom. Young people with older sex partners may be at increased risk for HIV. HIV education needs to take place before young people engage in sexual behaviours that put them at risk. Parent communication and monitoring may play an important role in reaching youth early with prevention messages.

Male-to-male sex: CDC data have shown that young gay, bisexual, and other MSM, especially young African American and young Latino MSM, have high rates of new HIV infections. Another CDC study showed that young MSM and minority MSM were more likely to be unaware of their HIV infection, a situation that puts their health and the health of their partners at risk. Young MSM may be at risk because they have not always been reached by effective HIV interventions or prevention education—especially because some sex education programmes exclude information about sexual orientation. A CDC study of MSM in 15 cities found that 80 per cent had not been reached in the past year by HIV interventions known to be most effective. Young MSM may also have increased risk factors for HIV (such as risky sexual behaviours) due to isolation and lack of support.

Sexual abuse: Young adults, both male and female, who have experienced sexual abuse, are more likely to engage in sexual or drug-related risk behaviours that could put them at risk for HIV infection.

Sexually transmitted infections (STIs): The presence of an STI greatly increases a person's likelihood of acquiring or transmitting HIV. Some of the highest STI rates in the country are among young people, especially young people of minority races and ethnicities.

Substance Use: Young people in the US use alcohol, tobacco, and other drugs at high rates. CDC's 2009 National YRBS found that 24.2 per cent of high school students had had five or more drinks of alcohol in a row on at least 1 day during the 30 days before the survey, and 20.8 per cent had used marijuana at least one time during the 30 days before the survey. Both casual and chronic substance users are more likely to engage in high-risk behaviours, such as unprotected sex, when they are under the influence of drugs or alcohol. Runaways, homeless young people, and young persons who have become dependent on drugs are at high risk for HIV infection if they exchange sex for drugs, money, or shelter.

Lack of Awareness: Research has shown that a large proportion of young people are not concerned about becoming infected with HIV. This lack of awareness can translate into not taking measures that could protect their health. Abstaining from sex and drug use is the most effective way to avoid HIV infection, but adolescents need accurate, age-appropriate information about HIV and AIDS, how to reduce or eliminate risk factors, how to talk with a potential partner about risk factors and how to negotiate safer sex, where to get tested for HIV, and how to use a condom correctly. Parents also need to reinforce health messages, including how to protect oneself from HIV infection.

HIV/AIDS Education

HIV and AIDS education for youth plays a vital role in global efforts to end the AIDS epidemic. Despite the fact that HIV transmission can be prevented, each year hundreds of thousands of young people become infected with the virus. In 2009 alone, there were 890,000 new HIV infections amongst young people aged 15-24 UNAIDS/UNICEF (2010) and in 2010. 5 million 15-24 year olds were living with HIV. WHO/UNAIDS/UNICEF (2011) "In 2009 alone, there were 890,000 new HIV infections amongst young people aged 15-24."

Providing young people with basic AIDS education enables them to protect themselves from becoming infected. Youth are often particularly vulnerable to sexually transmitted HIV, and to HIV infection because of drug-use. Acquiring knowledge and skills encourages young people to avoid or reduce behaviours that carry a risk of HIV infection. UNESCO (2009, May), Even for young people who are not yet engaging in risky behaviours, AIDS education is important for ensuring that they are prepared for situations that will put them at risk as they grow older UNESCO, Director-general (2008), AIDS education also helps to reduce stigma and discrimination, by dispelling false information that can lead to fear and blame. This is crucial for prevention, as stigma often makes people reluctant to be tested for HIV and individuals that are unaware of their HIV infection are more likely to pass the virus on to others.

Educating young people about HIV and AIDS necessitates discussions about sensitive subjects such as sex and drug use. Many people believe that it is inappropriate to talk to young people about these subjects and fear that doing so will encourage young people to indulge in risky behaviours. Such attitudes are often based on moral or religious views rather than evidence, and severely limit AIDS education around the world. Substantial evidence shows that educating young people about safer sex and the importance of using condoms does not lead to increases in sexual activity S.L., (2008).

The belief that young people should only be taught about sex and drugs in terms of them being 'wrong' may perpetuate stigmatization of people who are living with HIV. If young people are taught that indulging in 'immoral' sex and drugs will lead to HIV infection, educators risk implying that anyone who has HIV is therefore involved in these 'immoral' activities. In order to prevent becoming infected with HIV, young people need comprehensive information about how HIV is transmitted and what they can do to stop themselves from becoming infected. This information should be delivered without moral judgment.

Schools play a pivotal role in providing AIDS education for young people. Not only do schools have the capacity to reach a large number of young people, but school students are particularly receptive to learning new information. Therefore, schools are a well-established point of contact through which young people can receive AIDS education. At the same time, in many countries HIV and AIDS are significantly weakening the capacity of the education sector, and greater investment in education is vital for the provision of effective HIV prevention for young people. The World Bank (2002), A UNESCO study in 2009 found that in Eastern and Southern Africa, children had 'low levels of knowledge' regarding HIV/AIDS which was attributed to, among other factors, lack of teacher training, lack of examination for students on the topic (and therefore little incentive to teach it) and unease teaching the subject resulting from embarrassment UNAIDS/UNICEF, (2010).

Teachers Training

AIDS education requires detailed discussions of subjects such as sex, death, illness and drug use. Teachers are not likely to have experience dealing with these issues in class, and require specialised training so they are comfortable discussing them without letting personal values conflict with the health needs of the students. UNESCO (2009, May), Teacher training is fundamental to the successful delivery of AIDS education in schools, and yet efforts to train teachers are often inadequate, if in place at all. For example, teachers in Malawi report not receiving any training on HIV and AIDS, and in Kenya many teachers have opted out of teaching about HIV and AIDS as a result of inadequate training. UNESCO (2008)

HIV/AIDS Education Outside the School

Although offering HIV/AIDS education at school is a principal method of reaching large numbers of young people, there are 75 million children around the world who are either unable to go to school or choose not to. In order to ensure that all young people are reached with basic AIDS education programmes that target youth outside of school are essential. The youth who are in school also benefit from receiving further information about HIV and AIDS from other sources, adding to and reinforcing what they learn in school. Families, friends, the wider community, mass media and popular culture all influence youth, and it is important that they convey accurate educational information about HIV and AIDS.

Tribal Development Programmes for Tribal Youth
An Overview

– Mr. **Azimuddin F. Sherkar**

Introduction

Government of Maharashtra through the Tribal Development Department is implementing several schemes for tribal youth. Some of the major ones are – Ashram Schools, Tribal Hostels, Scholarships Schemes, Income generation schemes under nucleus budget, under Article 275 of the Constitution of India, special Central Assistance Schemes etc. The present paper throws light on the 2 schemes namely pre-service training programmes where tribal youth are being groomed, oriented and trained to appear for the various competitive examinations held by MPSC and various other similar agencies. The second scheme is "Tribal Youth Leadership Programme". These two programmes are in force since 1985. Tribal Research and Training Institute, Pune is implementing these two schemes successfully.

Objectives of the Study

The main objective of this paper is to highlight two schemes that are being implemented by the Tribal Research and Training Institute, Pune for youth.

The Schemes

A. Appearance for various competitive examinations

1. *Preparation for appearance to various competitive examinations*

All the programmes related to competitive examinations are held in the Tribal Research and Training Institute, Maharashtra State, Pune at various points of time during the year. Total 5 batches are constituted for imparting training. In each batch 40 tribal youth are selected. The time span of each programme is of one month duration. In all 200 tribal youth are groomed, oriented and trained during the year. Formerly, the programme was conducted for two weeks duration; wherein, 12 batches consisting of 40 tribal youths were held. In other words, 480 youths were trained during the year. Formerly, the number of tribal youths for such type of training was big but the duration of the time limit was short i.e. of 2 weeks. Therefore, in such a short time span, the participant students could not get much benefit. Considering this situation, the time span was increased so that the quality training could be imparted to the participant students. It is observed, now, that during the span of 25 years, more than 20,000 have been trained so far by Tribal Research and Training Institute, Pune. Many of them have been successfully placed in various jobs.

2. *Facilities for the programme*

The tribal students selected from all over tribal areas of Maharashtra are reimbursed to and fro transportation charges. They are provided with free lodging and boarding amenities. Free reading material worth to Rs. 500/- to 900/- is distributed free of cost to each and every students. Experts from various fields having qualification and experience are roped in to groom these tribal youth on modern lines.

3. *Feedback from these students*

The tribal youth so groomed are required to submit their response regarding the utility of the training. It is observed that students who attend these training programmes have expressed their faith in this Institute's endeavour. They have appreciated the efforts of the Tribal Research and Training Institute, Pune and thanked the Government of Maharashtra for such type of trainings.

B. Tribal Youth Leadership Training Programmes

1. *The need for Tribal Youth Leadership Training Programmes*

There is a need that there should be awareness amongst the tribal people about the various schemes implemented by the Government of Maharashtra so that they could benefit from these schemes. The tribal people should know what schemes are being implemented for their benefits in various spheres such as health, agriculture, economic development, education, etc. It was felt by the Government that the young educated tribal students should be aware about the various competitive examinations held by various agencies such as UPSC, MPSC, Staff Selection Commissions, Banking Recruitment Boards etc. in order that they can appear, compete and make their entry into Government service on the posts reserved for Scheduled Tribes. In short, it was felt by the Government that the educated tribal youths can play a major role in bringing about awareness amongst the tribals. Considering this factor, a scheme "Tribal Youth Leadership Programmes" was formulated and was allotted to the Tribal Research and Training Institute, Pune, for its implementation.

In this programme, the initiative is taken by the educated tribal youth themselves and they create awareness amongst the tribals and the tribal society. Various meetings, workshops, seminars etc. are held at Integrated Tribal Development Project level and in such types of workshops, experts in the various fields, mainly those government officers who implement the various schemes, local functionaries etc. people are called in to guide the tribal people. The tribal people like to attend such types of programmes because they know what is being done by the Government of Maharashtra for them.

2. *Facilities for the programme*

At the project level, one batch of 40 tribal students is selected and they are given all sorts of information so that they can go in their village and inform, help and assist the tribals to take the benefit from these schemes. There are 24 Integrated Tribal Development Projects (ITDPs) functioning in the state of Maharashtra. Just recently i.e. in the year 2012, five more I.T.D.Ps. have been created newly at Solapur, Bhandara, Dhule, Kalamnuri in Hingoli district and Pusad in Yeotmal district. Considering this fact, 24 POs X 40 students = 960 students are being trained every year. Till 2012, more than 20,000 students have been trained and they are giving their services in the tribal field.

An amount of Rs.15,000/- is placed at the disposal of each Project Officer of the concerned ITDP, to organize the programme. An amount of Rs.3,60,000/- is spent every year by the Government of Maharashtra on this scheme in all the 24 ITDPs.

3. *Feedback from these students*

Focused group discussion with the beneficiaries revealed that the leadership programme certainly helped them to understand the basic concept regarding the subject. Secondly, the trained beneficiaries make efforts to spread this message to their fellow tribals by word of mouth. The tribal girls have also been benefited and empowered through this programme.

Concluding Remarks

It is evident from the data presented above, that over 40,000 tribal youth have been benefited from the above two training programmes. The

Tribal Development Department is simultaneously implementing several programmes to support the tribal youth. For example the Department has established 1008 Asrham Scholls in the state of Maharashtra in the tribal pockets of Maharashtra which cater educational, health, nutritional, lodging and boarding services to over 4,50,000 tribal students. Similarly, there are 480 tribal hostels for boys and girls at taluka places which cater the above mentioned services for the graduates and post graduates. For further details one can log on to mahatribal.gov.in.

Tree Plantation Plan for Schools and Colleges

– Dr. **Robin D. Tribhuwan**

The Research Problem

The Concern over the balance between human life and environment assumed international dimensions during the 1950's. The new environment movement was sparked off by two famous books-Rachel carson's. Silent spring (Carson, 1962) and Garret Hardin's, The tragedy of Commons. (Hardin, 1968)

In the early seventies, there developed two schools of thought about the causes of environmental degradation : One School blamed greed and relentless economic growth; whereas the other blamed unstabilized population growth. As apathy pointed out by Stanely Foundation (1971), the unabated pollution and unstabilized population are the real threats to our way of life and life itself.

As the world becomes inter-dependent and fragile, the future of humanity holds great peril and great promise. The dominant patterns of production and consumption are causing environmental devastation, the depletion of resources, and the massive extinction of species. Communities are being under mined. The benefits of development are not shared equitably and the gap between the rich and the poor is widening. Injustice, poverty, ignorance and violent conflicts are wide spread and cause the great suffering.

An unprecedented rise of human population has over burdened ecological and social systems. The foundations of global security are threatened.

The United Nations conference on Human Environment, held in June 1972, was the event that turned the environment into a major issue at the international level.

The measurement by British researchers of the size of the ozone hole, first reported in 1985 shocked the world. (Farnharn, Gardiner and Shanklin 1985). The global 2000 report recognized for the first time that species extension was threatening biodiversity as an essential component of Earth's ecosystem (U.S. Government 1980).

The World summit on sustainable Development, in Johannesburg, South Africa from 2-4 September 2007, where in 21,000 delegates, including 104 heads of the states and governments gathered to draw up a plan to eradicate poverty, change unsustainable patterns of production and consumption, plan and manage the natural resource base preservation strategies and work out the requirements of sustainable development.

Concept of Sustainable Development

The most commonly used definition of Sustainable Development comes from the 1987 report by World Commission on Environmental and Development (WCED also known as Brut land Commission) titled our common future.

"Sustainable development is that which meets the needs of the present, without compromising the ability of future generations to meet their needs."

It is an anthropocentric concept, which desires to seek a balance between social, economic and ecological aspects of a community.

The United Nations Conference on Environment and Development (UNCED), held in Rio, in 1992 declaration stated that, "Human beings are at the centre of concerns for sustainable development" They are entitled to a healthy and productive life in harmony with nature"

There are several definition of sustainable development relating to social, economic and ecological variables. However, all definitions of sustainable development has environment as an integral component, but how it fits into different interpretation is the main concern. The goal of sustainable development is to maximize the three systems namely ecological system, social system and economic system. It is all about ensuring a better quality of life for everyone, now and for generations to come. This paper is based on secondary data and aims at unveiling the need to balance social, economic and ecological resources with references to Maha.

Why care about Ecosystems ?

Eco systems sustain us. They are earth's primary producers – solar – powered factories that yield most basic necessities : Food, Fibre, Water and all at efficiency unmatched by human technology. Eco-systems also provide essential functions – services like air and water purification, climate control, nutrient cycling and soil production – that we can't replace at any reasonable price.

Why care for stabilizing social, economic and ecological systems ?

There is a very close relationship between social, economic and ecosystems. The existence of a state or country depends a lot on the quantity and quality of social, economic and ecological resources they have secondly it is equally important that the quality and quantity of the above mentioned three resources and systems is stable and balanced, for the survival of its citizens.

Forest Cover in Maharashtra

If one has to analyze the stability of social, economic and ecological resources in Maharashtra with reference to forest cover its use by the rural and tribal population one gets an idea that the demand for forest resources is high both in tribal, rural and urban areas, but the supply is less.

For instance,the total population of Maharashtra is 112.37 million as per 2011 census which constitutes 9.29 per cent of the country's population.

Out of this, rural population is 54.77 per cent and Urban population is 45.23 per cent. The population density is 366 persons per square kilometer. The live stock population of 35.95 million (Live stock census 2007).

As against this, the forest cover in the state, based on interpretation of satellite data of October-December 2008 in 50,646 km^2 which is 16.46 per cent of the state's geographical area that is 307,713 Km^2 (India state of forest Report). It is pertinent to note that the 16.46 per cent forest cover includes land covered with trees, shrubs, grass and fallow land as well.

The India, state of Forest report 2011 gives a breakup of forest cover in Maharashtra, which is as follows:

Forest Cover in Maharashtra

1. Non-forest area : 82.19%
2. Very Dense Forest area : 2.84%
3. Moderately dense forest area : 6.76%
4. Open Forest : 6.86%
5. Scrub Forest area : 1.35%

The same report provides us information stating that only Gadchiroli, has the highest very dense forest area cover among all 35 districts in the state followed by Chandrapur, Gondia and Amravati. The above statistics certainly shows an imbalance of social, economic and forest resources.

Dependency on Forest Resources

It is pertinent to note at this juncture that the tribal and rural populations depend a lot on forest resources for fuel wood, bamboo, timber, medicine, leaves, flowers, fruits, gum, honey etc.

There are 45 tribes in the state of Maharashtra, having a population of 85.77 lakhs, which amounts to 8.85 per cent to the total population of the state. In his book captioned Tribal Housing Issues, Tribhuwan Robin (2004) has revealed that tribals use maximum forest resources for building their houses. The houses of Koknas, Koli Mahadeo, Halbi, Gonds are large as compared to the houses of Katkaris, Koli Dhor, Dubla, Dhodia etc. The timber and other wall material required for building the house of course comes from the forest.

Besides this, there is a great demand for timber, bamboo and other forest resources in the cities required for furniture, construction, paper mills etc. This means there is a rapid depletion of forest in the state. This alarming warning hints at the imbalanced situation. There is an urgent need to assess the status of social, economic and ecological balance, if the goal of sustainable development has to be achieved.

1. What can schools and colleges do ?

The network of Zilla Parishad, Tribal Ashram and Private schools is really vast in the country. So is the case with colleges. In fact in Maharashtra itself there are 1008 aided and Government Ashram Schools, providing education to over 4,50,000 tribal children. These children, under the supervision of the teachers and head masters can plant trees. If every child and Youth in Government and private college plants a tree, millions of trees will be planted every year. The Tribal and Rural Development Department, including Forest Department should provide funds to the schools and colleges.

2. Role of Farmers

The agriculture Department must involve farmers in tree plantation. Saplings of plants should be provided along with funds before rainy season.

3. Self-help Groups

NGO's and Government Departments have established several Micro-Credit Unions in rural, urban and tribal areas. Women self Help Groups should be funded to plant trees on their farms, fallow land, around their houses, and around village grazing lands.

4. Motivate builders

Motivate builders to plant trees in their societies and building compliances.

5. Role of NGO's

Indentify good NGO's to promote tree plantation. These NGO's should be provided with funds to plan, implement, monitor and follow-up the plantation programme.

6. Farm house owners

It is observed that farm house owners have promoted tree plantation on their farms. More can be done by them.

7. National social service

The NSS can certainly take up tree plantation programme in the rural and tribal areas. The college youth can contribute a lot in this venture.

Concluding Remarks

If school children, college and N.S.S. youth, under the supervision of their teachers take up tree plantation programme, millions of trees can be planted and taken care of every year. The different departments of government can fund this programme.

Environmental experts and Botanists can be involved in planning this programme, so as to make it scientific and sustainable. Its high time we think of sustaining the biodiversity of our nation.

REFERENCES

India State of Forest Report, 2011, Forest Survey of India, Ministry of Environment & Forests, Government of India, Dehradun.

Census of India 2001 and 2011 Government of India, Maharashtra.

Live Stock Census, 2007, Maharashtra State.

Interpretation of Satellite Data of October-December 2008.

Tribhuwan Robin, 2004. Tribal Housing Issues, Discovery Publishing House, New Delhi.

Leadership Course in Biodiversity Conservation Notes on Sustainable Development, Bombay Natural History Society, 2008-2009.

Index

H

I

Z